MEN OF

OUR TIME

The

University

of

Georgia

Press

Athens

and

London

An
Anthology
of Male
Poetry in
Contemporary
America

Men
of Our Time

Edited by

Fred Moramarco

and Al Zolynas

© 1992 by the University of Georgia Press

Athens, Georgia 30602

All rights reserved

Designed by Richard Hendel

Set in 10/14 Ehrhardt

by Tseng Information Systems, Inc.

Printed and bound by Braun-Brumfield

The paper in this book meets the guidelines

for permanence and durability of the

Committee on Production Guidelines for

Book Longevity of the Council on Library

Resources.

Printed in the United States of America

96 95 94 93 92   C   5 4 3 2 1

Library of Congress Cataloging in
Publication Data

Men of our time : an anthology of male

poetry in contemporary America / edited

by Fred Moramarco and Al Zolynas.

p. cm.

Includes index.

ISBN 0-8203-1404-8 (alk. paper)

ISBN 0-8203-1430-7 (pbk.: alk. paper)

1. American poetry—20th century.

2. American poetry—Men authors.

3. Men—United States—Poetry.

I. Moramarco, Fred S., 1938–   .

II. Zolynas, Al, 1945–   .

PS590.M4   1992

811'.50809286—dc20   91-31462

CIP

British Library Cataloging in Publication
Data available

THIS BOOK IS DEDICATED
TO THE MEN OF OUR TIME

CONTENTS

FATHERS AND THEIR DAUGHTERS

MEN AND WOMEN

ACKNOWLEDGMENTS

There are a lot of people to thank for their help in locating poets and poems and for other good advice: Philip Levine, Robert Bly, Rita Dove, W. D. Ehrhart, and Steve Kowit were especially helpful, pointing out poets and poems we might have missed; Sam Hamill made useful suggestions for revising the introduction; Philip Levine deserves a special thanks for his careful reading of the collection in an earlier form and his suggestions for revision. Suzanne Colby's absolutely invaluable clerical and administrative assistance, corresponding with the poets and generally getting the manuscript in order, needs special mention as well: thanks, Suzanne. Thanks also to Karen Orchard, the executive editor of the University of Georgia Press, who believed in the work from the outset. We're both grateful for support from our institutions: San Diego State University for a Summer Faculty Fellowship for Research or Creative Activity and United States International University for released time from teaching. The archive at the University of California, San Diego, was also an extremely useful resource.

For a book of this sort it seems appropriate to acknowledge some men who are particularly important in one or another of our lives: Pete LaBarbera, Bill Sullivan, Clint Walcott, Walt Herd, Dan Danner, Bill Kleinman, Dave Davis, Chuck Moran, Mark Wyland, Steve Maranto, Steve and Nicholas Moramarco, Steve Kowit, David Bardwick, Ken Richardson, Peter Skrzynecki, Floyd D. Williams ("The Colonel"), and Kostas and Brian Zolynas. Finally, we'd like to give an extra-special thanks to the women in each of our lives who provided inspiration, support, advice, criticism, and sometimes even lunch: Arlie Zolynas and Frances Payne Adler.

Unless otherwise specified, all the poems in this anthology appear by permission of their authors.

Jack Agueros: "Parting Since" from *Correspondence Between the Stonehaulers* by Jack Agueros (Hanging Loose Press, 1991).
Antler: "Hot Summernight Cloudburst Rendezvous" appeared in *Erotic by Nature, Long Shot, Church-Wellesley Literary Review, Chiron Review,* and

O mores!" from *You Get So Alone at Times That It Just Makes Sense,* © 1986 by Charles Bukowski. Used by permission of Black Sparrow Press.

Raymond Carver: "My Dad's Wallet" and "My Daughter and Apple Pie" from *Where Water Comes Together with Other Water* by Raymond Carver, © 1984, 1985 by Raymond Carver. Reprinted by permission of Random House, Inc.

Philip Cioffari: "Breaking Bones" and "Home" appeared in *Worcester Review.*

David Citino: "Mario Lanza Defeats Luciano Pavarotti in a Tenor Competition Held on a Turntable in My Father's Living Room" and "Night Journey" from *Last Rites and Other Poems* by David Citino, © 1980 by the Ohio State University Press. Reprinted by permission.

Horace Coleman: "A Black Soldier Remembers" first appeared in *New Letters* (1976); "OK Corral East" appeared in *Obsidian* (1975).

Robert Creeley: "Memory, 1930" and "Mother's Voice" from *Mirrors,* © 1983 by Robert Creeley. Reprinted by permission of New Directions Publishing Corporation.

Philip Dacey: "One of the Boys" from *The Boy Under the Bed* (Johns Hopkins University Press, 1981); "Porno Love" from *How I Escaped from the Labyrinth and Other Poems* (Carnegie-Mellon University Press, 1977); "Crime" from *The Man with Red Suspenders* (Milkweed Editions, 1986).

Leo Dangel: "Passing the Orange" from *Old Man Brunner Country* (Spoon River Poetry Press), © 1987 by Leo Dangel; "My Father in the Distance" originally appeared in *Poetry Now.*

Peter Davison: "Mother & Child #3" and "At Sixty" from *The Great Ledge* by Peter Davison, © 1989 by Peter Davison. Reprinted by permission of Alfred A. Knopf, Inc.

James Dickey: "The Hospital Window" and "Adultery," © 1962 and © 1966 by James Dickey. Reprinted from *Poems, 1957–1967,* Wesleyan University Press by permission of University Press of New England. "The Hospital Window" first appeared in *Poetry.*

Emanuel di Pasquale: "My Mother's Nightmares," © 1989 by Emanuel di Pasquale, with the permission of BOA Editions, Ltd., 92 Park Ave., Brockport, N.Y. 14420.

Stephen Dobyns: "Wind Chimes" and "Black Dog, Red Dog" from *Black Dog, Red Dog* (Henry Holt & Co., 1984).

Joseph Duemer: "Burn Victim" originally appeared in *MSS* and was reprinted in *Customs* (University of Georgia Press, 1987).

Alan Dugan: "Love Song: I and Thou," "To a Colleague, From the Country," "Letter to Donald Fall," from *New and Collected Poems 1961–1983* by

David Mura: "The Emergency Room" and "Grandfather-in-law" appeared in *After We Lost Our Way* (E. P. Dutton, 1989).

Leonard Nathan: "Family Circle" from *Dear Blood* by Leonard Nathan, reprinted by permission of the University of Pittsburgh Press. © 1980 by Leonard Nathan. "Toast" from *Holding Patterns* by Leonard Nathan, reprinted by permission of the University of Pittsburgh Press. © 1982 by Leonard Nathan. "Just Looking, Thank You" from *Carrying On: New and Selected Poems* by Leonard Nathan, reprinted by permission of the University of Pittsburgh Press. © 1985 by Leonard Nathan.

John Frederick Nims: "The Evergreen" from *Selected Poems* by John Frederick Nims (University of Chicago Press, 1982), © 1982 by the University of Chicago. Reprinted by permission of the University of Chicago Press.

Perry Oldham: "Noon" first appeared in *Carrying the Darkness: American Indochina—The Poetry of the Vietnam War*, edited by W. D. Ehrhart (Avon Books, 1985).

Antony Oldknow: "Talking with Her," ©Antony Oldknow, appeared in *Cream City Review* (1985).

Simon J. Ortiz: "My Father's Song" was published in *A Good Journey* (University of Arizona Press, 1985).

Basil T. Paquet: "Basket Case" first appeared in *Winning Hearts and Minds*, ed. Jan Barry, Basil T. Paquet, and Larry Rottman (1st Casualty Press, 1972).

Walter Pavlich: "On the Life and Death of Stan Laurel's Son" first appeared in *Mānoa* (University of Hawaii Press, 1989) and subsequently appeared in *The Pushcart Prize XV* (Pushcart Press, 1990) and in *The Lost Comedy* (Howlet Press, 1991). © by Walter Pavlich.

Mark Perlberg: "The Floating World" reprinted by permission from *Hudson Review* 42 (Spring 1989). © 1989 by Mark Perlberg.

Robert Peters: "The Butchering" from *The Sow's Head and Other Poems* (Wayne State University Press, 1968); "Song for a Son" from *Song for a Son* (W. W. Norton, 1967). © by Robert Peters.

Robert Pinsky: "History of My Heart," from *History of My Heart*, © 1984 by Robert Pinsky, was first published by The Ecco Press in 1984. Reprinted by permission.

Charles Potts: "Raspberry," © by Charles Potts, was previously published in *A Rite to the Body*, ed. Hugh Fox (Ghost Dance Press, 1989).

Bin Ramke: "*Mater Dolorosa*" from *White Monkeys* (University of Georgia Press, 1981).

Michael Rattee: "Long Fingers" appeared in *Calling Yourself Home* (Cleveland

W. D. Snodgrass: "A Friend" from *After Experience* (Harper & Row, 1968), © 1968 by W. D. Snodgrass.

Gary Snyder: "Axe Handles" excerpted from *Axe Handles*, © 1983 by Gary Snyder. Published by North Point Press and reprinted by permission.

Gary Soto: "The New Movies" and "Shopping for a Woman" reprinted from *Black Hair* by Gary Soto, by permission of the University of Pittsburgh Press. © 1985 by Gary Soto.

Peter Spiro: "Tone Deaf" previously published in *Third Lung Review*.

William Stafford: "A Memorial: Son Bret" appeared in *American Scholar*.

Frank Steele: "October, 1987" and "Untitled" from *The Salesman* (Plainsong Press, 1988).

Gerald Stern: "Bob Summers' Body" and "Magritte Dancing" from *Leaving Another Kingdom* (Harper and Row, 1990), © 1990 by Gerald Stern.

Barry Sternlieb: "Bathing the Girls" appeared in *Thinning the Rows* (Brooding Heron Press, 1990); "For Kyla, Age 3" appeared in *Fission* (Adastra Press, 1986).

Frank Stewart: "The Dance" first appeared in *Ironwood* (1987); "To a Friend Killed in Dragon Valley, Vietnam" first appeared in *The Paper* (1981) and then in *The Open Water* (Floating Island Publications, 1982).

Austin Straus: "L.A. Morning" appeared in *POETRY/LA* (1984).

Barton Sutter: "Rochester" and "My Parents Bought Me Comic Books" from *Pine Creek Parish Hall and Other Poems*, © 1985 by Barton Sutter. Published by Sandhills Press and reissued by Greysolon Press (1990).

Nathaniel Tarn: "The Mortal Wife" first appeared in *Seeing America First* by Nathaniel Tarn (Coffee House Press, 1989). Reprinted by permission of the publisher. © 1989 by Nathaniel Tarn.

Henry Taylor: "At the Swings" and "The Aging Professor Considers His Rectitude" reprinted by permission of Louisiana State University Press from *The Flying Change* by Henry Taylor, © 1985 by Henry Taylor.

David Trinidad: "Night and Fog (San Francisco)" originally appeared in *Pavane* by David Trinidad (Sherwood Press, 1981), © 1981 by David Trinidad.

Lloyd Van Brunt: "Wanda Pickles" original version first published in *Working Firewood for the Night* by Lloyd Van Brunt (The Smith, 1990), © 1990 by Lloyd Van Brunt.

John Vernon: "Boy Watering Fuchsias" first appeared in *Roberson Poetry Annual* (Spring 1980).

Mark Vinz: "Passages" first appeared in *Mixed Blessings* (Spoon River Poetry Press), © 1989 by Mark Vinz.

INTRODUCTION

American men living in the waning years of the twentieth century have experienced remarkable psychological transformations beyond the obvious changes brought about by the media explosion, the computer revolution, or any of the other technological alterations of human life. These changes are more deeply rooted and have to do with the male inner life and its relationship to the outer world—how men relate to women and to one another, how they deal with and experience fundamental male roles such as father, son, brother, husband, lover, and friend. Many contemporary men are exploring masculinity and male roles in a way that previous generations of men would have found appalling or at least unacceptable. Evidence of this introspective turn is a spate of recent books, films, television programs, magazine articles, and other cultural events and artifacts that examine male experience in this new way. A few examples are Sam Keen's *Fire in the Belly: On Being A Man*, Anthony Astrachan's *How Men Feel*; Warren Farrell's *Why Men Are the Way They Are*; Mark Gerzon's *A Choice of Heroes, The Changing Face of American Manhood*; Harry Brod's *The Making of Masculinities*; Robert Bly's highly successful men's retreats as well as his best seller, *Iron John: A Book About Men*; regular national conferences on male issues sponsored by men's organizations such as The Coalition of Free Men, The National Organization of Changing Men, and The National Congress of Men, and the establishment of national magazines, journals, and newsletters dealing exclusively with men's issues. Men are turning inward in large numbers and in ways that previous generations of men would have considered self-indulgent.

At their best and most productive, these new explorations are neither a reaction to feminism (though obviously influenced by it) nor a reversion to previous male dominant modes of cultural investigation. They build upon the feminist view that traditionally men have regarded their experiences as "universal" and have largely excluded consideration of gender from the examination of the major issues in their lives. Instead of regarding male experience as universal, these explorations seek specifically to understand men in relation to those aspects of our culture that shape and define the male roles within it. Contemporary men—more than men of previous generations—seem willing to explore and express their feelings without embarrassment. Because of this, both men and women are discovering that male life in our time brings with it burden as well as privilege, pain as well as power, failure and disappointment more often than success and patriarchal authority.

And what has poetry to do with all this? For one thing, many American men have been reasserting the *primary* function of poetry as the most exact verbal expression of a personal inner world. This essential quality of poetry has been deflected in twentieth century America, largely as a result of modernism that saw personal poetry as embarrassing and maudlin. Ever since T. S. Eliot defined twentieth century poetry as "an escape from emotion" (in that landmark essay of modernism, "Tradition and the Individual Talent") and Ezra Pound took refuge from the personal in a series of personae and a dense thicket of literary and scholarly allusion, a substantial number of influential American poets have regarded poetry of the feeling self with suspicion. The only cardinal literary sin of modernism is sentimentality; an excess of ideas (such as the deluge of fragmented "gists and piths" we experience in *The Cantos*) is not only acceptable, but valued as a kind of intellectual macho; an excess of feelings, however expressed, is not. In some sense, it can be argued that Pound and Eliot made it more acceptable for men to write poetry at all. Poetry in America has always been regarded as a kind of sissified activity for a man; intellectualizing it and distancing it from personal emotional expression made it more "manly." Because the repression of personal feelings has been a hallmark of conventional American maleness from the dark supressions of our Puritan ancestors through the uncomplaining toughness of Hemingway's heroes or the monosyllabic stoicism of movie stars like Gary Cooper or John Wayne, the modernist tradition was as American as apple pie. For contemporary American men, the intellectual, literary, and pop-culture heritage all reinforced the idea that public self-expression is unmanly.

Since the emergence of contemporary feminism in the late 1960s, many anthologies of poetry by contemporary women have articulated and defined a distinctive sensibility attuned to the particulars of a woman's life in our time—a sensibility characterized by speaking things previously unspoken and requiring, as Adrienne Rich puts it, "a whole new language beginning here." Though it's obvious that changes in women's lives and their ways of being in the world have had an enormous impact on men's lives and the deeply embedded traditions by which they have lived, virtually no attention has been paid to the poetry of men as a distinct entity, other than in a negative way to dismiss it as "phallocentric" and insensitive to the alternate views of human experience revealed in women's poetry. A few years ago, Alicia Ostriker (who has written a book about women's poetry called *Stealing the Language*) wrote in the *New York Times Book Review* that women's poetry is where the action is in contemporary writing, and that men, for the first time in American literary history, were not in the forefront of innovation.

But a quiet revolution has been taking place in men's poetry as well over the past few decades, as men also have been chronicling the "history of their hearts" (to borrow the title of Robert Pinsky's book) and have been examining those relationships central to their being in the world: their connections to their fathers and mothers; their own sense of fatherhood and of being sons and brothers; their marriages, divorces, and other aspects of their love lives; as well as the ways they conceive of maleness and femaleness. Though there are precedents for this kind of self-examination in American poetry, for many male poets this has been unexplored territory.

The personal introspective mode in American poetry comes mainly from Emily Dickinson and until recently was not widely extended to depictions of male experience. As so many feminist writers have shown, Dickinson's work was the source and inspiration for many twentieth century women poets— enabling them "to speak the unspeakable" (Rich), to verify their internal reality as outward truth. For European and Latin American male poets, the internal life has always been a primary source of poetic imagery—the poetry of Rainer Maria Rilke, Arthur Rimbaud, Federico García Lorca, Antonio Machado, Pablo Neruda, and so many others creates a modern male tradition tied deeply to personal life and inner reflection. And while there is a male poetry of introspection in America—e e cummings, Randall Jarrell, Kenneth Rexroth, Theodore Roethke come immediately to mind—these writers, until recently, have not shaped the canon of American literature as much as the less inwardly directed poets.

Not until the mid-1950s did this state of affairs change. When Allen Ginsberg wrote in the famous opening lines of "Howl": "I saw the best minds of my generation destroyed by madness," he spoke for a generation of American men—both homosexual and heterosexual—whose individual experiences were not being authenticated in the poetry of the time. Since poetry remains the closest we can come to externalizing verbally the experience of the private self, Ginsberg's "Howl" struck a major chord in many of the writers of the time. The poetry of the late 1950s in America, by both men and women alike, was dominated by what has been called the "confessional" impulse. Poets like Sylvia Plath, Anne Sexton, Robert Lowell, John Berryman, and W. D. Snodgrass, among others, reacted vigorously to the emotional restraints of the Pound-Eliot generation, giving us startling and memorable personal lines like:

My mind's not right

A car radio bleats,
'Love, O careless Love . . .' I hear
my ill spirit sob in each blood cell,
as if my hand were at its throat. . . .
I myself am hell;
nobody's here—
    (Robert Lowell, "Skunk Hour")

There sat down, once, a thing on Henry's heart
so heavy, if he had a hundred years
& more, & weeping, sleepless, in all them time
Henry could not make good.
    (John Berryman, "Dream Song 29")

A chicken hawk floats over, looking for home.
I have wasted my life.
    (James Wright, "Lying in a Hammock . . .")

Such frank confessions of personal inadequacy were startling coming from men. Vulnerability and self-doubt are not socially supported masculine qualities, and as poets began looking inward, the collective voice of male poets in America began to change. Robert Bly and James Wright began to examine the deep images that haunt the male psyche and to translate introspective European and Latin American male poets. Robert Pinsky and Robert Hass expressed the troubled anxiety lurking beneath the surface of complacent American middle-class life while poets like Amiri Baraka gave voice to the seething anger of African Americans; Phil Levine, Richard Hugo, Donald Justice, and many others became mentors for a new generation of male poets who felt freer to explore the inner life—to make it the central subject of their poetry.

We call this anthology *Men of Our Time* because we intend it to reflect both the diversity and commonality of male experience today. We also intend it to counter the negative image of male poetry projected by otherwise reasonable attempts at cultural revision. One contributor notes that his manuscript was returned by a major publisher with a reader's report remarking that his poetry had "surprising integrity despite its male orientation." Early along we decided to reprint a number of poems by well-established poets mentioned above and others like them because these poets seemed to write out of a distinctly male sensibility that has simply not been acknowledged. We then solicited new poems with four basic criteria in mind. First of all, we wanted only first-rate poetry, which for us means poetry with memorable lines, strong emotional impact, and resonance. Secondly, we sought poems that reflect particularly male experience. We were interested in not only obvious expressions of this experience, like poems about fathers and sons, but also in more subtle nuances of various male relationships: with women, with other men (both as friends and as lovers), and with the deeper realities of their interior lives. Third, we wanted to achieve some generational mix in the volume—poems by young, middle-aged, and older men that express the preoccupations of various life stages. And fourth, we sought to achieve an ethnic and racial mix that reflects the diversity and multicultural tenor of American life.

As we collected these poems, we began to realize how impressively poetry has captured the changes in men's lives over the past few decades. For example, the depth and intensity of the father-son connection and the deep fissure in human experience that occurs when it's breached is movingly expressed in the section of poems by sons about their fathers. These poems speak with more authority and power than a long litany of social statistics about single parents or absent fathers. In fact, the contemporary male poet who hasn't written a poem about his father is rare, and these poems resonate with the unmistakable sound of truth. They seem to give voice to a vast unspokenness that hangs in the air between generations. As Gary Young puts it in his lovely poem "Loch Lomond":

> What we wanted to say escaped us,
> moved ceaselessly away like ripples
> from the boat which seemed
> to lose its buoyancy as the day went on.

Just reading these words and others like them in the section of poems about fathers seems to restore some of that buoyancy as "what we wanted to say" is finally said. These poems seem to reinforce what Robert Bly, who has spent the last several years traveling around the country talking with thousands of American men in great depth, has identified as the primary submerged emotion of contemporary men: grief between fathers and sons.

We found poems about brothers far less common than those about fathers, although brotherhood in its broader sense of a common bond between males of a given generation seems as much a part of contemporary male life as it has always been. Philip Levine's powerful "Baby Villon" and "You Can Have It" remind us of this continuity, as does Peter Spiro's tender expression of brotherly love in "Trying to Gain Folds." And while homophobia is still widespread in the society, more men seem willing to write about their love for other men, sometimes with a celebrative zeal, as Antler does in "Hot Summernight Cloudburst Rendezvous" and sometimes with the courageous self-revelation of David Trinidad's "Night and Fog."

For most contemporary men, Vietnam has left an indelible mark on their consciousness, whether they went or stayed at home, whether they endorsed or protested the war. The poems in the war section are some of the most painful and moving to read, not only for the pain and horror they embody, but for the love that comes through, sometimes in the most impossible situations. For example, in Yusef Komunyakaa's "We Never Know," a soldier approaches a dead body on the battlefield:

> I pulled the crumbled photograph
> from his fingers.
> There's no other way
> to say this: I fell in love.

It is a paradox that the most destructive of human activities continues to produce poetry of eloquence and grace. Whether this will continue to be so after the technological devastation of the Persian Gulf War remains to be seen. While it seems more and more evident that fighting in war is no longer an exclusively male behavior, for many centuries the experience of going to war has shaped men's perception of the world. As a tragic consequence of this latest war, it will likely shape some women's perception as well.

While not all men share the experience of war (or are fathers or brothers, for that matter) every male is born into this world a son. Yet the relationship between the son and his own adult life can be also problematic in American society for economic reasons (it is increasingly difficult for young people to establish financial independence from their parents) and because of the loss of initiation rituals marking the transition between boyhood and manhood in our society. When these rituals do occur—see Stuart Dybek's "Brass Knuckles," Philip Cioffari's "Breaking Bones," for example—they're often tied to macho and narrow definitions of masculinity that exclude men who do not define their manliness in terms of violence and physical strength. And when they're not violent, these initiations in the contemporary world are often enacted alone or in desperation and are ultimately ineffective and self-negating, as in Michael Rattee's "The Runaway" or Louis Jenkins's "The Lost Boy."

But one aspect of male life more than all others seems increasingly volatile: the relationship between men and women. As Anthony Astrachan has pointed out, while many men intellectually support the women's movement and women's equality, "most men tend to have more and stronger painful feelings than pleasurable ones about these changes." This ambivalence has played havoc with traditional relationships. Although there are a good number of warm and touching love poems in this collection, the more characteristic note is one of desire for union and intimacy coupled with a recognition of distinction and "distances." As Michael Rattee expresses it in "Distances,"

> he begins to think that everything
> comes down to distances
> that how far one thing is from another
> is what defines each of them

Men recognize these distances while at the same time they seem to be searching for ways to bridge them. In our selections about men and women we have news from the front of the struggle between the sexes to understand one another. The shifting role of both sexes in the contemporary world has sharply altered relationships between men and their wives, lovers, sisters, daughters, and mothers. While men seem to be writing a great deal about their wives, lovers, daughters, and to a lesser extent about their mothers, we found poems about sisters in extremely short supply—not one is included in this anthology!

The last section of the book is called "The Hearts of Men" and, for us, captures the essence of male inner life as it is experienced today. The poems reveal men's most intimate feelings about the loss of childhood, sexual anxieties and fantasies, aging, self-sufficiency and dependency, and the perennial quest for a masculine identity. As Michael Blumenthal puts it,

> . . . they pour
> their grief like tide
> into the air
> and move out again,
> like Odysseus,
> into the deep sea
> of disconnectedness. . . .

The poems in this section embody the quality we were most seeking: an un-apologetic grounding in distinctly male experience or imagination. Not every poem written by a man has this quality. Men, like women, write about a wide variety of subjects not connected to their gender. On the other hand, sometimes the connection to gender, while not obvious, is unmistakable. For example, we recognized that connection in the poem which concludes the volume, Jack Grapes's playfully mysterious, "My Rodeo":

> I am a man who comes home depressed, lonely
> frustrated, who tries to smother his rodeo,
> his cheap rodeo.
> And I haven't even the courage to do that.
> Imagine smothering one's rodeo.
> The shame would haunt me the rest of my life.

This poem became for us a kind of emblem for the anthology. The men we have included here do not smother their rodeos; they speak out in clear, sometimes comic, sometimes tragic, and often eloquent voices.

Any anthology reflects the biases of its editors, and this one is no different. Throughout, we have preferred poems that speak directly, with a minimum of "artifice." We have avoided poems that sacrifice emotional honesty for lin-guistic acrobatics. We aimed instead for a broad range of men's voices, from the post-punk, raw, youthful, urban energy of Eric Brown (who publishes a magazine called *Rats with Keys* in East Los Angeles) to the seasoned sophis-tication of Peter Davison; from the philosophical kibitzing of Gerald Stern to the stately cadences of Henry Taylor; from the unrestrained directness of Charles Bukowski to the soulful dignity of Joseph Bruchac. We were inter-ested primarily in poems that grow out of and speak from life experiences, especially formative and major life experiences: Robert Bly writing a poem in his father's presence for the first time; W. D. Snodgrass writing about the anguish of an adulterous relationship; Raymond Carver looking through his father's wallet after his death; Jimmy Santiago Baca and Galway Kinnell watching the births of their children; William Stafford, Michael S. Harper, John Frederick Nims, or Robert Peters grieving over the deaths of their chil-dren; David Trinidad coming to terms with his homosexuality; Etheridge Knight "feeling fucked up" at the loss of a sweetheart; James Broughton musing about senility and "defective wiring" in his old age. These, of course, are just a few examples.

Any anthology is also an act of recontextualizing. The cumulative effect of reading these poems in this new context is to recognize a subtle strength in men's voices that is not "universal," but distinctly male. The traditional male claim to universality has justly aroused the anger of many women who often feel alienated from the experiences described in much male poetry. Finally, we felt it important to include poems that reflect and reveal men as they are, not as they ought to be or might be in a world less flawed than ours. This is not a poetry that speaks for all human experience, but it does speak, in its variety, diversity, and individuality, for the emerging community of male poets in our time. What Walt Whitman said of himself is true of that community: it is large and contains multitudes.

BOYS BECOMING MEN

"He thought he could hear voices,

far away, calling his name"

THE LOST BOY

When Jason did not come home from school on the bus Barbara began to worry. She went next door to ask if Bobby, who rode the same bus, had seen Jason. Bobby remembered seeing Jason but didn't think he got on the bus. Bobby's mother, Teresa, said "Oh, he probably just decided to walk." Teresa thought Barbara was a silly woman who fussed over her children. Bobby and Chris set out to look for Jason. It was an adventure, a search through the dark continent. Barbara used Teresa's phone to call the school. Meanwhile, Jason returned home, went in the back door and up to his room. Through the open window he could hear his mother in the next yard. He flopped down on the bed and looked at comics. He could hear his mother talking about calling the police. He lay looking at the big crack in the ceiling. He thought about what it was like to be lost. He thought he could hear voices, far away, calling his name.

Louis Jenkins

BOY AT THE WINDOW

Seeing the snowman standing all alone
In dusk and cold is more than he can bear.
The small boy weeps to hear the wind prepare
A night of gnashings and enormous moan.
His tearful sight can hardly reach to where
The pale-faced figure with bitumen eyes
Returns him such a god-forsaken stare
As outcast Adam gave to Paradise.

The man of snow is, nonetheless, content,
Having no wish to go inside and die.
Still, he is moved to see the youngster cry.
Though frozen water is his element,
He melts enough to drop from one soft eye
A trickle of the purest rain, a tear

For the child at the bright pane surrounded by
Such warmth, such light, such love, and so much fear.

Richard Wilbur

THE RUNAWAY

He imagines a world without excuses
where a boy can board a bus with no fare
and ride as far as he wants
getting off where there's snow in summer
or at a swimming hole in mid-winter
in either case there is a rope
to help him up in one place
or down in the other
and no one will ask him
all those questions he's so tired of
why is he going there
or what is he up to
why is he traveling alone
and does his mother know where he is
he just rides the bus
holding his piece of rope like a friend
who will do whatever he wants
pretending he's old enough at last
not to need permission for anything
that if he winked at the woman beside him
she would smile and settle in her seat
making her skirt rise on her legs
the way he'd seen once in a movie
about soldiers leaving their hometown
to fight in a foreign country
he remembers thinking then
that that was the thing to do
just pack up and go off
to where everything is unfamiliar

4

it would be just like in a dream
where no matter how strange
or dangerous things become
it's always all right when you wake up
but now his mother's voice
forces him out of the bus
trying desperately to think
how he can say nothing
and make her believe that it's all right
that no excuses are needed
to make him fit in the world

Michael Rattee

THE LESSON (*from* Stoic Pose)

for David Politzer

At dawn, they splashed his cheeks with cold saké.
Then they led him to a room—brusquely
sliding back the panels—
where a man's, a peasant's body
lay on the mat, naked
except for stripes of shadow
across the flesh:
This was his introduction
to death.
They positioned him near the corpse, saying:
The boy is samurai;
he must learn.
In his hands they placed
the heavy sword,
as quietly he began to cry. . . .

Later, they hung his small, blood-flecked kimono
on a bamboo pole:

He was five when they taught him
to quarter the bodies.

Cyrus Cassells

STREET KID

I stand before the window that opens
To a field of sagebrush—
California country northeast of San Francisco.
Holding to the earth and its shield of silence,
The sun burns my thirteen years into the hill.
The white breath of twilight
Whirrs with insects crawling down the glass
Between the bars. But it is the meadowlark
Warbling at the end of the fence
That sets me apart from the rest of the boys,
The cool toughs playing ping pong
And cards before lock-up.
When this new home stops calling on memory,
As well as my nickname, Injun Joe,
Given to me by the brothers,
The Blacks, the Chicanos, the others growing
Lean as this solitude, I step
From the window into the darkness,
Reach my soul building a nest against the wall.

Duane Niatum

ALAN VALERIANO SEES A LYNCH MOB

This morning, Alan wraps a rust and verdigris
paisley scarf around his do, a bouffant
Elvis coxcomb. I'm sitting on

his bed with his little brother
Jose, my best friend in fifth grade.
On KDIA, the Tempts croon about sunshine
on a cloudy day while Alan's getting on
his finest threads. Later, the requisite black
leather hip-length coat, but first,
starched Levi's steam-ironed between newspapers.
Jose asks about the cut on Alan's forehead.
Here's the thing, blood. I'm styling down Fillmore
yesterday. The old men, they standing round
the liquor store, and old Mr. Page, he ask,
"Where you going, my man?" But I keep on strutting.
Ladies on corners with they twenty dollars of White
Rain hair spray, they pivot to watch me go by, yeah.
Alan slips a flamingo knit over
a sleeveless turquoise undershirt. Then
silk stockings ribbed in maroon. In the mirror,
he rehearses the strut: left index finger
slung inside the pants pocket,
the other arm swinging free from right shoulder
cocked slightly lower than the left.
Anyway, I seen my partner Jackson
across the street, dig? And he yells,
"Say, Al! Check out my new ride, man!"
And his buddy Rolando, he yelling too,
"That's a '57 Chevy, nigger!
Sweet, sweet, sweet." So I yell back,
"Let's go for a spin, man," and Jackson,
he give me the wheel. We burning rubber
now, blood, heading for the Sunset.
Jose and I look at each other. Both
thinking the same thing: the Sunset District
might as well have its own white
pages—MacInerny, Petrovsky, Puccinelli, Ryan.
Well, maybe some Changs and Wongs. A Gomez or two.
We doing it, boy! Rubber smoking
every time we come round a corner.
But, hell, that cheegro Jackson, he got gypped.
Some mother-fucking thing wrong with the brakes, and boom!

the car's up against a garage door.
Jesus Christ, man. Got blood dripping
in my eyes, and we drawing a crowd now.
Blonde hair, freckles everywhere. Rolando
and Jackson, boy, they gone. And I'm seeing
axe handles, shotguns, a burning goddamn cross.
So I rip off my scarf, man, show them straight
hair. "I ain't a nigger! I'm flip! Filipino!"
Jose glances at me, but I'm
looking out the window. Now
Alan adds the final touches: sky-blue
Stacy Adams shoes, the leather coat,
one last glimpse into the mirror.

Vince Gotera

SHAKING

For us a handshake was a duel:
two boys in a friendly clasp
of greeting were fighting the test
of power. Who squeezed first might have
an advantage, unless the cold
tendons got strained, and the grip,
so big and cruel at once would
weaken from the quick exertion
as the other built up a grasp
that overrode and then melted
the opposing hand, while we both
kept grinning hello. But the best
defense was to cup your palm so
knuckles weren't aligned for grinding
but curled under the hostile force.
It was the feint of giving in,
while the rival bore down and thought
himself near victory that was

the last strategy. And when he
crunched you toward acquiescence and
withdrawal from the lethal shake,
you put everything, your whole weight
and blood and warmth and thought, pumped down
through shoulder and elbow and wrist
on the opponent's paw as his
smile registered surprise and pain
and you broke down his control in
the vise of your own gesture of
reciprocation, serious welcome.

Robert Morgan

FIRST PRACTICE

After the doctor checked to see
we weren't ruptured,
the man with the short cigar took us
under the grade school,
where we went in case of attack
or storm, and said
he was Clifford Hill, he was
a man who believed dogs
ate dogs, he had once killed
for his country, and if
there were any girls present
for them to leave now.
               No one
left. OK, he said, he said I take
that to mean you are hungry
men who hate to lose as much
as I do. OK. Then
he made two lines of us
facing each other,
and across the way, he said,

is the man you hate most
in the world,
and if we are to win
that title I want to see how.
But I don't want to see
any marks when you're dressed,
he said. He said, *Now*.

Gary Gildner

BREAKING BONES

Take his lunchbox.
Pass around the peanut butter sandwich, the apple, the chocolate cookies.
Pull the bread apart, grind each half into the cement.
Play stickball with the apple.
Scale his cookies, one by one, at passing cars.
Grab his book bag, tear out the pages for tonight's homework,
write dirty words in red crayon on all the covers.
Load his gloves with stones,
sink them in the black muck of a sewer.
Swipe his hat and piss in it;
if he fights back, everyone jump him at once.
Track him down after school, on Saturdays and Sundays.
Gang up on him at all the following places:
street corners, bus stops, movie theatres, bars, offices, parties, dreams.
Fix it so when you're not around, he'll do it for you.
Fix it so he spends lunch hours, a lifetime by himself.
Fix him good.

Philip Cioffari

BRASS KNUCKLES

Kruger sets his feet
before Ventura Furniture's plate glass window.
                    We're
            outlined in streetlights,
        reflected across the jumbled livingrooms,
bedrooms, diningrooms,
                        smelling fresh bread
            from the flapping ventilator down the alley
            behind Cross's Bakery.

His fist keeps clenching
(our jaws grinding on bennies)
                    through the four thick rings
            of the knuckles he made me in shop
        the day after I got stomped
                    outside St. Sabina's.

    "The idea is to strike like a cobra. Don't follow through. Focus
total power at the moment of impact."
                    His fist uncoils
                            the brass
whipped back a centimeter from
                    smashing out my teeth,
        the force waves
                        snapping my head back.
                        "See?" he says,

sucking breath like a diver, toe to toe
with the leopard-skin sofa;
                    I step back
        thinking how a diamond ring cuts glass;
his fist explodes.
                The window cracks for half a block,
                knees drop out of our reflections.
An alarm
is bouncing out of doorways,
                        we cut

down a gangway of warm bread,
boots echoing
through the dim-lit viaduct on Rockwell
where I see his hand
flinging orange swashes off the concrete walls,
blood behind us
like footprints,
spoor for cops;
in a red haze of switches
boxcars couple,
we jump the electric rail
knowing we're already caught.

Stuart Dybek

RITE

Some of the guys on the team wanted to give the cocky freshman a pink belly. When he came out of the shower holding a white towel around his waist, the guys grabbed him and forced him down to the wet cement floor of the locker room, the towel falling from his waist.

Once on the floor, they held his arms and legs down, while he kicked and twisted his body and his limp penis jounced from side to side. While the others held him down, the team captain kneeled down next to him and began slapping his taut stomach hard with both hands like a drum skin. He slapped harder and harder and the sound rang off the cement walls like gunshot. His white stomach turned pink and then crimson and inflamed and then the captain stopped.

They let go of him and got up and everyone was smiling. Sweat glistened on their cleansed faces in the half-light.

Richard Oyama

THE BUTCHERING

1

Dad told me to hold the knife
and the pan. I heard the click
on wood of the bullet inserted,
rammed. Saw a flicker thrash
in a tree beside the trough,
saw a grain in the sow's mouth,
felt my guts slosh.

"Stand back," dad said.
Waffled snow track
pressed by his boots and mine.
Blood and foam. "Keep the knife
sharp, son, and hold the pan."
One of us had shuffled,
tramped a design,
feet near the jackpine.
"She'll bleed slow.
Catch all the blood you can."

A rose unfolded, froze.
"Can't we wait?" I said.
"It should turn warmer."

Spark, spark buzzing
in the dark.

"It's time," dad said, and waited.

2

Bless all this beauty! preacher
had exclaimed; *all sin and beauty
in this world! Beast and innocent!*

Fistbones gripped the foreshortened
pulpit rim. Thick glasses drove
his furious pupils in.

3
Dad brought the rifle to the skull.
The sow's nose plunged into the swill,
the tips of her white tallow ears as well.
Splunk! Straight through the brain, suet
and shell. Stunned! Discharge of food,
bran. Twitch of an ear. Potato, carrot,
turnip slab. "Quick. The knife, the pan."

He sliced the throat.
The eye closed over.
Hairy ears stood up, collapsed.
Her blood soured into gelatin.
She had begun to shit.

4
We dragged her
to the block and tackle rig.
We tied her tendons, raised her,
sloshed her up and down.
We shaved her hair,
spun her around, cut off
her feet and knuckles,
hacked off her head,
slashed her belly
from asshole down through
bleached fat throat.
Jewels spilled out
crotches of arteries
fluids danced and ran.

We hoisted her
out of dog reach
dumped her entrails
in the snow
left the head
for the dogs to eat—
my mother disliked head-meat.
The liver, steaming monochrome,

quivered with eyes.
We took it home.

5
I went to my room.
Tongues licked my neck.
I spread my arms,
threw back my head.
The tendons of a heel
snapped.
What had I lost?
bit   bridle   rage?

Preacher in his pulpit
fiddling, vestments aflame.
He, blazing, stepping down
to me. Hot piss came.
I knelt on the floor,
bent over, head in arms.
Piss washed down, more.
I clasped my loins,
arm crossed over arm.
And I cried
loving my guts,
O vulnerable guts,
guts of creatures.

Robert Peters

DAVID

I think Caravaggio has seen it right,
shown anyway with the boy and the head
(Is it really his *own* face, the giant's,
slack-jawed, tormented? Another story.)
the look of the lean boy, the lips

pursed to spit or kiss, the head held
at arm's length from him by the hair,
the eyes, if they show anything, reading
pity and contempt, hatred and love,
the look we keep for those we kill.
He will be king. Those fingers twined
in dark will pluck the hair of harps,
golden, to sing the measure of our joy
and anguish. By hair will Absalom
dangle from a limb, his tongue a thoroughfare
for flies, and the man grown old and soft
will tear his from the roots to make lament.
The look you give Goliath on that day
will flicker on your weathered face
when you spy bare Bathsheba on the roof
(O the dark honey, liquor of strange flesh,
to turn a head to birds, a heart to stone!)
and you will live to learn by heart
the lines upon this alien face.
So I say that Caravaggio
saw it right, that at the moment when
the boy has killed the man and lifts the head
to look at it is the beginning and the end.
I, who have pictured this often and always
stopped short of the miracle, seen David stoop
to feel for smooth stones in the filmy brook,
the instant when palm and fist
close like a beggar's on a cold coin,
know now I stopped too soon.
Bathed in light, the boy is bound
to be a king. But the sword . . .
I had forgotten that. A slant
of light, its fine edge rest across
his thigh. Never again a rock will do.
It fits his hand like a glove.

George Garrett

I don't remember the name of the story,
but the hero, a boy, was lost,
wandering a labyrinth of caverns
filling stratum by stratum with water.

I was wondering what might happen:
would he float upward toward light?
Or would he somersault forever
in an underground black river?

I couldn't stop reading the book
because I had to know the answer,
because my mother was leaving again—
the lid of the trunk thrown open,

blouses torn from their hangers,
the crazy shouting among rooms.
The boy found it impossible to see
which passage led to safety.

One yellow finger of flame
wavered on his last match.
There was a blur of perfume—
mother breaking miniature bottles,

then my father gripping her,
but too tightly, by both arms.
The boy wasn't able to breathe.
I think he wanted me to help,

but I was small, and it was late.
And my mother was sobbing now,
no longer cursing her life,
repeating my father's name
among bright islands of skirts
circling the rim of the bed.

I can't recall the whole story,
what happened at the end . . .

Sometimes I worry that the boy
is still searching below the earth
for a thin pencil of light,
that I can almost hear him

through great volumes of water,
through centuries of stone,
crying my name among blind fish,
wanting so much to come home.

Michael Waters

MY FATHER'S SHOW

I remember hiding there in the dark
                    in the Scotch
                    in being a kid
while they danced
out front in the spotlights
a hulking dark man
in a black tuxedo
whirling his small partner overhead
        curves of her torso
molded in pink sequins

They were just a warmup act
for the singer and the comedian
I had met them backstage
aging show business athletes
                    never going to be stars

but my feeling of terror
the impossible perfection
                    of being a man
of cigarette smoke   neon lights on the cars
of key rings   sex   and bank accounts
coalesced on them
the dark bull man
                hunched and stiff
holding up the arching salmon body
of the woman to the light

Richard Silberg

WHOREHOUSE

my first experience in a whorehouse
was in Tijuana.
it was a large place on the edge of
the city.
I was 17, with two friends.
we got drunk to get our guts
up
then went on
in.
the place was packed with
servicemen
mostly
sailors.
the sailors stood in long
lines
hollering, and beating on
the doors.

Lance got in a short
line (the lines indicated the
age of the whore: the shorter the

line the older the
whore)
and got it over
with, came out bold and
grinning: "well, what you guys
waiting for?"

the other guy, Jack, he passed me
the tequila bottle and I took a
hit and passed it back and he
took a hit.

Lance looked at us: "I'll be
in the car, sleeping it
off."

Jack and I waited until he was
gone
then started walking toward the
exit.
Jack was wearing this big
sombrero
and right at the exit was an
old whore sitting in a
chair.
she stuck out her leg
barring our
way: "come on, boys, I'll make
it *good* for you and
cheap!"

somehow that scared the
shit out of Jack and he
said, "my god, I'm going to
PUKE!"

"NOT ON THE FLOOR!" screamed
the whore
and with that

Jack ripped off his
sombrero
and holding it
before him
he must have puked a
gallon.

then he just stood there
staring down
at it
and the whore
said, "get out of
here!"

Jack ran out the door with
his sombrero
and then the whore
got a very kind look upon her
face and said to me:
"*cheap!*" and I walked
into a room with her
and there was a big fat man
sitting in a chair and
I asked her, "who's
that?"
and she said, "he's here to
see that I don't get
hurt."

and I walked over to the
man and said, "hey, how ya
doin'?"

and he said, "fine,
señor . . ."

and I said,
"you live around
here?"

and he said, "give
her the
money."

"how much?"

"two dollars."

I gave the lady the two
dollars
then walked back to the
man.

"I might come and live
in Mexico some day," I
told him.

"get the hell out of
here," he said,
"NOW!"

as I walked through the
exit
Jack was waiting out there
without his
sombrero
but he was still
wavering
drunk.

"Christ," I said, "she was
great, she actually got my
balls into her
mouth!"

we walked back to the car.
Lance was passed out, we
awakened him and he drove us

out of
there

somehow
we got through the border
crossing

and all the way
driving back to
L.A.

we rode Jack for being a
chickenshit
virgin.
Lance did it in a gentle
manner
but I was loud
demeaning Jack for his lack of
guts
and I kept at it
until Jack passed out
near
San Clemente.

I sat up there next to
Lance as we passed the last
tequila bottle back and
forth.

as Los Angeles rushed toward
us
Jack asked, "how was
it?"
and I answered
in a worldly
tone: "I've had
better."

Charles Bukowski

BURN VICTIM

When I was a dumb boy, this girl
a little older undressed alone
and got in bed before I was allowed
in the dark room, or in under darker

sheets. I was not to see her arms
laced with long scars, and rough
some places, like the silver bark
of sapling elms. But she moved

toward me, softening like fire,
opening like burned wood, and pulled
me safely through the smoldering air
every day for one long summer.

It was hot inside of her, and sweet
as a garden drenched with rain.
We hardly spoke—how could we,
doing each other this distant,

elemental favor? I must have felt
to her, the way, at night, my own heart
feels—reliable, thumping quietly.
It doesn't know what it is doing.

Joseph Duemer

THE DANCE

There was no trusting for anyone in her hair,
it wound tight, braided, and bore
terrible hooks and silver pins
barely concealed beneath the surface,
whose coldness grazed my cheek

as I took her in my cautious arms. But her body
at once became a brook, blue and flowing long
around me as the dance began—or tangible
atmosphere, clothed in small wings that brushed
my body, in a way so gentle for a moment
I couldn't feel my own coarseness anymore, though
I searched for it. Perhaps this
was the mystery—that she affirmed the air
even in me, at sixteen, who to that point
had been all earth. The severity of the braids
was her mother's touch, I saw,
for as we spun they slowly unwound,
the small strands fell about her ears, then
strayed along her neck, her face
tilted back, her eyes closed, and she
never thought to rearrange them. Though young,
I knew it wasn't me that made her smile,
but the dance and her own light wildness
—nothing in my power could create
that smile—and I held on, the way
the rocks hold a current, or a flag
a swirling wind. We danced
and she passed through me, and I was finally
lost to boyhood and myself, and became,
in the turning, a man, completed and inconsolable
when she let me go.

Frank Stewart

ROCHESTER

My senior year we did *Jane Eyre*.
Rita Johannsen was Jane,
And I was Rochester.

The way the story goes
I've got this crazy wife,
And I keep her locked away
In a distant wing of the house
Because I'm rich as hell.
In the end she burns the house
And burns herself, as well.
That's how I get to be blind
And marry the governess.

Of all the lines I memorized
I only remember one.
It's at the end, I'm blind,
And I turn to Jane and say:
"You have given me the light."
Blackout. Pause.
Thunderous applause.

When I think about it now, I feel
Rochester was cheated, kind of
Castrated, you know? I mean
At first he's sort of ornery
And makes these sharp remarks,
But in the end he's whipped
And tied up with this governess.

The audience just loved it,
The way that he was tamed.
I get so mad to think of it
That I've thought up
This version of my own
In which, I call it *Rochester*,
What happens is Jane Eyre
Dies of influenza. Rochester
Is forced to learn to love his ugly wife,
And they're unhappy ever after

Because women think we're dumb.
They think we can't feel anything.
They think that we can't see
The sneaky way they run things.
But I can see, and I
Don't hesitate to lie. Say
Some woman lights my cigarette?
I'll use that line, I'll tell her:
"You have given me the light."
She laughs but half believes it,
And half is good enough.

Or say she wonders how she looks,
And I see grey and wrinkles
And feel for both of us.
You think I tell her that?
I tell her: "You
Just look terrific."

They like to think we're blind.
That audience believed I was
When I was Rochester,
But I was just pretending,
And they were in the dark,
Applauding and applauding.

This was years ago,
But I can close my eyes
And still see everything:
My parents, sitting separately,
The faces of my friends.
I'm Rochester,
And Rochester sees everything:
Rita's mouth and teeth,
Delicious little ears,
And how the silver sweat runs
Trickling down her neck.

Barton Sutter

The boy waits on the top step, his hand on the door
to the screen porch. A green bike lies in the grass,
saddlebags stuffed with folded newspapers. The street
is lined with maples in full green of summer, white houses
set back from the road. The man whom the boy has come
to collect from shuffles onto the porch. As is his custom,
he wears a gray dress with flowers. Long gray hair
covers his shoulders, catches in a week's growth of beard.
The boy opens the door and glancing down he sees yellow
streaks of urine running down the man's legs, snaking
into the gray socks and loafers. For a year, the boy
has delivered the man's papers, mowed and raked his lawn.
He's even been inside the house, which stinks of excrement
and garbage, with forgotten bags of groceries on tables:
rotten fruit, moldy bread, packages of unopened hamburger.
He would wait in the hall as the man counted out pennies
from a paper bag, adding five extra out of kindness.
The boy thinks of when the man's mother was alive.
He would sneak up to the house when the music began
and watch the man and his mother dance cheek to cheek
around the kitchen, slowly, hesitantly, as if each
thought the other could break as simply as a china plate.
The mother had been dead a week when a neighbor found her
and even then her son wouldn't let her go. The boy sat
on the curb watching the man hurl his fat body against
the immaculate state troopers who tried not to touch him
but only keep him from where men from the funeral home
carried out his mother wrapped in red blankets, smelling
like hamburger left for weeks on the umbrella stand.

Today as the boy waits on the top step watching the urine
trickle into the man's socks, he raises his head to see
the pale blue eyes fixed upon him with their wrinkles and
bags and zigzagging red lines. As he stares into them,
he begins to believe he is staring out of those eyes,
looking down at a thin blond boy on his front steps.
Then he lifts his head and still through the man's eyes

he sees the softness of late afternoon light on the street
where the man has spent his entire life, sees the green
of summer, white Victorian houses as through a white fog
so they shimmer and flicker before him. Looking past
the houses, past the first fields, he sees the reddening
sky of sunset, sees the land rushing west as if it wanted
to smash itself as completely as a cup thrown to the floor,
violently pursuing the sky with great spirals of red wind.

Abruptly the boy steps back. When he looks again into
the man's eyes, they appear bottomless and sad; and he
wants to touch his arm, say he's sorry about his mother,
sorry he's crazy, sorry he lets urine run down his leg
and wears a dress. Instead, he gives him his paper
and leaves. As he raises his bike, he looks out toward
red sky and darkening earth, and they seem poised
like two animals that have always hated each other,
each fiercely wanting to tear out the other's throat:
black dog, red dog—now more despairing, more resolved.

Stephen Dobyns

PRIMER

This kid got so dirty
Playing in the ashes

When they called him home,
When they yelled his name over the ashes,

It was a lump of ashes
That answered.

Little lump of ashes, they said,
Here's another lump of ashes for dinner,

To make you sleepy,
And make you grow strong.

Charles Simic

PUER ETERNIS

We still play. And pray that our legs will last.

For we would be that boy again, alone in the school yard, his heart filled with the sky and the vision of the hoop. The winter clouds explode with his longing, his feet numb on the frozen pavement, his hands red and swollen.

Step light, sweet child, weave through the cold air and glide for your lay-up. Make it.

He practices, he practices.

Driven by his legs and the dream of flying, he prays: Please let me make it.

Not for fame, not for fortune, not even for a girl, but himself deep in the vision of his own magnificence. There is no end to his desire. He must be perfect from every side. The clouds wait for him to reach their thunder, and he pivots, leaps, and twirls into the twilight.

He dribbles dark streets and shoots to himself through the market town. Swish, swish, he never misses.

And comes home exhausted, ball at his side, hungry for a huge dinner to grow immense. He pores over the sports page and tapes his heroes on the bedroom wall. He adventures into the night to watch them close. They are gods in their luminous uniforms and he's in love with them. The time will come when he too will carry a duffle and wear a letter on his coat. Beautiful girls will cheer his name and he too will take his place on the great court.

It happens, the glow of the moon on the snowy walk and flash of the bright gym. Earth odor of the locker room and his genitals snug in the jock strap. Squeak of the magic floor and the drum of balls in warm-up. His heart leaps.

And now his arms will shine and his face will flush and throb. He bobs. He shakes his hands.

Will he make it? Will he float beatific through the wild chanting?

Please, he prays, please let me make it.

And become beautiful like the deer and the wolf and even the eagle, the innocent animal he would worship in himself, eternally hunting and hunted, body to body in the sacred dance.

Please.

But neither struggle nor desire nor the clouds themselves can help him, and no boy escapes the inevitable wound.

For he's not as good as he wants to be and someone is always better.

He learns to hate in order to win.

He can't stand to lose.

He turns and punches his best friend.

The crowd is merciless and he lets go of his vision.

He falls.

He becomes a man.

And the years pass by on a long journey of retreat.

Yet always beneath the scar in his eyes there lives the image of that angel who once ran to get chosen in every Saturday morning, the longing to be great and the joy of pretzels and soda while he waited.

And now we have passed forty.

And come to the court from a troubled marriage or money problems, from the suicide of a friend and a painful failure in the mirror when we shave.

Now there is no crowd as we walk into the gym and undress. The butcher, the baker, the lawyer, the teacher, the writer, the painter, the cabinet-maker, the builder, the salesman and the therapist. Cigarette smokers, beer drinkers. Dreamers of beautiful women and perfect work. Praising athletes half our age.

We want him back, the boy now bald and grey who puffs and grunts up court, gluttonous for another shot. Our knees won't last forever and yet we still keep driving. Not for fame, not for fortune, but to share whatever it is that keeps us alive.

Now we need each other to make sides.

Now we apologize for bursts of rage.

And recognize each other's wounds.

Dear life, we are humble in your grace and praise our breath.

Send us now to each other and the vision of the boy who once roamed a strange neighborhood in search of a hoop.

Peter Najarian

SONS SEEING FATHERS

"Wolf silence between them"

INTIMATE MEN

Age-bitten father,
son, sip
nursing home coffee, send
clouds from smuggled cigars
out the room's pried view.

Their smiles are quarter moons.
Their eyelids pat the drowsy
wolf silence between them.

Irvin Moen

MEMORY, 1930

There are continuities in memory, but
useless, dissimilar. My sister's

recollection of what happened won't
serve me. I sit, intent, fat,

the youngest of the suddenly
disjunct family, whose father is

being then driven in an ambulance
across the lawn, in the snow, to die.

Robert Creeley

YOUR FATHER OVER YOUR RIGHT SHOULDER
for Phil Woods

He watches quietly,
floats above you to prove
the dead are active,
waits for you to cross the street
toward a woman's house
he once entered,
pushes his weight
on your back when he rings
the doorbell and no one answers.

Your father hides
over your shoulder,
but you finish the letter to him
that could kill you
if you sent it,
sentences around many questions,
a few words misspelled in the late night.

He bothers you when
you look over your shoulder,
and is good at getting back in place
when you go on and try
to shake him off,
that breathing on your neck.

He follows you everywhere
and you want to reach back
and touch him, feel
sharp whiskers on his chin,
a face you never touched,
the head that rests on your shoulder
right before you fall asleep.

Ray Gonzalez

MY FATHER'S SONG

Wanting to say things,
I miss my father tonight.
His voice, the slight catch,
the depth from his thin chest,
the tremble of emotion
in something he has just said
to his son, his song:

We planted corn one spring at Acu—
we planted several times
but this one particular time
I remember the soft damp sand
in my hand.

My father had stopped at one point
to show me an overturned furrow;
the plowshare had unearthed
the burrow nest of a mouse
in the soft moist sand.

Very gently, he scooped tiny pink animals
into the palm of his hand
and told me to touch them.
We took them to the edge
of the field and put them in the shade
of a sand moist clod.

I remember the very softness
of cool and warm sand and tiny alive mice
and my father saying things.

Simon J. Ortiz

LOCH LOMOND
                    for my father

You were struck first
by the trees, how they came
to the very edge of the water,
and how, in certain shallow inlets,
the top branches of madrone
broke through the surface of the lake.
We followed the shoreline fishing.
Loose beads of lead weights
rolled from one side of the boat
to the other, bouncing as we
shifted ourselves gracelessly
from seat to seat. The wind,
wrinkling the water like a sheet
of paper, kept us cool and dry.
We said little. The thin air,
the worried hum of the electric motor
seemed to silence us, limit
our speech to reflections on lures,
casts, the inscrutable nature of fish.
What we wanted to say escaped us,
moved ceaselessly away like ripples
from the boat, which seemed
to lose its buoyancy as the day went on.
I felt we were sinking. When the light
began to fail I turned the boat

Gary Young

THOSE WINTER SUNDAYS

Sundays too my father got up early
and put his clothes on in the blueblack cold,
then with cracked hands that ached
from labor in the weekday weather made
banked fires blaze. No one ever thanked him.

I'd wake and hear the cold splintering, breaking.
When the rooms were warm, he'd call,
and slowly I would rise and dress,
fearing the chronic angers of that house,

Speaking indifferently to him,
who had driven out the cold
and polished my good shoes as well.
What did I know, what did I know
of love's austere and lonely offices?

Robert Hayden

MY FATHER IN THE DISTANCE

You crossed the pasture to the cornfield.
I cultivated toward the end of the row
where you waited in your faded overalls,
your hand resting on a fence post.
Your hand, only once, had rested on my head,
while we stood at the parlor window
and watched sparrows hopping on the porch.
As the corn rows shortened between us,
I saw again man and boy photographed
on glass, framed in the window.

Your hand dropped from the post.
I thought you had come with new orders.
Go home and fix the well pump?
Grind some hog feed?
I stopped the tractor and climbed down.
We talked. Talked about how the cockleburs
were almost gone, how the field
looked greener after that last rain,
how the corn should be knee high
by the 4th of July—important things.

Leo Dangel

MY FATHER'S FIGHTS

His best
were the two
between Chuck Davey
& Chico Vejar:

Davey, balding,
insurance man
in trunks
with a jab
precise as a surgeon;

Vejar, Latin legs,
legs from where
they grow up playing soccer,
that don't fold,
his own blood
shiny on his gloves;

My father,
in the stuffed chair
facing the Zenith,
throwing so many punches
no one could
get near.

Stuart Dybek

MY FATHER'S KITCHEN

I don't know when he started hating Blacks or why,
though we argued hours in his kitchen,
fake brick pasted to one wall like grief.

In '65, when riots started to blister
and he drove close enough to get spotted,
I don't know if any rocks hit the car,
just that he threw it into reverse
and hauled ass back to this side of the river.

And I didn't know my flesh would take on his age and wrinkles,
as we sat facing each other, his bitterness become mine
until neither my mother nor my wife could pry us apart
from our friable mass of English—
that I would match him mask for mask
as we glared in those black vinyl chairs.
Dirty Commie, he hissed.
I raised my beer and smiled in his face.

How many generations back in Poland,
a farmer's hovel with dirt floor
and dirtier logic, did they also think
there could be a winner? There was only mirror
and reflection. The dark
rose from the bottom of the river.

We were the last ones awake, we had forgotten
the others, could have gone on sitting there
for a hundred years without moving,
without any sign of surrender.

John Minczeski

MERLE BASCOM'S .22

"I was twelve when my father gave me this .22
Mossberg carbine—hand-made, with a short octagonal
barrel, stylish as an Indian fighter posing
for a photograph. We ripped up Bokar coffee cans
set into the sandbank by the track—competitive
and companionable. He was a good shot, although
his hands already trembled. Or I walked with my friend
Paul who loved airplanes and wanted to be a pilot,
and carried my rifle loosely, pointing it downward;
I aimed at squirrels and missed. Later I shot woodchucks
that ate my widowed mother's peas and Kentucky
Wonders when I visited on weekends from college,
or drove up from my Boston suburb, finding the gun
in its closet behind the woodstove. Ten years ago
my mother died; I sold up, and moved here with my work
and my second wife, gladly taking my tenancy
in the farmhouse where I intended to live and die.
I used my rifle on another generation
of woodchucks that ate our beans. One autumn an old friend
from college stayed with us after a nervous breakdown:
trembling from electroshock, depressed, suicidal.
I wrapped the octagonal Mossberg in a burlap
bag and concealed it under boards in the old grainshed.
In our quiet house he strengthened and stopped shaking.
When he went home I neglected to retrieve my gun,
and the next summer woodchucks took over the garden.

I let them. Our lives fitted mountain, creek, and hayfield.
Long days like minnows in the pond quickened and were still.
When I looked up from Plutarch another year had passed.
One Sunday the choir at our church sang Whittier's hymn
ending with 'the still small voice of calm.' Idly I thought,
'I must ask them to sing that hymn at my funeral.'
Soon after, I looked for the .22 in the shed,
half expecting it to have vanished, but finding it
wrapped intact where I left it, hardly rusted. I spent
a long evening taking it apart and cleaning it;
I thought of my father's hands shaking as he aimed it.
Then I restored the Mossberg to its accustomed place
in the closet behind the stove. At about this time
I learned that my daughter-in-law was two months pregnant:
It would be the first grandchild. One day I was walking
alone and imagined a granddaughter visiting:
She loved the old place; she swam in the summer pond with us;
she walked with us in red October; she grew older, she fell
in love with a neighbor, she married . . . As I daydreamed,
suddenly I was seized by a fit of revulsion:
I thought: 'Must I go through all that again? Must I live
another twenty years?' It was as if a body
rose from a hole where I had buried it years ago
while my first marriage was twisting and thrashing to death.
One night I was drunk and lost control of my Beetle
off 128 near my ranchhouse. I missed a curve
at seventy miles an hour and careened toward a stone wall.
In a hundredth of a second I knew I would die;
and, as joy fired through my body, I knew something else.
But the car slowed itself on rocks and settled to rest
between an elm and a maple; I sat breathing,
feeling the joy leach out, leaving behind the torment
and terror of my desire. Now I felt this affliction
descend again and metastasize through my body.
Today I drove ninety miles, slowly, seatbelt fastened,
to North Andover and Paul's house, where he lives flying
out of Logan for United. I asked him to hide
the firing pin of an octagonal .22.

He nodded and took it from my hands without speaking.
I cannot throw it away; it was my father's gift."

Donald Hall

MENTOR

In this version Odysseus was just too busy,
so his son went instead,
a little disgusted at how comfortable
the old man had become.

And it was fun living by his wits,
wryly observing the passing scene
with the smugness of all travelers,
but after ten years even Troy
made him think of dust and ashes.

So when the world had finally shrunk
to his satisfaction,
he returned to discover the city free of plots,
his mother still mistress of the house,
and there on his table
the book he had always wanted to read,
with some passages underlined
by his father.

Mark Osaki

HE WANTED TO SHOW ME

I stayed out all night and was drunk.
My mother called my father
and my father came

to wait, sitting out the night
in silence like two monks seeking Nirvana.
They found it when I arrived. Me,
I was that spiritual thing
they were waiting for. My father smiled
and grabbed my neck like he would
a lobster claw trying to squeeze the tender
meat from the joints. I looked in his mouth
past the brown tartar on his teeth
past the vapors rising from too much Scotch
past the bumps on his tongue
past that sprig of meat which hangs in the back of your throat.
I looked way down
into his gut and saw a pool of black
scummy stuff boiling.
He punched me in the eye because he
wanted to show me.
He kneed me in the groin because he
wanted to show me.
He pulled my hair and threw me to the floor because he
wanted to show me.
Then he up-chucked the boiling black scummy stuff
from his belly all over me because he
wanted to show me
what a young man's life was really worth.

Peter Spiro

THE SPRING FATHER STOPPED SNOWING

That spring, Father stopped snowing.
He let out a long sigh, the last gust of wind
after a blizzard. He dropped his newspaper,
turned his palms upward, his face flushed pink again.

None of us believed he had stopped—
the TV screen still vibrated with white flecks,
countertops were covered by flakes of pie dough,
the dining room table was drifted over with lace.

But it was true—all that snow began to melt,
the basement filling with a foot of water.
After the lights went out, he waded toward the fuse box,
a candle in front of his forehead.
Not dangerous at all, he told us, water up to his waist.

We believed him, until the flood lifted the house
from its foundation.

He looked thinner
as he took us to the swaying attic, opened closets,
showed us family photo albums:
great grandmothers and grandfathers we'd never seen,
their eyes frosted over.

Trying to lighten the house, he dropped them
out the window
as water climbed the steep stairs.

On the roof, he handed us each our baby picture,
gave Mom their wedding photo.
Keep these in your pockets, he told us,
they might buoy you up.

He slid down the shingles onto a cake of ice,
pushed away from the house with a gaunt smile.

Bill Meissner

Father Gladly

Father in the shower
gladly recalls his son
Here a remnant of the yard
the white rose
his son pulled down
One petal
bruised by small son-hands
still shivers
Ahhh
There were days when
whack whack whack
his heart
was never silent
At night
Good night
father
built himself a house of stars
Son son
father was not so far
Father sniffs
the lather flower
between his breasts
The smell reaches up
with small son-hands
father gladly
pushes away again

Father Guiltily

eats himself to sleep
Sunflower seeds secret scoops
Night's face gets long
Father's beard pops out
Father swallows
under a small white sky

Sleeps
Sticky peach halves
family lives
Father poles a barge
Father poles very far
Back and forth
a key turns in a lock
The clock

Father Gravely

prepares to scold his son
Lightning dribbles from his lips
In his wake
a line of fathers
leaps up straight
Beneath his brows
the blue cheek
blackens
When it is done
father's fathers
gravely touch
their son

Father Grossly

underestimates his tax
Debits his assets multiplies
divisions
On father
the world depends
Father deducts it
Through thick dollar snow
father crunches
slowly slowly
toward the nothing
he owes

Father Gently

Sticks sticks
we gather
There are webs everywhere
he and I
Wet webs
All the spiders are gone
he says
I look down and there
spider-white
he is
I reach down I
touch something
sticky
wet dirty
mine
Sticks become branches
up up and up
Oh yes
When I touch sky
he is gone

Jay Ladin

PASSAGES

The first poem in the book
I just happen to open
is about a dead father—
how many like it I've read
before I knew what they meant.
And now, every book I pick up
has one of those poems in it—
every book in every room.

Listen: sometimes he and I would
sit alone, for hours, not talking.
I couldn't leave—he wanted me home,
not to talk to or listen to,
just to sit there, two aging men . . .
Do you know how it is
to hate somebody for leaving
when you need him there?

Mark Vinz

MORNING

He cradled his head in those hands
which might have kept it,
which might have grown into part of his head
but I would come in, and call him, *daddy*,
and they would let go.
Every day I saw a man
who wore one suit
and had a beard hid under his skin.
It was black.
I could see it in the light
see its darkness
as it came out first through his eyes
precisely in their centers
when he looked at me.
Under his suit, under his shirt
and undershirt, it started coming
through his chest too, and on his back.
He thought about his beard
because it was tangled in his head.
It made him unhappy,
his head was heavy
and sometimes he rested it in those hands
letting his beard come out through

their backs, through the backs
of his palms, the backs of his fingers,
through the backs of things lost.

Alberto Rios

EPIGRAMS FOR MY FATHER
(John Henry Redmond, Sr.)

I
Fatherlore: papa-rites, daddyhood;
      Run & trapsong: Search & dodgesong.
Steelhammeringman.
Gunbouter; whiskeywarrior.
Nightgod!
Moonballer/brawler grown old.
Slaughterhouse/river mackman:
Hightale teller & totempoleman.

II
Wanderer across waters:
Folkbrilliance & Geniusgrit;
Railraging railsplitter:
Railrage! Railrage!
IC & *BM&O* & *MoPac* & *Midnight Special:*
Freight train . . . . . . bring my daddy back!

III
Stone-story. The story of stone, brokenbricks—
Rocks hurled in pleasure & rage,
Pebbles soft & silent:
Home-dome is a blues-hard head.

IV

45-degree hat, Bulldurham butt bailing from lips;
Gabardine shining shining shining
Above white silk socks—
        satin man
        satin man
        silksure & steelstrong
        hammerhold on life
        hammerhold on life

V

Sun-son. Stonebone. Blackblitz.
Fatherlore. Struggledeep: Afridark, Afrolark,
        daddydepth—
        Riverbottom song.

Eugene B. Redmond

(U N T I T L E D)

Walking along, he was nearly always happy.
Coming down a street, he moved
by letting himself go, not quite
boat motion but some way
his shoulders (in spite of those boxy suits!)
used to occupy the air in curves.
Other people walk, but my father
sort of gathered as he came,
a natural heavyweight,
feet pumping a secret treadle
that only he understood, gait conducted
by the delicate slabs of his hands.
Others move like burglaries
in progress, songs lifting, or street drills,
but Daddy walked like hospitality,
like warmth in motion. The sky rippled around him

as he came, so that I really thought
the parted air was somehow changed
because he passed through it, happy.
And remembering this, I find myself happy.

Frank Steele

MARIO LANZA DEFEATS LUCIANO PAVAROTTI IN A TENOR COMPETITION HELD ON A TURNTABLE IN MY FATHER'S LIVING ROOM

Selections
M'Appari; La donna è mobile; Celeste Aida; Vesti la giubba.

Range
Pavarotti, while unmistakably Italian and a great tenor,
can't match the range of Lanza, who, having fallen apart
into stereo after his death, now ranges wraith-like through
my father's mind, throaty and full, high-low as siren.

Class
Pavarotti's got class, takes lessons, kisses hands
and while singing in French sounds like he's singing in French.
Lanza's got no class at all, often drank pints of scotch
and chianti during four loud plates of pasta, touched
greasy lips to silk sleeve, perspired freely.

Size
Pavarotti looks, father says, "wide as he is tall."
Lanza, long dead and still, now most likely's raw cold bone,
thin and sere, insubstantial, thin black discs
twirling on a spindle.

Tragedy
Pavarotti lives, eats, bows, appears on television, while Lanza—
father often told us as we grew up sober, middle-class

and Catholic—Lanza, having been dressed in corsets
like some swollen crone during his most intimate love scenes,
finally ate himself to death in Hollywood, buffeted about
by shame and his great gifts, the veins
in his head and heart popping like flashbulbs.

Results
Pavarotti's good, but he's not dead. He can't sing to father
of his youth, a vast lovely war and the world in uniform,
a beauty dim and constant, the stumbling rush to age.

David Citino

OFF THE RECORD

In the attic I find the notes
he kept in college
over forty years ago: *Hooray*
for Thanksgiving vacation! he wrote
in the margin of Psych 102.
And for a moment I can see him there,

feel the exuberance surge through
that odd cell of his body
where I am still
a secret code uncompleted, a piece
of DNA, some ancient star-stuff.
And then I find a recording of me

from 1948, when he was twenty-two
and I was three, and I can see,
from my perch up on his shoulders,
him stopping at the gaudy arcade,
plugging his lucky quarter into
the future where we'd always be.

Maybe imagination is just
a form of memory after all, locked
deep in the double helix of eternity.
Or maybe the past is but one more
phantasmagoric invention we use
to fool ourselves into someone else's shoes.

It is not my voice I want to hear
on memory's fading page, on imagination's disk.
It is my father's in the background
prompting me, doing his best
to stay off the record, his hushed
instructions vanishing in static.

Ronald Wallace

THE HOUSES

Up on the mountain where nobody is looking
a man forty years old in a gray felt hat
is trying to light a fire in the springtime

up on the mountain where nobody
except God and the man's son are looking
the father in a white shirt is trying
to get damp sticks to burn in the spring noon

he crumples newspaper from the luggage compartment
of the polished black Plymouth parked under the young leaves
a few feet away in the overgrown wagon track
that he remembers from another year
he is thinking of somewhere else as the match flame blows

he has somewhere else in mind that nobody knows
as the flame climbs into the lines of print and they curl
and set out unseen into the sunlight
he needs more and more paper and more matches
and the wrapping from hot dogs and from buns
gray smoke gets away among the slender trees

it does not occur to the son to wonder
what prompted his father to come up here
suddenly this one morning and bring his son
though the father looks like a stranger on the mountain
breaking sticks and wiping his hand on the paper
as he crumples it and blowing into the flames
but when his father takes him anywhere they are both strangers

and the father has long forgotten that the son
is standing there and he is surprised
when the smoke blows in his face and he turns
and sees parallel with the brim the boy looking at him
having been told that he could not help and to wait there
and since it is a day without precedents the son
hears himself asking the father whether he may
please see what is down the wagon track and he surprises
himself hearing the father say yes but don't go far

and be very careful and come right back
so the son turns to his right and steps over
the gray stones and leaves his father making
a smoky fire on the flat sloping rock
and after a few steps the branches close overhead
he walks in the green day in the smell of thawed earth
and a while further on he comes to a turn to the right
and the open light of cleared ground falling away
still covered with the dry grass of last year
by a dark empty barn he can see light through

and before the barn on the left a white house
newly painted with wide gray steps leading
up to the gray floor of the porch where the windows

are newly washed and without curtains so that he
can look into the empty rooms and see the doors
standing open and he can look out
through windows on the other side into the sky
while the grass new and old stands deep all around the house
that is bare in readiness for somebody
the wind is louder than in the wood
the grass hissing and the clean panes rattling

he looks at rusted handles beside bushes
and with that thinks of his father and turns back
into the shadowy wagon track and walks
slowly tree by tree stone by stone under
the green tiers of leaves until he comes
to the smell of smoke and then the long pile of stones
before the clearing where his father is bending
over the fire and turns at the son's voice and calls him
a good boy for coming back and asks whether
he's hungry and holds out a paper plate
they stand in the smoke holding plates while the father
asks the blessing and afterwards the son tells him

of the white house the new paint the clean windows
into empty rooms and sky and nobody in sight
but his father says there is no such house along there
and he warns the son not to tell stories
but to eat and after a moment the son
surprises them both by insisting that he has
seen it all just as he said and again the father
scolds him this time more severely returning
from somewhere else to take up his sternness
until the son starts to cry and asks him
to come and see for himself after they have eaten

so when the plates have been burned and the fire
put out carefully and the car packed they walk
without a word down the wagon track where the light
seems to have dimmed as though rain might be on its way
and the trees are more remote than the boy

had thought but before long they reach the opening
where the track turns to the right and there is
the glare of the dry grass but no house no barn
and the son repeats I saw them but the father says
I don't want to hear any more about it

in a later year the father takes the boy
taller now and used to walking by himself
to an old farm in the middle of the state
where he busies himself in the small house he has bought
while the son having been told that he cannot help
walks down the lane past the vacant corn crib and barn
past the red shale banks where the lane descends
beside unkempt pastures with their springs and snakes
into the woods and onto a wooden bridge

still on his father's land he watches the dark water
flow out from under low branches and the small fish
flickering in glass over the black bed and as he
turns and climbs the lane on the far side he sees
to his right below him on the edge of the stream
a low house painted yellow with a wide porch
a gun leaning beside the front door and a dog's chain
fastened to the right of the steps but no dog visible

there appears to be no one in the house and the boy goes
on up the lane through the woods and across pastures
and coming back sees that nothing has changed
the gun still by the door the chain in the same place
he watches to see whether anything moves
he listens he stares through the trees wondering
where the dog is and when someone will come home

then he crosses the stream and returns to his father
indoors and in the evening he remembers
to ask who is living in the yellow house
in the woods on the far side of the stream
which he had understood was his father's land
but his father tells him there is no house there

by then they have left the farm and are driving home
and the son tells the father of the gun by the door
the dog's chain by the front steps and the father
says yes that is his land beyond the stream
but there is no building and nobody living there

the boys stops telling what he has seen
and it is a long time before he comes again
to walk down the lane to the woods and cross the bridge
and see on the far side only trees by the stream

then the farm is sold and the woods are cut and the subject
never brought up again but long after the father
is dead the son sees the two houses

W. S. Merwin

BRIEFCASES

Fifteen years ago I found my father's
    in the family attic, so used
        the shoemaker had to
repair it, and I kept it like love

until it couldn't be kept any more.
    Then my father-in-law died
        and I got his, almost
identical, just the wrong initials

embossed in gold. It's forty years old,
    falling apart, soon
        there'll be nothing
that smells of father-love and that difficulty

of living with fathers, but I'd prefer
    a paper bag to those
        new briefcases
made for men living fast-forward

or those attaché cases that match
    your raincoat and spring open
        like a salute
and a click of heels. I'm going

to put an ad in the paper, "Wanted:
    Old briefcase, accordion style,"
        and I won't care
whose father it belonged to

if it's brown and the divider keeps
    things on their proper side.
        Like an adoption
it's sure to feel natural before long—

a son without a father, but with this
    one briefcase carrying
        a replica
comfortably into the future,

something for an empty hand, sentimental
    the way keeping is
        sentimental, for *keep-*
sake, with clarity and without tears.

Stephen Dunn

PRAYER FOR THE MAN WHO MUGGED MY FATHER, 73

May there be an afterlife.

May you meet him there, the same age as you.
May the meeting take place in a small, locked room.

May the bushes where you hid be there again, leaves tipped with
    razorblades and acid.
May the rifle butt you bashed him with be in his hands.
May the glass in his car window, which you smashed as he sat stopped at a
    red light, be embedded in the rifle-butt and on the floor to break
    your fall.

May the needles the doctors used to stitch his eye, stab your pupils every
    time you hit the wall and then the floor, which will be often.
May my father let you cower for a while, screaming for the mercy you never
    showed.
May he laugh, unload the gun, toss it away; then
May he take you with bare hands.

May those hands, which taught his son to throw a curve and drive a nail and
    hold a frog, feel like cannonballs against your jaw.
May his arms, that powered handstands and made their muscles jump to
    please me, wrap your head and grind your face like stone.
May his chest, thick and hairy as a bear's, feel like a bear's snapping
    your bones.
May the legs, which showed me the flutter kick and carried me miles
    through the woods, feel like tree trunks crushing your only claim to
    manhood as he chops you down.

And when you are down, and he's done with you, which will be soon, since,
    even one-eyed, with brain damage, he's a merciful man,
May the door to the room open and let him stride away to the Valhalla he
    deserves.
May you, bleeding and broken, drag yourself upright.

May you think the worst is over;
You've survived, and may still win.

Then may the door open once more, and let me in.

Charles Harper Webb

A R E Q U I E M

My father, listening to music, that's me,
my legs outstretched upon the bed
as I lean back in my chair. I think of him
in his chair, legs crossed carelessly
and with his musing smile recalling his first wish,
to become a baritone, his smile seeking
after his youth or watching it in the distant past,
untouchable. I am alone, and the opera playing
heightens my loneliness, without son, without father,
without past or present, and my future a problem.

Eh, father, as I listen to your favorite opera
you would have enjoyed my listening and approved
emphatically, while I'd withhold myself,
tentative towards opera, as other matters burned in me,
such as the need to be free,
and so we would argue but soon fall silent
and go our separate ways.

I am alone in my apartment, alone as you were
without me in your last days at about my age.
I am listening to Rossini and thinking of you
affectionately, longing for your presence once more,
of course to wrestle with your character,
the game once again of independence,
but now, now in good humor
because we already know the outcome,

for I am sixty-six, going on sixty-seven,
and you are forever seventy-two.
We are both old men and soon enough
I'll join you. So why quarrel again,
as if two old men could possibly settle
between them what was impossible
to settle in their early days?

David Ignatow

DON'T GROW OLD

I

Old Poet, Poetry's final subject glimmers months ahead
Tender mornings, Paterson roofs snowcovered
Vast
Sky over City Hall tower, Eastside Park's grass terraces & tennis courts
    beside Passaic River
Parts of ourselves gone, sister Rose's apartments, brown corridor'd high
    schools—
Too tired to go out for a walk, too tired to end the War
Too tired to save body
too tired to be heroic
The real close at hand as the stomach
liver pancreas rib
Coughing up gastric saliva
Marriages vanished in a cough
Hard to get up from the easy chair
Hands white feet speckled a blue toe stomach big breasts hanging thin
hair white on the chest
too tired to take off shoes and black sox
                    Paterson, January 12, 1976

I I

He'll see no more Times Square
honkytonk movie marquees, bus stations at midnight
Nor the orange sun ball
rising thru treetops east toward New York's skyline
His velvet armchair facing the window will be empty
He won't see the moon over house roofs
or sky over Paterson's streets.

New York, February 26, 1976

I I I

Wasted arms, feeble knees
    80 years old, hair thin and white
        cheek bonier than I'd remembered—
head bowed on his neck, eyes opened
    now and then, he listened—
I read my father Wordsworth's *Intimations of Immortality*
"*. . . trailing clouds of glory do we come*
    from God, who is our home . . ."
        "That's beautiful," he said, "but it's not true."

"When I was a boy, we had a house
    on Boyd Street, Newark—the backyard
        was a big empty lot full of bushes and tall grass,
    I always wondered what was behind those trees.
When I grew older, I walked around the block,
    and found out what was back there—
        it was a glue factory."

May 18, 1976

I V

Will that happen to me?
Of course, it'll happen to thee.

Will my arms wither away?
Yes yr arm hair will turn gray.

Will my knees grow weak & collapse?
Your knees will need crutches perhaps.

Will my chest get thin?
Your breasts will be hanging skin.

Where will go—my teeth?
You'll keep the ones beneath.

What'll happen to my bones?
They'll get mixed up with stones.

June 1976

V

FATHER DEATH BLUES
Hey Father Death, I'm flying home
Hey poor man, you're all alone
Hey old daddy, I know where I'm going

Father Death, Don't cry any more
Mama's there, underneath the floor
Brother Death, please mind the store

Old Aunty Death Don't hide your bones
Old Uncle Death I hear your groans
O Sister Death how sweet your moans

O Children Deaths go breathe your breaths
Sobbing breasts'll ease your Deaths
Pain is gone, tears take the rest

Genius Death your art is done
Lover Death your body's gone
Father Death I'm coming home

Guru Death your words are true
Teacher Death I do thank you
For inspiring me to sing this Blues

Buddha Death, I wake with you
Dharma Death, your mind is new
Sangha Death, we'll work it through

Suffering is what was born
Ignorance made me forlorn
Tearful truths I cannot scorn

Father Breath once more farewell
Birth you gave was no thing ill
My heart is still, as time will tell.

July 8, 1976 (Over Lake Michigan)

VI

Near the Scrap Yard my Father'll be Buried
Near Newark Airport my father'll be
Under a Winston Cigarette sign buried
On Exit 14 Turnpike NJ South
Through the tollgate Service Road 1 my father buried
Past Merchants Refrigerating concrete on the cattailed marshes
past the Budweiser Anheuser-Busch brick brewery
in B'Nai Israel Cemetery behind a green painted iron fence
where there used to be a paint factory and farms
where Pennick makes chemicals now
under the Penn Central power Station
transformers & wires, at the borderline
between Elizabeth and Newark, next to Aunt Rose
Gaidemack, near Uncle Harry Meltzer
one grave over from Abe's wife Anna my father'll be buried.

July 9, 1976

VII

What's to be done about Death?
Nothing, nothing
Stop going to school No. 6 Paterson, N.J., in 1937?
Freeze time tonight, with a headache, at quarter to 2 A.M.?
Not go to Father's funeral tomorrow morn?
Not go back to Naropa teach Buddhist poetics all summer?
Not be buried in the cemetery near Newark Airport some day?

Paterson, July 11, 1976

Allen Ginsberg

66

MY FATHER AT 85

His large ears hear
everything.
A hermit wakes
and sleeps
in a hut underneath
his gaunt cheeks.
His eyes blue,
alert, dis-
appointed and suspicious
complain
I do not bring him
the same sort of jokes
the nurses do.
He is a small bird
waiting to be fed,
mostly beak,
an eagle or a vulture
or the Pharoah's servant
just before death.
My arm on the bedrail
rests there,
relaxed, with new love.
All I know of the Troubadours
I bring
to this bed.
I do not want
or need
to be shamed
by him
any longer.
The general of shame
has discharged him
and left him in this
small provincial
Egyptian town.
If I do not wish
to shame him, then

why not
love him?
His long hands,
large, veined, capable,
can still retain
hold of what he wanted.
But is that
what he desired?
Some powerful
river of desire
goes on flowing
through him.
He never phrased
what he desired,
and I am
his son.

Robert Bly

OPENING UP

"Breathe deeply now." Dr. Cooley fits the
black inhalation mask above my father's face the
chrome fittings, the varicolored tanks of oxygen, the
cyclopropane and nitrous oxide the
sweet cool mist the
mask's expensive rubber bends like soft leather my
father's body going limp the
women's hands press needles into his hot arms the
white tape creases over locked in steel and blood they
are forcing something down his throat it
is a plastic crowbar quickly the
table expands

Cooley touches the knife to your chest
splits the skin going red

blade scraping bone
down the length of your body
Cooley receives the bone saw
thaaaaaa, thaaaaaaaaaaap
wisps of blue smoke rise
moist dust powders the doctor's sleeve
as he strains, strains the
electric buzzing weakens, whines
your breast bone separates
from bottom to top

Cooley fits a retractor along the
raw edges of your ribcage
inch by inch
he opens this cavity
revealing 15,000 packs of Camels later the
slick mottled surfaces of your lungs

Now Cooley lifts the pink pericardial membrane
scissors it carefully open and
there like a dark fist
is your heart its
scarred, irregular bulk
still undulating
still undulating

Joe David Bellamy

WATER

The sound of 36 pines side by side surrounding
the yard and swaying all night like individual hymns is the sound
of water, which is the oldest sound,
the first sound we forgot.

At the ocean
my brother stands in water
to his knees, his chest bare, hard, his arms
thick and muscular. He is no swimmer.
In water
my sister is no longer
lonely. Her right leg is crooked and smaller
than her left, but she swims straight.
Her whole body is a glimmering fish.

Water is my father's life-sign.
Son of water who'll die by water,
the element which rules his life shall take it.
After being told so by a wise man in Shantung,
after almost drowning twice,
he avoided water. But the sign of water
is a flowing sign, going where its children go.

Water has invaded my father's
heart, swollen, heavy,
twice as large. Bloated
liver. Bloated legs.
The feet have become balloons.
A respirator mask makes him look
like a diver. When I lay my face
against his—the sound of water
returning.

The sound of washing
is the sound of sighing,
is the only sound
as I wash my father's feet—
those lonely twins
who have forgotten one another—
one by one in warm water
I tested with my wrist.
In soapy water
they're two dumb fish
whose eyes close in a filmy dream.

I dry, then powder them
with talc rising in clouds
like dust lifting
behind jeeps, a truck where he sat
bleeding through his socks.
1949, he's 30 years old,
his toenails pulled out,
his toes beaten a beautiful
violet that reminds him
of Hunan, barely morning
in the yard, and where
he walked, the grass springing back
damp and green.

The sound of rain
outlives us. I listen,
someone is whispering.
Tonight, it's water
the curtains resemble, water
drumming on the steel cellar door, water
we crossed to come to America,
water I'll cross to go back,
water which will kill my father.
The sac of water we live in.

Li-Young Lee

ALVEOLI

> (Tooth sockets in the jaw. Cells in a honeycomb.
> Formed with the tongue touching the ridge at the
> roof of the mouth. Air sacs in the lungs.)

Going down over what's left
of Coney Island pavillions with the sun that's lasted this long
before sinking into blood-orange sandbar rim
of child's paradise not so far away

it can't be walked in
                    as we used to . . .
                                        Nat and I now drive
through snow on the Belt Parkway from the hospital
where Pop, finally retired at 88 and fading fast, had said
to me of all he might have said to me
about dying: "This is my job,"
and I recall his favorite quote from the gospel
of the clock-watching god:
        "Time is money, and money is time.
        Make money in good time,
        but don't do time for making money."

Last here 5 years ago, I flew
to Nat's side after his VW was crushed
by a speeding car at an intersection in Brownsville.
The STOP sign—down since the days of O'Dwyer—had been left
facing skyward . . . to warn off what?—fallout? UFO's? highflying
suicides whose vision would grow
sharper midway in their dive?

While I flew the friendly skies—the only creature
able to eat chicken-soup 30,000 feet in the air—
Nat lay eleven hours under the knife,
being pieced together; a quarter-
sized scar at the base of his throat
is all you can see
when he has his clothes on.

Since then he's had six cars—all Cadillacs—
stolen from him.
To no longer draw attention, he explains,
he's bought the Lincoln Continental—two-tone,
with wire wheels, CB radio, and armor
shaped like grillwork—we're riding in. He lifts the CB and,
by his grin, I know
he's going to clown for me:
                        "Breaker, breaker, this is

One Crazy Kibbe* calling the Jewelery King. Hey good buddy,
what's my traffic like on the ol' Skyline to Starret City?
Can you read me? This is One Crazy Kibbe, just outta the bin,
lost in the frost, calling the Jewelery King for some info.
Can you give me a copy, good buddy?"

                                 "It's poetry," I say, and mean it,
then hear a squawk of voices cooked from transcontinental grits and static
crisscross the channel, but no Jewelery King.
We're headed toward south Jersey where Nat and his wife, once more trying
for a girl, have just had their fourth boy in a row.

I think of Pop; my first sight of his sleeping
face so hollowly melted down; yellow
wrist-tag on hand holding bedsheet and loose white hair-tuft
give him the look of a shrewd rakish lifer. Opening his eyes,
I am surprised he recognizes me, then gets startled.
I take his hand and, tipping forward, feel myself pour
into a long last-minute kiss of hopeless retrieval, and lean
over him as over an edge
of a roaring high wind I have seen in times of stress before, but
no person had been in it,
and now there was a person.

We've brought some things—money, stamps, electric shaver—
"Don't," he says; his eyes I don't ever remember being so
nearly all black and worn out with ardor and fear
stare at the open doorway.
"Don't leave anything. They come when I sleep and steal everything.
They don't come when I call them to help me
take three steps to the toilet."

I wonder about the cancer in his prostate and the pain he's feeling
not allowing the doctors to remove his testicles.
The germ acts on the cell like a spermatozoon, taking
shape like foetal tissue, like a child never completed,

Kibbe: a meat-filled Arabic pastry.

that goes on, never reaching a limit. The tumor
spreads—spreading is all it can do; it would spread
to infinity in the cells if infinity could spread
in the body and the body with it.

"I want to go home," he says. "Take me, sneak
me out, tell them you're taking me for a walk.
I have money, I'll let you
have money so you won't be miserable like me."
He turns to Nat: "He'll go soon,
like always. You take me out of here. If not,
you're leaving me a dead man.
I'll throw myself from the window."

                              For a moment, I forget
we're on the ground floor, recalling
the man on a panel of survivors who told of capsizing
with his three children in a storm at sea,
and having to choose, chose to hold onto the two youngest . . . a choice,
luckily, he did not have to carry through, though
the guilt was still with him long after they were all rescued.

Follows a moment which feels like centuries
breathing down our necks as Pop awaits
a reply he won't receive in a silence with no end,
and I feel us slowly enclosed in a lowering cone
fitting tight as a phone-booth, where nothing moves
while something is sifted; nothing stirs
while something is shaken; nothing distracts
from his tilted face lifting toward me
on a shifty hot wind that can't be trusted; that has
roared through time in a sudden overcharge of current;
and, rolling all the light in its path up behind him, opens
a hole through which air rushes out,
and the infinite distance closer.
This is no dream,
unless the eyes, too, are a dream.
If he fell back now, it would take years
for his head to hit the pillow.

Something swift, final, not fully understood
passes between us. Too late, I think, but how
can I be sure since that day, on Van Ness Avenue, when what
I thought were char-broil fumes from Hamburger Heaven
were from Delmore's Mortuary behind me.

Now I carefully bring his legs around and down
to the floor, encircle him with my arms under his arms and lift him,
deadweight, to standing position.
Nat comes over and helps but it's no good, the three of us together
can't make it halfway to the door.

                 Just then, the face of a pretty black
                             nurse
appears from around the doorframe, teasingly, as if it were a burlesque
                             curtain,
and she, cinnamon candy. Smiling, she comes in, checks us over,
her flashing black eyes looking blacker, brighter
for being set in all the surrounding white, and motions us time's up.
We ease him back into bed, make a date to return,
and walk out to where the leafless fossil-tips of trees
sway delicately stiff and curved in a driving wind and drive back
to the living of winter.

Jack Marshall

THE HOSPITAL WINDOW

I have just come down from my father.
Higher and higher he lies
Above me in a blue light
Shed by a tinted window.
I drop through six white floors
And then step out onto pavement.

Still feeling my father ascend,
I start to cross the firm street,
My shoulder blades shining with all
The glass the huge building can raise.
Now I must turn round and face it,
And know his one pane from the others.

Each window possesses the sun
As though it burned there on a wick.
I wave, like a man catching fire.
All the deep-dyed windowpanes flash,
And, behind them, all the white rooms
They turn to the color of Heaven.

Ceremoniously, gravely, and weakly,
Dozens of pale hands are waving
Back, from inside their flames.
Yet one pure pane among these
Is the bright, erased blankness of nothing.
I know that my father is there,

In the shape of his death still living.
The traffic increases around me
Like a madness called down on my head.
The horns blast at me like shotguns,
And drivers lean out, driven crazy—
But now my propped-up father

Lifts his arm out of stillness at last.
The light from the window strikes me
And I turn as blue as a soul,
As the moment when I was born.
I am not afraid for my father—
Look! He is grinning; he is not

Afraid for my life, either,
As the wild engines stand at my knees
Shredding their gears and roaring,
And I hold each car in its place
For miles, inciting its horn
To blow down the walls of the world

That the dying may float without fear
In the bold blue gaze of my father.
Slowly I move to the sidewalk
With my pin-tingling hand half dead
At the end of my bloodless arm.
I carry it off in amazement,

High, still higher, still waving,
My recognized face fully mortal,
Yet not; not at all, in the pale,
Drained, otherworldly, stricken,
Created hue of stained glass.
I have just come down from my father.

James Dickey

TO MY FATHER, DYING IN A SUPERMARKET

At first it is difficult
to see you
are dropping dead—

you seem lost
in thought, adjusting your tie
as if to rehearse

some imaginary speech
though of course beginning
to fall,

your mouth opening wider
than I have ever seen
a mouth,

your hands deep
in your shirt,
going down

into the cheeses, making the sound
that is not
my name,

that explains nothing
over and over,
going away

into your hands
into your face,
leaving this great body

on its knees,
the father
of my body

which holds me
in this world,
watching you go

on falling
through the Musak,
making the sound

that is not my name,
that will never
explain anything, oh father,

stranger, all dressed up
and deserting me
for the last time.

Wesley McNair

---

1 9 3 3

My father entered the kingdom of roots
    his head as still as a stone
    (Laid out in black with a white tie
    he blinked
    and I told no one
    except myself over and over)
    laid out long and gray

The hands that stroked my head
    the voice in the dark asking
    he drove the car all the way to the river
      where the ships burned
    he rang with keys and coins
    he knew the animals and their names
      touched the nose of the horse
      and kicked the German dog away
    he brought Ray Estrada from Mexico in his 16th year
      scolded him like a boy, gave him beer money
      and commanded him to lift and push
    he left in October without his hat
    who answered to the name Father

Father, the world is different in many places
    the old Ford Trimotors are gone to scrap
    the Terraplane turned to snow
    four armies passed over your birthplace
      your house is gone

all your tall sisters gone
your fathers
everyone
Roosevelt ran again
you would still be afraid

You would not know me now, I have a son taller than you
    I feel the first night winds catch in the almond
        the plum bend
        and I go in afraid of the death you are
    I climb the tree in the vacant lot
        and leave the fruit untasted
    I blink the cold winds in from the sea
        walking with Teddy, my little one
        squeezing his hand I feel his death
    I find the glacier and wash my face in Arctic dust
    I shit handfuls of earth
    I stand in the spring river pissing at stars
    I see the diamond back at the end of the path
        hissing and rattling
        and will not shoot

The sun is gone, the moon is a slice of hope
    the stars are burned eyes that see
    the wind is the breath of the ocean
    the death of the fish is the allegory
        you slice it open and spill the entrails
        you remove the spine
        the architecture of the breast
        you slap it home
        the oils snap and sizzle.
        you live in the world
    you eat all the unknown deeps
    the great sea oaks rise from the floor
    the bears dip their paws in clear streams
        they hug their great matted coats
        and laugh in the voices of girls
    a man drops slowly like brandy or glue

In the cities of the world
   the streets darken with flies
   all the dead fathers fall out of heaven
      and begin again
   the angel of creation is a sparrow in the roadway
   storks rise slowly pulling the houses after them
   butterflies eat away the eyes of the sun
   the last ashes off the fire of the brain
   the last leavening of snow
   grains of dirt torn from under fingernails and eyes
   you drink these

There is the last darkness burning itself to death
   there are nine women come in the dawn with pitchers
   there is my mother
      a dark child in the schoolyard
      miles from anyone
      she has begun to bleed as her mother did
   there is my brother, the first born, the mild one
      his cold breath fogging the bombsight
   there is the other in his LTD
      he talks to the phone, he strokes his thighs
      he dismisses me
   my mother waits for the horsecart to pass
   my mother prays to become fat and wise
      she becomes fat and wise
   the cat dies and it rains
   the dog groans by the side door
   the old hen flies up in a spasm of gold

My woman gets out of bed in the dark and washes her face
   she goes to the kitchen before we waken
   she picks up a skillet, an egg
   the kids go off to school without socks
   in the rain the worms come out to live
   my father opens the telegram under the moon
      Cousin Philip is dead
      my father stands on the porch in his last summer

he holds back his tears
he holds back my tears

Once in childhood the stars held still all night
the moon swelled like a plum but white and silken
the last train from Chicago howled through the ghetto
I came downstairs
my father sat writing in a great black book
a pile of letters
a pile of checks
(he would pay his debts)
the moon would die
the stars jelly
the sea freeze
I would be a boy in worn shoes splashing through rain

Philip Levine

OCTOBER, 1987

At the funeral home they hand me
Daddy's watch, the silver Swiss one
I bought him at the P-X in Germany
twenty-eight years ago. He must have
had it on, or Mama put it on him
that last day when he didn't know
anybody and his arms jerked so.
The funeral home people are asking
if I'd like it buried with him.
Standing by the open casket,
I think back to that last afternoon
when these folded hands were still
his hands, their violent motion reaching
for what? For some way out? The watch
on the wrist that was still his wrist—
it's still running, face browned over

like year-old newspaper, and the second-hand
completing its thin circular slice
back to noon—it can
saw down so many things.
I decide to take back the watch.

Frank Steele

MY DAD'S WALLET

Long before he thought of his own death,
my dad said he wanted to lie close
to his parents. He missed them so
after they went away.
He said this enough that my mother remembered,
and I remembered. But when the breath
left his lungs and all signs of life
had faded, he found himself in a town
512 miles away from where he wanted most to be.

My dad, though. He was restless
even in death. Even in death
he had this one last trip to take.
All his life he liked to wander,
and now he had one more place to get to.

The undertaker said he'd arrange it,
not to worry. Some poor light
from the window fell on the dusty floor
where we waited that afternoon
until the man came out of the back room
and peeled off his rubber gloves.
He carried the smell of formaldehyde with him.
He was a big man, this undertaker said.
Then began to tell us why
he liked living in this small town.

This man who'd just opened my dad's veins.
How much is it going to cost? I said.

He took out his pad and pen and began
to write. First, the preparation charges.
Then he figured the transportation
of the remains at 22 cents a mile.
But this was a round-trip for the undertaker,
don't forget. Plus, say, six meals
and two nights in a motel. He figured
some more. Add a surcharge of
$210 for his time and trouble,
and there you have it.

He thought we might argue.
There was a spot of color on
each of his cheeks as he looked up
from his figures. The same poor light
fell in the same poor place on
the dusty floor. My mother nodded
as if she understood. But she
hadn't understood a word of it.
None of it had made any sense to her,
beginning with the time she left home
with my dad. She only knew
that whatever was happening
was going to take money.
She reached into her purse and brought up
my dad's wallet. The three of us
in that little room that afternoon.
Our breath coming and going.

We stared at the wallet for a minute.
Nobody said anything.
All the life had gone out of that wallet.
It was old and rent and soiled.
But it was my dad's wallet. And she opened
it and looked inside. Drew out

a handful of money that would go
toward this last, most astounding, trip.

Raymond Carver

THE SHOEBOX

I finally broke down and opened the shoebox
which arrived just weeks after my father died.
All winter I had put it out of sight on top

of the bookshelves where I wouldn't be tempted.
The box was not, as I would have expected,
stuffed with photographs, but packets,

wallet-sized, each with a dozen
"snaps," each sequence a kind of story,
and I couldn't have predicted how they would spring out

once I removed the rubber bands
wound tight as bowstrings around the top—
too late now to put them back,

to stop what I had set in motion—
there is no love in them, only
a memorializing will.

A predictable cast, my father's six
older sisters, their several (only three
between them!) issue.

It wasn't that everyone looked demented,
those spinster aunts, those whiz kid cousins,
but that no one looked like they wanted

to be where they were, in that parking lot fronting the beach,
in front of that penny arcade or movie marquee,
clutching that bulging suitcase. . . .

Only one glossy found its way into the box,
the only shot not taken with my father's Minolta:
a puppet without strings, no,

a ventriloquist's dummy, all shocked innocence—
me, glassy-eyed, open-mouthed, plenty of space
between my teeth, dangling above

my father, a rotund, baby-faced, leering man,
and his mother, a slack-jawed, toothless old woman,
greedily gazing up at the child as if she were its mother. . . .

The passersby on Times Square look happy
in a miserable sort of way.
In the mid-fifties laissez-faire seems

to extend everywhere except the family.
I plucked the images I didn't like
but when, after a few hours,

I tried to stuff the slender packets back in
and close the box, even with half
of the photographs smoking in the wood stove

they wouldn't smash down, the rubber bands
would not stretch beyond the limit
they had held for a decade,

yet I felt if I was to sleep, to have peace,
the box had to be shut.
The top had to fit snug around the edges.

Mark Rudman

POEM WITHOUT A METAPHOR
for Father, dead seven springs

the seventh robin
lights on the thumb
of my son

my lilac bush
is doing its
white explosions

a south breeze
stirs my unnamed tree

the Missouri
swells far from the
bluff of your grave

a Dakota farmer
inverts a corn field

a rock
will soon go skimming
the perfectly round
pond of childhood:

seven springs
and still I lack
the metaphor
of your death

David Allan Evans

SONS AND THEIR MOTHERS

"The way you tell it, it took you

all morning to fall"

WAR STORY: 1942

I was too young to remember
the year of your heroic fall,
Mama, the strength of purpose
that possessed you when you lost
your footing on the stair but lifted
me above your head, a bundled flag
you would keep from the enemy's hands,
a live bomblet that might explode
upon contact with the planet.
The way you tell it, it took you
all morning to fall, as if you
had stumbled near the top of a glacier
—had slowly toppled, caught in a fugue
of gravity.
            Later, you wept.
Your legs had taken the full weight
of your patriot's body: beautiful
Janet Gaynor legs, Lillian Russell
legs. Now you could count your losses:
what motherhood, what marriage had cost
you. Even now, in Florida, as you waltz
with my white-haired father, supported
by his sun-bathed arms, by the charm
of the dance and the music, you feel
the pain of that moment when you knew
I was safe and you could claim
your wounds.

Charles Fishman

CHOPPING A MOTHER'S PIANO

Three sons and a father did it:
they used axes and a saw
and the youngest a small hammer.
Too many broken keys to play or sell;
it was too heavy to haul for junk.
On a snowing night they'd agree
to turn it to firewood and wire;
even she had nodded from her chair.

In April they dragged it out to the yard,
laid it on one side like a brown bear
prodded from winter. It rested there
humped up in the morning light;
but they remembered when it was master—
the years of lessons sullenly tapped,
pounded into those stained keys,
the chipped chords they knew by touch.

They swarmed over it—pulled, pried,
split the bone-brittle wood inside,
bleached by a hundred indoor winters.
They stripped ridges of fine dust
from its exposed ribs with fingers;
watch for splinters, the father said,
and keep the dog clear of the ax.
At noon they fixed their own lunch.

>   Before them there'd been music;
>   they knew it without her saying, as if
>   her fingers, when she towelled them dry,
>   remembered a more responsive chord.
>   She listened beyond their bawdy jokes
>   to what they could hear just faintly
>   at night when glissandoes drifted
>   upstairs to the fuzzy edge of sleep.

They'd played for her, or tried.
The First Red Book. The Second.
On into minuets, even a nocturne.
But after dinner the father would be home;
he'd take them up the dirt driveway—
his grounders hopped crazily in the gravel,
his fly balls threaded the phone wires
till it was too dark to see.

They stacked the last slivers in bundles.
Then the youngest came back from the house,
thought she was crying on her bed, quietly.
So they stood around the bristly piles,
tried to kick them straight, then dug out
the bat and gloves and wandered up the drive
while it was still light. None of them,
not even she, has mentioned this until today.

Charles Atkinson

MY MOTHER'S NIGHTMARES

Horses gallop on her body.
Black shades flay her.

Hissing snakes
coil inside her mattress,
breeding cankers and blindness.

Lizards, flying
like hands of rough lovers,
sound the depth of her blood.

In the night, drunken friends
of her dead husband
break down her doors.

Red-hatted monks leer.

Emanuel di Pasquale

SARAH CORNISH

my mother lives
through

the burning of
her city

in smoky skin
sleeps

without radio
away from the window

windows fall
through the silent
darkness

in the ruins
my brother carries
a case of beer

his back open to the street

there is not
a sleep deep enough
for her tonight

Sam Cornish

Mother, I'm sure you remember
when I almost hanged myself in the kitchen?
I was fourteen and had just inherited
milking the cows from Allen
whose time doing chores must have ended
when he graduated from high school.
I wasn't mad about doing them.

Anyway, that night I came in from milking,
after feeding hogs, calves, chickens,
and hung myself. Of course you remember.
In the kitchen by the sink
we had that towel—I haven't seen one since—
a single cotton loop,
four feet long, a foot wide,
hanging from a wooden spool or dowel
affixed to the wall.
The lower loop must have been
not quite sink-high: I hung from that.

You came from your radio program
to find me, still wearing my mackinaw,
chore-cap and buckle overshoes.
My feet were behind me, on the scatter rug.
I was face down and slung forward.
the towel was under my chin,
my hands just off the floor.
dead still.

You said as soon as you got me free
I started to breathe and get my color.
Thank God I came in when I did thank God,
you cried and cried, rocking
my head and shoulders to you,
sitting on the floor. It may have been
the last time you held me so.

When I could talk I told you
that I remembered slipping on the rug and falling,
that I must have hit my head on something
and, throat-first, fallen into that loop.

Mother, this month I'm going to be forty-nine,
I've never told you the truth about that night,
and I want to tell you now.
I don't think I meant to die,
but I did hang myself—not quite by accident:
I came in, set the milk pail down, and,
perfectly idly, deliberate and purposeless,
I put the towel under my chin,
stretched out, keeping my overshoes on the rug,
lowered my body, then my hands,
and swung there, as I'd done before—often.
Dreaming, I suppose, but about what?
I don't know any more, maybe I never knew.
The last thing I remember was
a kind of tingling all over
and a sound—like time. Maybe
I was trying to dream about hanging myself,
how it would be, or acting out a movie fantasy
of my execution by the lynch-mob—
maybe it was something like that—
but it's possible I was thinking of nothing.

What a nightmare I was to you—
I might have died many times,
from carelessness or experimenting:
I almost drowned when I was seven.
It was just luck I didn't fall twenty-five feet
to the concrete floor of the potato warehouse.
I was side-swiped twice by cars, hit by a truck.
All from recklessness, all my fault.
When I was fifteen, I dove
from a tree and knocked myself out
on a rock in the river's bottom.
I played on the tops of moving freight cars.

Dove into snow-banks from the roof of a store.
Three times, once driving,
I was in cars or trucks that rolled over.
And once, with a bellyful of beer
I tried to chugalug a (stolen) fifth of
Seagram's whiskey. All this before I was nineteen.
And before I became as I have now become
very careful and willing to live,
as you are doing, for a long time.

I have been brooding on all those we know
who have been killed in a few seconds' surprise.
And about altering this one incident for you—
if not quite removing it
from that list you must have made by now
of the merciless tricks freak accidents can pull.
We don't have to name our dead, do we?

I'm sorry I lied. I must have thought
I'd catch hell. I know it gave you nightmares.
And I've had mine: when Elizabeth was two
she was standing on the car seat beside me,
I was driving, we were taking a big curve,
and the passenger door swung open.

She did not quite fall,
but I've dreamed it over, waking and sleeping,
ever since—and she's almost nineteen now.
I'm also sorry I waited
thirty-five years to tell you.
I hope it makes a difference to you,
it does to me: it reminds me to say
Thank God you came in when you did,
mother, for the life you gave,
what it's been, what it will be.

Roland Flint

MY MOTHER, IF SHE HAD WON FREE DANCE LESSONS

Would she have been a person
With a completely different outlook on life?
There are times when I visit
And find her settled on a chair
In our dilapidated house,
The neighborhood crazy lady
Doing what the neighborhood crazy lady is supposed to do,
Which is absolutely nothing

And I wonder as we talk our sympathetic talk,
Abandoned in easy dialogue,
I, the son of the crazy lady,
Who crosses easily into her point of view
As if yawning
Or taking off an overcoat.
Each time I visit
I walk back into our lives

And I wonder, like any child who wakes up one day to find themself
Abandoned in a world larger than their Bad dreams,
I wonder as I see my mother sitting there,
Landed to the right-hand window in the living room,
Pausing from time to time in the endless loop of our dialogue
To peek for rascals through the
Venetian blinds,

I wonder a small thought.
I walk back into our lives.
Given the opportunity,
How would she have danced?
Would it have been as easily
As we talk to each other now,
The crazy lady
And the crazy lady's son,
As if we were old friends from opposite coasts
Picking up the thread of a long conversation,

Or two ballroom dancers
Who only know
One step?

What would have changed
If the phone had rung like a suitor,
If the invitation had arrived in the mail
Like Jesus, extending a hand?

Cornelius Eady

(U N T I T L E D)

I last saw my mother a week after her suicide, in a dream. She was so shy;
she was only there a moment. I'd called her stupid. How could you be so
stupid? Eight years later she's back. What do you want, I ask her, what do
you really want? I want to sing, she says. And she sings.

Gary Young

N I G H T   J O U R N E Y

A man clothed in memories
that no longer fit him well,
his hair stained gray,
decides to return.

He rids the bedroom
of all light but his own
while singing softly
"On This Day O Beautiful Mother."

He sees her standing in the window
looking as he knows she looked
on the moon-bright night
his father knew her.

Her lips are moving, he hears
the Angelus prayers
inside his head, remembers
being gently bathed and fed.

Now he's ready to be old.

David Citino

TONE DEAF

It was a remark passed
like a breeze
on a muggy summer's night you never notice
but I did—like ice
so cold it burns. She said
I always sang out of tune
that I was tone deaf, with a chuckle.
But to me it meant the key I wore
around my neck, the t.v. dinners,
the strange men who'd wake me
with a flush late at night
the naked bulb in my room
and the cold plaster walls,
the cold plaster walls.
I curled into a wounded ball
then uncoiled like a cobra.
Hard and without mercy
I stung at her most vulnerable part
around the belly button
closest to the womb.

My words, loosening the dry skin
around her jaw. Her ears
reaching for the sky like bad guys—I give.
She slumped into the same wadded mess
my father used to beat her into
with the leg of a chair
or his fist.
She began biting her bottom lip raw,
tasting the blood and enjoying it
while her top lip trembled like the reed of a flute
playing the same sad tunes,
the dirge of my childhood.
And so I sang to my mother,
sang with my bones and my toes,
loud and high enough
to shatter the wine glasses
saturating the table cloth red
as our common bond
and my song was forgiveness
and the notes were
all out of tune.

Peter Spiro

LIPSTICK

Who can hurry past the five-and-dime,
the cardboard Max Factor ad

fading in the yellow light
of the abandoned, fly-littered window,

without recognizing the miniature skyline—
spires, smokestacks, the blinking, red antennae—

his mother's lipsticks etched
on the powdered, greenhouse air of her bedroom?

Only God or someone taller could count them!
I wanted to explore that foreign city,

hold her hand across the cinnabar avenues,
whisper in libraries of peach frost and ruby.

Gray school mornings in the railroad flat,
pretending to be still asleep,

I'd watch my mother dress
for the subway ride into Manhattan.

She'd sit in her bra and half-slip,
elbows propped on the vanity top,

brushing the flames across her lips,
first one flavor, then another—

forbidden strawberry, crushed orange, cafe au lait—
then close her lips on a tissue.

I'd steal the paper from the wicker
basket to taste the exotic

spices, the delicious
mocha, creme caramel, glazed papaya,

and when I was older, ten or twelve,
I'd wrap tissue after tissue

around my small, preening member,
smudging the lipstick on my flesh.

I never wrestled any desire
to smear the lipstick on my face,

touch the tubes
to my own parched lips,

but was touched by the story of Rilke,
poor Rainer, whose suffocating mother

painted the lips of her dear Maria!
O the poems! His problems with women!

Was his mother drawing out,
as she layered shade upon shade,

the lovely woman who lived inside him,
or was she blotting out,

dyeing his lips a deeper red, deeper
till almost black,

the boy who peeked
from behind his eyelids, feverish and weak?

Michael Waters

SECRETS

Each room except the room you're in
is empty. No need to check.
How many times in forty-five years
did you wish for such a silence,
just a moment to collect yourself
amid the chaos of a life too full
with other people's needs?

And now you've got more silence
than you'll ever need, more time
than anyone should ever have
alone, each memory another moment
in a world where time holds
nothing but the past
and someone else's future.

What do you dream of?
What do you fear each time
you turn to hear Dad stirring
and you realize that what you hear
is just the silence of an empty house,
an absence permanent as stone?

Surely such a silence turns
the heart back in upon itself.
Do you find your husband there?
Four sons and four grandchildren?
Some little Brooklyn girl
in pigtails skipping rope
that once was you?

Mother, does it all come down
to empty rooms and half-imagined sounds
of someone familiar? So many hopes
and disappointments make a life.
What were yours? I'd like to know.

W. D. Ehrhart

RASPBERRY
                    for Sarah G. Potts

My mother was born on Bastille Day
The year the Wright Brothers finally flew
Their bike with wings over Kitty Hawk
While Henry Ford assembles his line of Model T's
In any color you want so long as it's black.

Changes in the external world
Too numerous to catalog
Much less care about
Our peculiar mechanical ineptitude
For the things we've come to prefer over people.

TV, Computers, Cat Scanners,
Artificial hearts for millionaire dentists
And any number of less vital organs
Transplanted from body to body
By well-healed doctors manipulating death
In the so-called health care delivery system.

I love you, Mom, and all the wonderful
Moves you made for me beyond the obvious
Rocking me to sleep in your womb.

I remember raspberries
Where you taught me how to care for them
At altitudes in Idaho
Where none but the native
Bramble fruit dare grow.

On Saturday at Pioneer Park
The 4th of July leaves of the sycamore,
Otherwise rooted to the spot,
As I stare up thru their canopy,
Walk into the sky.
At the end of many branches

Out from under the upside down
Crotch of the semi-barkless tree
The leaves at maximum extension say,
"This is as far as we go."

Six weeks later on my birthday
Which I have reasons to believe
You recall more vividly than your own
Judy & Emily & I picked a few
Gallons of huckleberries
On the road to Jubilee Lake
Made large by the late spring rains
Turned ripe in the Blue Mountain sun.

I turn back with tears in my eyes
Where other men fail to keep the spark
Of love at home alive, to face the music of
My mother, wife, and daughter.

There is no road to be on
That can tell us more or make us feel better.

I'd like for you
To have my love
Not one last time
But always as you sail
From your body sick with age and medicine
Into the unknown.
Relax
And let peace be on your side
As I am by your side
500 miles away.

I'm up early on Labor Day
To run my two miles into shape
With tears streaming down my face
You will always be with me.

Like the raspberries bouncing
Off my face in the late morning dream of driving,
Road turned into snow and then to melting water.
As two white bulls appear,
I speak to my friends:
"Get my bike and wagon,"
As we ford past them
In the chilling runoff water of the stream.

Charles Potts

MOTHER & CHILD #3

Nothing below the wrist? Hands are missing?
No way to thread a needle, grasp a hammer,
pluck strings, stir kettles, tease the drooping
curl of a lover's hair? Never a palm
against the cheek, never a pen between the fingers?
No hands, we finish second to the ape.

In the nightmare my mother's hands, lopped off,
left me helpless to be lifted up. A door
chillier than time would close between us,
thicker than the fact of her early death
over uneaten breakfast on her birthday.

Her face has faded, unfamiliar
as photos yellowing for fifty years.
Touch faded long since: "How can I keep in touch
when there is nothing to touch?" I asked myself.
Answer? Can't. No voice to recognize.
No face to smile at. No hands to lift me up.
Nothing's remembered but lips, the fleeting posture
of a woman crouching, the knot of a red bandanna,
the smell of a body powdered in the morning.

Time's accidents entrap and then release
the tiny puffs of memory that arrive
like signals sent in smoke from a distant tribe
whose messages we might have understood
if only we had spoken the right language.
All children learn the ways that breast and milk
and hands lift up the body of a baby.
Hands spoke the truth, and when they spoke we heard.

Peter Davison

GETAWAY

My mother,
Who held like a rivet
For 20 years,
Snapped one day
And left us for jazz
And Willy Sutton,
Lover and 50's gunman. She
Didn't go far or often,
Just closed off the living room
And dolled up,
Wore the dress with no back,
The clear Cuban heels.
She'd open the keyboard, the lid
Of a dream,
And beat out rolling
Getaway jazz,
Or punchy white Chicago club stuff
Improvising and reaching
For the high roller. Willy
Her lover of fast pianos
Who filled her lap with hot gold,
Whose fingers found the one hundred triggers
Of her skin. Willy her purpose,

Her wheelman out of Pawtucket
Away from my father,
From me.

She'd come back. In the pink, in time
As though never away. Into the arithmetic
Of clocks, the correct dress,
Resigned, but never finally,
To the equation of rooms. To sit
And play contained, fit piano.
To be this way for months. Then begin again.
Blue pools in her skin quickened,
The piano picked up,
And Willy'd lift out
Of her fierce keys
To be hers.

Mother, light as a whiff of lemon oil,
Took Willy for all he had. When
He got stupid and went to prison
She kicked his ass
Out of her dream
And took up with someone else,
Anything to distance her
From the fixed and safe,
Those little metered joys,
Plagues of Sunday.

Norman Hindley

HOSPITAL THOUGHTS, LAST YEAR
AND TODAY

Last Christmas Eve, I woke to see Mama, dead
twelve years, bending over me in that strange bed,

but no, it was just those pale hospital green
walls, the yellow daze of fever. I'm seeing

things, I thought. But it must have been like that
for my father, a woman with blue-black hair in whites

bending over him during morning rounds,
like the Tenente and Cathy in *A Farewell to Arms*.

Around them—like a 1940s black-
and-white flick—the war. Sirens and ack-ack

guns, Manila covered with a shroud of smoke
again. General MacArthur returning like

an iron bloodhound, the Japanese kneeling by the sea.
When I was nine, that's how I'd wanted it to be.

I didn't want my parents to meet in a bank
in San Francisco, Tagalog words like magnets

drawing them together. But that Florence
Nightingale bedside scene never took place.

Those knotted hospital sheets tight around my chest,
I recalled Mama's cancer. How doctors christened

her a "model" patient. Once a pediatrician,
she had already fingered all their talismans:

chemotherapy, radiation treatment,
her hair falling out, her body shucking off weight.

At Carew and English, Papa and I found
she'd already ordered a shiny cedar coffin.

Now my father lies in a VA ward in
California—when I visit, he is skinny

as a nine-year-old boy, legs like useless sticks.
He speaks of the war, the Bataan death march,

how thin he'd gotten in the concentration camp.
He tells me how he misses Mama sometimes.

More desperately than his hand on my hair, I want
to see my mother in white, next to the window,

the stethoscope gleaming round her neck.
The sun glints in her hair, full and black.

Vince Gotera

MOTHER'S VOICE

In these few years
since her death I hear
mother's voice say
under my own, I won't

want any more of that.
My cheekbones resonate
with her emphasis. Nothing
of not wanting only

but the distance there from
common fact of others
frightens me. I look out
at all this demanding world

and try to put it quietly back,
from me, say, thank you,
I've already had some
though I haven't

and would like to
but I've said no, she has,
it's not my own voice anymore.
It's higher as hers was

and accommodates too simply
its frustrations when
I at least think I want more
and must have it.

Robert Creeley

MATER DOLOROSA

I

Pollen from the goldenrod rises
to the power lines. On wet days
a crackle echoes among pylons
frightening the cows: but this
morning, cold, dry, and gold,
you hear a faint hiss as if
from electric flowers.

My mother, at the dining room window,
sighs for the passing of power above her,
and for time, and for one more season.

*

For each of my sins she cried,
but that is the duty of mothers.

2

In Italy the rainwater drains
through a sluice in the garden wall.
A young man, slightly drunk,
steps delicately across the puddle
moving in the road below.
He thinks how his mother
before he wakes will clean his shoes
then not speak for three days.

　*

In the terminal in Texas
we sit drinking coffee, waiting;
we look at an airline poster of Montreal,
the city lighted at night,
and we say we would live there

if we could live only there,
among the lights and lucent air,
far above the streets. Or that
is what I say; my mother says:
It is late; your father
flies through bad weather.

3

I have her eyes, they say, and so
I turn away. I often close
our secret eyes.

Bin Ramke

MY MOTHER WOULD BE A FALCONRESS

My mother would be a falconress,
And I, her gay falcon treading her wrist,
would fly to bring back
from the blue of the sky to her, bleeding, a prize,
where I dream in my little hood with many bells
jangling when I'd turn my head.

My mother would be a falconress,
and she sends me as far as her will goes.
She lets me ride to the end of her curb
where I fall back in anguish.

I dread that she will cast me away,
for I fall, I mis-take, I fail in her mission.

She would bring down the little birds.
And I would bring down the little birds.
When will she let me bring down the little birds,
pierced from their flight with their necks broken,
their heads like flowers limp from the stem?

I tread my mother's wrist and would draw blood.
Behind the little hood my eyes are hooded.
I have gone back into my hooded silence,
talking to myself and dropping off to sleep.

For she has muffled my dreams in the hood she has made me,
sewn round with bells, jangling when I move.
She rides with her little falcon upon her wrist.
She uses a barb that brings me to cower.
She sends me abroad to try my wings
and I come back to her. I would bring down
the little birds to her
I may not tear into, I must bring back perfectly.

I tear at her wrist with my beak to draw blood,
and her eye holds me, anguisht, terrifying.
She draws a limit to my flight.
Never beyond my sight, she says.

She trains me to fetch and to limit myself in fetching,
She rewards me with meat for my dinner.
But I must never eat what she sends me to bring her.

Yet it would have been beautiful, if she would have carried me,
always, in a little hood with the bells ringing,
at her wrist, and her riding
to the great falcon hunt, and me
flying up to the curb of my heart from her heart
to bring down the skylark from the blue to her feet,
straining, and then released for the flight.

My mother would be a falconress,
and I her gerfalcon, raised at her will,
from her wrist sent flying, as if I were her own
pride, as if her pride
knew no limits, as if her mind
sought in me flight beyond the horizon.

Ah, but high, high in the air I flew.
And far, far beyond the curb of her will,
were the blue hills where the falcons nest.
And then I saw west to the dying sun—
it seemd my human soul went down in flames.

I tore at her wrist, at the hold she had for me,
until the blood ran hot and I heard her cry out,
far, far beyond the curb of her will

to horizons of stars beyond the ringing hills of the world where the
    falcons nest
I saw, and I tore at her wrist with my savage beak.
I flew, as if sight flew from the anguish in her eye beyond her sight,
sent from my striking loose, from the cruel strike at her wrist,
striking out from the blood to be free of her.

My mother would be a falconress,
and even now, years after this,
when the wounds I left her had surely heald,
and the woman is dead,
her fierce eyes closed, and if her heart
were broken, it is stilld

I would be a falcon and go free.
I tread her wrist and wear the hood,
talking to myself, and would draw blood.

Robert Duncan

FATHERS AND THEIR SONS

"I am standing somewhere

I may have been before"

Midafternoon in Norfolk,
late July. I am taking our two sons for a walk
    away from their grandparents' house; we have
    directions to a miniature playground,
        and I have plans to wear them down
            toward a nap at five,

        when my wife and I
will leave them awhile with her father. A few blocks
    south of here, my wife's mother drifts from us
    beneath hospital sheets, her small strength bent
        to the poisons and the rays they use
            against a spreading cancer.

    In their house now, deep love
is studying to live with deepening impatience
    as each day gives our hopes a different form
    and household tasks rise like a powdery mist
        of restless fatigue. Still, at five,
            my wife and I will dress

        and take the boulevard
across the river to a church where two dear friends
    will marry; rings will be blessed, promises kept
    and made, and while our sons lie down to sleep,
        the groom's niece, as the flower girl,
            will almost steal the show.

    But here the boys have made
an endless procession on the slides, shrieking down
    slick steel almost too hot to touch; and now
    they charge the swings. I push them from the front,
        one with each hand, until at last
            the rhythm, and the sunlight

that splashes through live oak
and crape myrtle, dappling dead leaves on the ground,
   lull me away from this world toward a state
   still and remote as an old photograph
      in which I am standing somewhere
         I may have been before:

      there was this air, this light,
a day of thorough and forgetful happiness;
   where was it, or how long ago? I try
   to place it, but it has gone for good,
      to leave me gazing at these swings,
         thinking of something else

      I may have recognized—
an irrecoverable certainty that now,
   and now, this perfect afternoon, while friends
   are struggling to put on their cutaways
      or bridal gowns, and my wife's mother,
         dearer still, is dozing

      after her medicine,
or turning a small thing in her mind, like someone
   worrying a ring of keys to make small sounds
   against great silence, and while these two boys
      swing back and forth against my hand,
         time's crosshairs quarter me

      no matter where I turn.
Now it is time to go. The boys are tired enough,
   and my wife and I must dress and go to church.
   Because I love our friends, and ceremony,
      the usual words will make me weep:
         hearing the human prayers

for holy permanence
will remind me that a life is much to ask
of anyone, yet not too much to give
to love. And once or twice, as I stand there,
that dappled moment at the swings
will rise between the lines,

when I beheld our sons
as, in the way of things, they will not be again,
though even years from now their hair may lift
a little in the breeze, as if they stood
somewhere along their way from us,
poised for a steep return.

Henry Taylor

THE FOURTH SON

Halfway through my life I've lived one quarter
of it to create the persistence of memory
in the memory of the rest. More and
more I lose my place, being lulled

Offguard as a sleepy reader: I blink
and discover between period and
capital that some part of my life has
flashed and gone—or that I've been somewhere and back.

I'm always most unprepared for my sons.
They flicker in and out in the random
stages of growth arrested for the rest
of my life by the six years between us

today. I carry four-year-old Josh
in one arm to preschool because it was
so cold and I want to get them there fast;

fathers sometimes need excuses to hold
the warmth they love, I never did; Jerry
I pull along with the other hand, such
long legs to be only six, was Dennis
on school patrol? yes Dennis the missing
son has left early for school patrol. When

I'm back on the page *this time I know
why you've come:* today: my new wife

was told that the child we carried
to the hospital two weeks ago
in the plastic bowl proved under the
microscope to have been a perfect

boy, naturally. This time then you'd
come for the son that would've been half your
brother. We hadn't told you. When you visit
next summer, I don't know if we will.

Gerald Barrax

SUN PRAYER (*from* Child of the Sun—Gabriel's Birth)
to Gabriel

She gives a half-choked sob
and upside down
suspended between her legs
surfacing from sunlight,
leaves and flowers,
a thousand-year-old face appears,
Gabriel! Gabriel!
Flying dark shape in sunlight,
God descending from sky
upside down
between woman's legs,

arms and face glisten darkly with uterine juice,
shimmery,
it wriggles free of mother skin,
fierce glum godhead stone face
I stare at through vine hair,
its dark eyes squinch-lidded
unwrinkle wide in haunting ferocity

Jimmy Santiago Baca

MARK

b. Mayday 1982

When, after the final push,
and pull of exasperated forceps,
when he slipped from my ripped wife,
the surprise was no surprise.

To my dumb, stunned eyes
he seemed strangely familiar.
Through the blood and business
of delivery, the recognition:
so that's the way it is; greetings.

In the clinical fluorescence
and the blizzard of misgiving
he seemed long, patched in
purple and gray, face squeezed Chinese,
head tapered like a raindrop.

And still the calligraphy of features
said surprise: I am no mystery.
I'm you, the people you know best.
You've always known me.

Paul Gianoli

PETER AND THUNDER

Your face when you heard it. How you looked up.
How, crouched over toy parts,
suddenly you stiffened. How then you turned,
how you stared up in the direction
of the thunder. *They are at the gates.*
How then you looked at me, as if
I might send them away, as if with a few
low-toned, well-chosen words I could
send the thunder-gangs scuttling back
through all the holes in the sky.
As if there were no thunder deep
down in my own bones, no thunder
in yours, little son.

Michael Dennis Browne

SON AND HEIR

You came uninvited, a stark
and slimy, inconvenient thing
we couldn't throw out,
two romantics as we are.
So we raise you in this sty,
this poverty without hope
of prospects or college
only words and food from cans.
You'll hate my guts,
I knew that from the beginning.
Maybe you'll even be the one
to finally punch me out, split my lip
when I pitch a fit, screaming
at your mother. You'll yell
you selfish pig, and I'll turn
and play my ace, saying
coldly, levelly

I never wanted you.
But for now I walk you
back and forth at 2 A.M.

Angry at this intrusion on my
liquor, late movies, and poems
I shake you a little too hard.
But you don't cow
you just wrinkle in your red face
and blow a scream
back at me, already letting
into my mouth
the bitterness of blood.

William Greenway

BOY WATERING FUCHSIAS

Fuchsias drip on the porch, their
red collars curl
and pale necks hang down.
My son waters them.
Holds the hose and stares.
When the wind blows the trees
thrash around, but he doesn't
move, he makes his mouth small.

I watch through a crack the fuchsias,
dead ones shriveled on the walk below
and my naked son who pisses out of
sympathy with the hose—

watch through a crack in the blinds
and write this out of love,
the words neither white nor red enough,
the eye disappears in the word.

Fuchsias drip and nothing moves.
The flowers, the hose.
The stream of water seems to freeze.
My son lets it flow.
His generosity empties it.
The puddle it forms fills with sky.

Charles waters the fuchsias.
This picture isn't frozen in time.
I describe it carefully, then eat dinner,
later we move to another town.
Nothing in it stays the same
except the water, except the words.

John Vernon

ONE OF THE BOYS

Wanting to lie down on a bed
to read a book,
I am drawn not to the usual
marriage-bed but to the
lower bunk in my sons' room.

I lie down where Austin lies
each night, a seven-year-old
starting fresh, who has not unlearned
weeping at hurt, nor unlearned
the wild gesture that is like
the flash of an animal
escaping into the woods.

This is the male room,
where the mail of my life
has been piling up, unopened, for years.
I want to read it now

as I bask here in the exclusion
of all wives, mothers, daughters, even
lovers, even
the very best of witches.

A week ago I shared the room
of our car with my wife
as she drove us for the first time
to a marriage counselor. How far apart
two people in a car can be!
A glassy cave, and two
prototypes of the human
staring straight ahead
at the centuries-long task
of learning how to speak.
I wept then to think of Emmett,
whose dreams each night
are clouds moving like prophecies
across Austin's sky.

Now I fly in this lower bunk
into the future, the pilot
not to be seen
but believed, and felt
all around me in the form
of a magic circle,
a space the wizard carries
at all times inside him,
its power the source of any feat,
including the amazing
dissolution of walls between rooms.

Philip Dacey

FROM PINETOP HILL
for John Colby

I look farther than the stone
flies, arcing a parabola
always more downward.
I enjoy its fall; it stretches
me down its swing to earth.

Stone does not fly. It falls,
explodes in the river's motions,
draws laughter from my child.
I push him ahead of me
to climb the ledge-stacked hill.

I arc stone after stone,
child waiting to see them fly,
reaching to point them to water.
I see farther than the stone
does not fly, as into years.

My son laughs. I arc
stone and stone to please him.

Don Eulert

L. A. MORNING

Maybe it's Ian. Maybe walking with him
to the sitter's, a kind of
religious exercise, his singing
counterpoint to mine as we walk
wakens the gods.
The fog dances more gently
into the trees. This ripest of
moments gives birth to amazement

so pure it hurts. That the world
arranges itself so vividly before me!
That all things, trees, houses,
weeds, stones, roses,
even porched pigeons and a flat
gray sky, everything
glows! And my woman loves me
and my son adores me
and these marvels were set out for us to
stroll through and for one sweet minute
I have absolutely nothing to regret.

Austin Straus

FAMILY CIRCLE

When I left Ithaca
for the great action
I was clean-cut, smartly
purposeful and nice
by inexperience.

I thought I'd be back soon
because the earth is flatly
a circle, but found,
though you want to go straight,
what survives is bent.

Well, here I am finally,
beat-up pilgrim to a homely shrine,
my bare rock and old woman
willing glumly to receive what I offer—
a scar and a tall story.

I see my son's eyes lift slyly
from his plate, asking what it was for—
struggle, shipwreck, and such lies.
It was for this, sonny, this:
my eating and your asking.

Leonard Nathan

THE SHADE

A summer cold. No fever. Nothing. But a dozen times during the night
    I wake
to listen to my son whimpering in his sleep, trying to snort the sticky
    phlegm out of his nostrils.
The passage clears, silence, nothing. I cross the room, groping for
    the warm,
elusive creature of his breath and my heart lunges, stutters, tries to
    race away;
I don't know from what, from my imagination, from life itself, maybe from
    understanding too well
and being unable to do anything about how much of my anxiety is always
    for myself.
Whatever it was, I left it when the dawn came. There's a park near here
where everyone who's out of work in our neighborhood comes to line up in
    the morning.
The converted school buses shuttling hands to the cannery fields in Jersey
    were just rattling away when I got there
and the small-time contractors, hiring out cheap walls, cheap ditches, cheap
    everything,
were loading laborers onto the sacks of plaster and concrete in the backs of
    their pickups.
A few housewives drove by looking for someone to babysit or clean cellars
    for them,
then the gates of the local bar unlaced and whoever was left drifted in out of
    the wall of heat
already rolling in with the first fists of smoke from the city incinerators.

It's so quiet now, I can hear the sparrows foraging scraps of garbage on
    the paths.
The stove husk chained as a sign to the store across the street creaks in the
    last breeze of darkness.
By noon, you'd have to be out of your mind to want to be here: the park will
    reek of urine,
bodies will be sprawled on the benches, men will wrestle through the surf
    of broken bottles,
but even now, watching the leaves of the elms softly lifting toward the day,
    softly falling back,
all I see is fear forgiving fear on every page I turn; all I know is every time I
    try to change it,
I say it again: my wife, my child . . . my home, my work, my sorrow.
If this were the last morning of the world, if time had finally moved inside
    us and erupted
and we were Agamemnon again, Helen again, back on that faint, beginning
    planet
where even the daily survivals were giants, filled with light, I think I'd still
    be here,
afraid or not enough afraid, silently howling the names of death over the
    grass and asphalt.
The morning goes on, the sun burning, the earth burning, and between
    them, part of me lifts and starts back,
past the wash of dead music from the bar, the drinker reeling on the curb,
    the cars coughing alive,
and part, buried in itself, stays, forever, blinking into the glare, freezing.

C. K. Williams

WALKING AT NIGHT WITH MY SON, JAMES

This summer he's grown to my own height.
Our shoulders almost touch as we walk,
flashlights dark, the path through the field.
We remember old games, knowing night by touch
rather than going, like tightrope walkers,
on a thin beam of light from one hand to the earth.

The moon is a golden apple sliced in half
by shadow, glazed by southern clouds.
We pause where the meadow grass is highest,
both stopped by the thick smell of campion blossoms.
They're all around us, my son says, look!
Their blossoms are like larger, paler stars
in the sky spread at our feet.

So we stand for a time, shoulders almost touching,
in the midst of this field off the Middle Grove Road,
in the midst of our lives, sharing late August darkness.
All around us night flowers.

Joseph Bruchac

B · R · M · Tz · V · H

      a poem from memory for Matthew Rothenberg's
      thirteenth birthday celebrated as a "bar mitzvah
      event" one month after the date three decades
      three years past my own

naming the day it comes
deep into March
Aquarius has shifted into Pisces
—Diane's time—
waters receded & warm days
hanging over San Diego
where never in my life I thought to end up
or thought to be here
standing in this western yard
to make bar mitzvah
as event—I stress—not
the ghost of ceremony
I recall from my own lost 13th year
middle of wartime & reports
first coming in that told

deaths of others curly-headed
cousins sacrificed
only their photos left to scan thru
later · "who is this?"
you asked
"a child" I answered
hair curled like your own
forget it
death's depressing after all
someone still dreams of
a universe   benign   & wakes
to stifled flesh
I wouldn't interrupt this day with
but wonder
how any sanity was possible
this century
o Matthew Matthew born once
in the glow of brother—Milton's—death
the mystery thus thrust
into our thoughts
—of light & dark
co-equals—
I was alone to greet you (as I hope
you will not be)
of those who shared the table
at our home back in the Bronx
by then I was
the one surviving
(as I knew it would be)
& thought: how could I
bring them to life for you
except the poems pictures
I began around
their deaths   your life
fathers mothers grandmothers
set there as titles
ancestors the imagination made
the shades all poetry
recalls back to Ulysses in the pit

voice of David out of Sheol
orphic Jew my master
de profundis I could see her wraith
—those mad poetic words!—
my mother enter in dark of
restless sabbaths
she who would call us "sweet face"
too much love
has spoiled her
I could never
answer that or answer
my father's angers
disappointments of his life in dry goods
peddling peddling
the old books forsaken
he dropped off in sleep & told me
"strange that it takes so long to die"
& she "the whole town's talking"
mysteries of death
& life
fantastic faces all we know
we love
bar mitzvahs happening
on sabbaths that divide
the day that Jesus died
from Easter
—Esther of my mother's name—
when all the dead arise
in mind they sing
song that first ushered in your birth
a man child   son
grown old & beautiful
at last
"joy   joy
"praise   praise

Jerome Rothenberg

134

from THE AGE OF REASON

I
To know you own the grown-ups,
That they depend on you,
Is power, pure and simple, over
This unnatural world where teenagers,
Lined up outside the Hung Jury Pub,
Wait, dull-eyed and spike-haired,
For the matinee performance
Of Sarcastic Orgasm. Just turned seven,
You walk with me, your Dad,
Past the fresh punks and say,
"They look to me as if they've just
Discovered drugs." Incredulous,
I remember watching, as a child,
Art Linkletter, during the long days
At home in breathless
Confinement. I feel the adrenalin
The pediatrician gave so freely
Make my heart rage
Against my sweaty surroundings,
Where no blankets were ever fresh,
Where, in enforced hypochondria,
I lived in the black and white
Of TV or exhausted the children's
Room of the public library.
Recalling the countless science-fiction
Tales I devoured, I hear you tell me,
"This kid at school got
Blue potato chips for Easter."
A thoroughly modern first
Communion, I thought.
A meal fit for an alien.
I'm cut off from you except
For weekends like this one,
When we go to a "Boring
Old poetry reading" (where you
Behave exceptionally well, because

You've reached the Age of Reason
And can sit still for more than five
Minutes). This short-sleeved day
Is already threatened by rain.
But it's an idle threat,
Like the empty plastic cup
You've perched on the bookstore's
Balcony. That cup captivates
The audience more than the stiff
Verses of the poet, who's doing her best.
It seems the cup stays perched
For so long, and the reading lasts
So long, till "So long!"
And the cup falls. The poet
Retrieves it mid-verse, smiling weakly,
As once again you steal the show,
Delighting the bigger grown-ups
Who sit on the floor like children.

II

We leave the bookstore. The thunderstorm
Starts as if on cue. Dodging the lightning,
You say, "It's like an Atari game."
You are fascinated by the uptown bus.
You look through its wet
Video-screen windows at the city
You love unconditionally.
To you the city is an escape
From the immaculate suburbs,
Where every lawn but yours is perfect,
Where every house but yours is owned.
You master our affections,
Command our attention. You look at this city
As your own, thinking it exists
For you alone. You can leave it any time,
And it will always be there for you.
At school, forced to keep a journal,
You write, "I like the weekends because
I get to go to my Dad's house in the city.

He lets me stay up late and play pocer,
And I always go to 7-11 too."

I V
Despite my obsession with baseball,
High summer wears thin after two weeks
In the high nineties. This morning we
Trek to the 7-11 for my Sunday
New York Times and your lime Slurpee.
On the way you say, "God is infinite.
That means he doesn't have to die.
God is lucky. I wish I were infinite—
I'd get to live longer." Later we board
The downtown bus to Grandaddy's
Office to take a charter from this hot
City bereft of baseball
To Baltimore where Charlie Leibrandt
Ends the O's winning streak. He's perfect
Through five and a third, when he allows a walk.
Oblivious to the double play that follows,
You bum a buck and a half from Grandaddy
For a Coke. When you make your way
Back to the hot stands, you give him a quarter
Change, and begin to beg me, incessantly,
For a batting glove. I tell you to wait till
The game is over, and, on a weak single to right,
There goes the no-hitter. After the game,
I spend my last three dollars on the glove.
But the law firm is taking us out
For unlimited crabs and beer, and, after all,
They took us out to the ballgame.
And on the bus back, having made a flirtatious
Friendship with Jessica, who's seven too,
You're a little less antsy. Having had
Your fill of chocolate sundaes, you're
Content almost. The bus drops us off,
And Grandaddy drops me at my
Rented row-house in my "transitional"
Neighborhood. Then you ride back

To the suburbs in the climate-controlled
Cadillac with vanity plates that read
FLYNN. You take my scorecard and the team-
Photos for kids 14 and under to show your mom,
Who calls to say you're exhausted but happy—
Happy, that is, till you remember you've left
The batting glove in Grandaddy's car.
Perplexed, you say, "Mommy, Grandaddy's rich,
Isn't he? You should see his car!"
Before you go to bed your mother asks you
Whether you like your life.
"Not very much," you say. "I never
Get to do what I want."

VI
Searching the aisles of bright toys
In the bright toy supermarket, we hunt
For Mattel's rubber aliens, MUSCLEs,
Which you tell me stands for "Millions
Of Unusual Small Creatures Lurking
Everywhere." Everywhere I look, other
Weekend fathers indulge their small
Creatures, as I indulge you.
The movies are full of children
Adopted by aliens when their parents
Aren't looking, children liberated
For a couple of hours from marriages,
Governments, and leisurely suburban days.
And you frighten me, because I'd
Forgotten childhood's pain, the nightmares
About the first grade, because you forgive me
Even my worst moments, because I don't
Know how to make up for my absence. Here,
In Toys 'R' Us, plastic trinkets
(For children who dream of worlds where
Parents are parents) seem appealing to us
Adults who refuse adulthood
Even as we dream of it. And you
Children, seeing the necessity of our fantasy,

Captivate us with your childishness
Till we almost believe that happiness
Can be manufactured the way
Your Little League team manufactures
Runs, till we almost believe that
There are special rules for us
Who can't quite master the real
Rules, the rules for grown-ups.

VII
"Everyone has a mission in life," you tell me
As we drive around Greensboro aimlessly.
"Yours is getting us lost." I am trying
To get us back to Chapel Hill,
To Aunt Kathy ("whose mission in life
Is forgetting things") and Uncle Rick's
("Whose mission in life is to play with me").
I ask you what your "mission in life" is,
And you tell me, "It's to be obnoxious
And beg for money all the time." Despite
Our having had a good day visiting *my*
Friends and you being on best behavior, I laugh
At the truth in what you're saying. You amuse
Yourself so much, you continue,
"Mommy's mission in life is to pick up
After me." This pisses me off, I tell you.
But, though I'm angry, it seems a wonder
How *adaptable* you are, facing constant
Disruption with equanimity. And here,
In the last vacation of a whirlwind summer,
After four camps, and days in our offices
Between camps, with the extended days
Of school imminent, you and I are both
Afraid of the cooling off into winter.
There's a renewed sadness over everything,
As in school you begin a new journal:
"I don't get to see my Dad that much
On the weekdays, so I have to imagine him.
I hope he doesn't have to move far away,

Cause I like his cats and the city too."
When I read this I know for sure
It isn't just *my* heart breaking.
As I pack to leave our city I'm afraid.
Afraid that we'll grow distant,
Afraid that you will hate me. I want
To tell you to take care, as I move
Carelessly through my mission in life.
Let us try to live out our alien
Existences hopefully. Let us pray
That wishing will make us better.

Better, if not transformed.

Richard Flynn

FOR NICHOLAS

In the walking light of Andalusia
where the water weeps through the night
I climb the cobbled steps of the Albacin
with my son. His eyes burn with poems.
The earth pulls at our blood.

We find a Moroccan teahouse,
sit in a corner and sip Pakistani tea
from tall, slim, silver-latticed glasses.
We talk of the strange turns of life
that have brought us to this place
in the shadow of the Alhambra
where cats roam the fabled stones.

Here, in Lorca's town, he is finding his life.
Our eyes meet in a glistening gleam.
I have always been here with him—
in Andalusia, where the light walks,
the water weeps, and my son's eyes burn with poems.

Fred Moramarco

ON THE LIFE AND DEATH OF STAN LAUREL'S SON

For nine days, two Stanleys, one funny,
one drowning, brain capsizing in its own blood,
lungs miscarrying air
from one breath to the next, a tenant
shut in its dissembling body,
incubator too much like a show room.

Stan's tired of crying on screen,
off, that's all he can do. The night nurse
steals his exhausted handkerchief, hides it
under her sleeve on her wrist-pulse.
Someday these tears might be worth something.

Stan Jr. dies without one chuckle
to smooth out its face, and is burned
into a little pile his father feels
he keeps in a clear candy jar.
Every morning for luck Stan rubs
a fingerprint on the glass

cold as a spoon, his son
neutral inside. Then off to the laughter
works where he invents the same smile
each day, and that way of walking,
as if the ground were a ledge, and he's strolling
alone, three steps off the earth.

Walter Pavlich

DEATHWATCH

Twitching in the cactus
hospital gown, a loon
on hairpin wings,
she tells me how
her episiotomy
is perfectly sewn
and doesn't hurt
while she sits in a pile
of blood
which once cleaned
the placenta
my third son should be in.
She tells me how early
he is, and how strong,
like his father,
and long, like a black-
stemmed Easter rose
in a white hand.

Just under five pounds
you lie there, a collapsed
balloon doll, burst in your
fifteenth hour, with the face
of your black father,
his fingers, his toes,

and eight voodoo
adrenalin holes in
your pinwheeled hair-lined
chest; you witness
your parents sign the autopsy
and disposal papers
shrunken to duplicate
in black ink
on white paper
like the country
you were born in,
unreal, asleep,
silent, almost alive.

This is a dedication
to our memory
of three sons—
two dead, one alive—
a reminder of a letter
to DuBois
from a student
at Cornell—on behalf
of his whole history class.
The class is confronted
with a question,
and no one—
not even the professor—
is sure of the answer:
"Will you please tell us
whether or not it is true
that negroes
are not able to cry?"

America needs a killing.
America needs a killing.
Survivors will be human.

Michael S. Harper

In the way you went you were important.
I do not know what you found.
In the pattern of my life you stand
where you stood always, in the center,
a hero, a puzzle, a man.

What you might have told me
I will never know—the lips went still,
the body cold. I am afraid,
in the circling stars, in the dark,
and even at noon in the light.

When I run what am I running from?
You turned once to tell me something,
but then you glimpsed a shadow on my face
and maybe thought, why tell what hurts?
You carried it, my boy, so brave, so far.

Now we have all the days, and the sun
goes by the same; there is a faint,
wandering trail I find sometimes, off
through grass and sage. I stop
and listen, only summer again—remember?—

The bees, the wind.

William Stafford

SONG FOR A SON

My son's image
was painted on sand.

The wind from off the lake
bears me no news of him,
nor of his impression.

Was it arrogance to think
I could hold his features?

I had set them in memory,
fashioned cameos for the
mind, had seen that face at will,
in various attitudes, transforming
me—when he was alive.

But I am blind!
Unable to create a brow,
a lash, the hollow down
the back of the neck,
the throat!

Look.
Those trees hold nothing
in their branches. Those rushes
by the lake, so rife with
blackbirds, hold nothing:
         Mist faces,
         faces in shrouds,
         faces in clouds . . .
Water has worn the cameos down

Robert Peters

a.

Under this stone, what lies?
   A little boy's thistledown body.
How, on so light a child
      Gravel hefted and hurled?
Light? As a flower entwined
   In our shining arms. Heavy
Laid in this scale—it set
   Wailing the chains of the world.

b.

What did you say? We said:
   Bedtime, dear, forever.
Time to put out the light.
   Time for the eyes to close.
What did he do? He lay
   In a crazyquilt of fever.
His hands were already like grasses.
   His cheek already a rose.

c.

How was that year? His voice.
   Over sun on the rug, slow-turning,
Hung like a seabird lost the
   Lorn and bodiless cry.
Haunting the house. *And then?*
   I remember *then*. One morning
Silence like knives in the ear.
   A bird gone over the sea.

d.

What of his eyes? Dark glow
   Furling the world's great surface.
Bubbles among tree lights;
   Bubbles of ferny dew.
And his kiss? On our cheek at evening
   Vintage: a fine bursting.

This, and never dreamed his
  Span was a bubble too?

e.

Little head, little head,
  Frail in the air, gold aster—
Why did the great king stoop
  And smoothe those ringlets down?
For a tinsel party-hat?
  It was Christmas then, remember?
I remember grown men wept
  And couldn't lift that crown.

f.

Mother, these tears and tears?
  The better to see you, darling.
Mother, your golden glasses—
  Have a sorry fault,
Being made for things, dear,
  Mostly: carts and marbles.
Mothers wear, for children,
  Better the stinging salt.

g.

What you remember most—?
  Is a way of death with fingers.
How they are cast in tallow
  —Fingers, webbed as one.
Where was he going, with webs?
  A flying child? or a swimming?
He knew, where he went,
  One way back to the sun.

h.

"Tesoro!" implored the maid.
  "Treasure!" the tall signora.
Under a distant heaven
  What struck the famous tower?

Faults in the earth despairing.
    Worlds away, an orchard
Offered violets early.
    And we returned a flower.

i.
Where does he lie? Hill-high
    In a vision of rolling river.
Where the dogwood curls in April
    And June is a dream of Greece.
Like a Christmas scene on china,
    Snow and the stubborn myrtle.
Those flakes from feathery heaven—?
    Deepen all in peace.

j.
Where does he rest, again?
    In a vision of rolling river.
What does he know of river?
    What do we know of sea?
Comfort?—when tomorrow's
    Cheek by jowl with never?
Never . . . in whose garden
    Bloomed the used-to-be.

k.
Under the snow, what lies?
    Treasure the hemlock covers—
Skysail of frost, and riding in
    Starlight keen and steep.
But the boy below? What's here is
    Gear in a sea-chest only.
Stowed for a season, then
    Pleasure-bound on the deep.

John Frederick Nims

BHOPAL

> I've often wondered how it is at times
> Good people do what are as bad as crimes.
> —Clough

Eyes open, glazed like isinglass, the fire
behind gone out, this child of Bhopal lies
in his shallow grave of cinders—no time
for weeping as when we lost our son Sam
and stood, hands joined, to wish him well in some
life beyond. In fact he might have gone on
to Bhopal just in time to die again
at just three months. Not likely, but who knows?
One thing that's certain though is this: Third World
or one beyond, they're all our children now,
though borne by millions in brown arms and black,
and not much mourned by those who think their own
are wonders, others somehow less. And thus
I'll say good-bye to this son too, and yours.

David Ray

AXE HANDLES

One afternoon the last week in April
Showing Kai how to throw a hatchet
One-half turn and it sticks in a stump.
He recalls the hatchet-head
Without a handle, in the shop
And go gets it, and wants it for his own.
A broken-off axe handle behind the door
Is long enough for a hatchet,
We cut it to length and take it
With the hatchet head
And working hatchet, to the wood block.
There I begin to shape the old handle

With the hatchet, and the phrase
First learned from Ezra Pound
Rings in my ears!
"When making an axe handle
        the pattern is not far off."
And I say this to Kai
"Look: We'll shape the handle
By checking the handle
Of the axe we cut with—"
And he sees. And I hear it again:
It's in Lu Ji's *Wên Fu*, fourth century
A.D. "Essay on Literature"—in the
Preface: "In making the handle
Of an axe
By cutting wood with an axe
The model is indeed near at hand."
My teacher Shih-hsiang Chen
Translated that and taught it years ago
And I see: Pound was an axe,
Chen was an axe, I am an axe
And my son a handle, soon
To be shaping again, model
And tool, craft of culture,
How we go on.

Gary Snyder

FATHERS AND THEIR DAUGHTERS

"The first night after your daughter is born,

you dream she has turned to ice"

I C E

The first night after your daughter is born,
you dream she has turned to ice,
that there is ice under the bed,
ice in your veins, a heart of ice,
a cold you will carry
locked inside each brain cell.
You dream how you will move for the next sixty years
to the sound of her body melting.

A cold day in late March:
millions of pounds of lake ice
floating on black water, so you go out
lay down and make angels
in the snow, and later, back at the house
you drink through a night storm,
sure you hear the sound of your own wings
moving against the ice,
as if your body were still out there,
flapping on the surface not sure of the way out,
the way in.

I watch the journey with Cousteau
inside the iceberg, begin to believe
they are drifting through a huge heart,
the veins blue and tight,
and think of holding my own frozen heart
in my hands, enough ice there to
cool several drinks, three women,
a small pond,
the forehead of a feverish daughter.

Michael Delp

UNDER THE MAUD MOON

I

On the path,
by this wet site
of old fires—
black ashes, black stones, where tramps
must have squatted down,
gnawing on stream water,
unhouseling themselves on cursed bread,
failing to get warm at a twig fire—

I stop,
gather wet wood,
cut dry shavings, and for her,
whose face
I held in my hands
a few hours, whom I gave back
only to keep holding the space where she was,

I light
a small fire in the rain.

The black
wood reddens, the deathwatches inside
begin running out of time, I can see
the dead, crossed limbs
longing again for the universe, I can hear
in the wet wood the snap
and re-snap of the same embrace being torn.

The raindrops trying
to put the fire out
fall into it and are
changed: the oath broken,
the oath sworn between earth and water, flesh and spirit, broken,
to be sworn again,
over and over, in the clouds, and to be broken again,
over and over, on earth.

2
I sit a moment
by the fire, in the rain, speak
a few words into its warmth—
stone saint smooth stone—and sing
one of the songs I used to croak
for my daughter, in her nightmares.

Somewhere out ahead of me
a black bear sits alone
on his hillside, nodding from side
to side. He sniffs
the blossom-smells, the rained earth,
finally he gets up,
eats a few flowers, trudges away,
his fur glistening
in the rain.

The singed grease streams
out of the words, the one
held note
remains—a love-note
twisting under my tongue, like the coyote's bark,
curving off, into a
howl.

3
A round-
cheeked girlchild comes awake
in her crib. The green
swaddlings tear open,
a filament or vestment
tears, the blue
flower opens.

And she who is born,
she who sings and cries,
she who begins the passage, her hair
sprouting out,

her gums budding for her first spring on earth,
the mist still clinging about
her face, puts
her hand
into her father's mouth, to take hold of
his song.

4
It is all over,
little one, the flipping
and overleaping, the watery
somersaulting alone in the oneness
under the hill, under
the old, lonely bellybutton
pushing forth again
in remembrance,
the drifting there furled in the dark,
pressing a knee or elbow
along a slippery wall, sculpting
the world with each thrash—the stream
of omphalos blood humming all about you.

5
Her head
enters the headhold
that starts sucking her forth: being itself
closes down all over her, gives her
into the shuddering
grip of departure, the slow,
agonized clenches making
the last molds of her life in the dark.

6
The black eye
opens, the pupil
droozed with black hairs
stops, the chakra
on top of the brain throbs a long moment in world light,

and she skids out on her face into light,
this peck
of stunned flesh
clotted with celestial cheesiness, glowing
with the astral violet
of the underlife. And as they cut

her tie to the darkness
she dies
a moment, turns blue as a coal,
the limbs shaking
as the memories rush out of them. When

they hang her up
by the feet, she sucks
air, screams
her first song—and turns rose,
the slow,
beating, featherless arms
already clutching at the emptiness.

7
When it was cold
on our hillside, and you cried
in the crib rocking
through the darkness, on wood
knifed down to the curve of the smile, a sadness
stranger than ours, all of it
flowing from the other world,

I used to come to you
and sit by you
and sing to you. You did not know,
and yet you will remember,
in the silent zones
of the brain, a specter, descendant
of the ghostly forefathers, singing
to you in the nighttime—
not the songs

of light said to wave
through the bright hair of angels,
but a blacker
rasping flowering on that tongue.

For when the Maud moon
glimmered in those first nights,
and the Archer lay
sucking the icy biestings of the cosmos,
in his crib of stars,

I had crept down
to riverbanks, their long rustle
of being and perishing, down to marshes
where the earth oozes up
in cold streaks, touching the world
with the underglimmer
of the beginning,
and there learned my only song.

And in the days
when you find yourself orphaned,
emptied
of all wind-singing, of light,
the pieces of cursed bread on your tongue,

may there come back to you
a voice,
spectral, calling you
sister!
from everything that dies.

And then
you shall open
this book, even if it is the book of nightmares.

Galway Kinnell

DARA

When they start pulling you out
The anesthesiologist tells me I may look.
I stand and look over the tent
That hides your mother's body from herself.
I look and see
The slick wet head, deceptively black,
That will dry to your nappy red.
Tugs at you. Cuts. Cuts.
I understand your fear, reluctance.
You had clung so tightly
Inside, attached so uncertainly to the womb
Against the tide of blood that threatened to sweep you away
Down the toilet where she sat, head bowed,
Watching the flood.
Bargaining for you (Yes: with that promise she keeps)
With the god she might as easily have cursed.
Except that it might be you who paid.
Cuts. Cuts. Your mother's flesh, muscle, fat, blood.
They tug and tug now
After you had held so tightly
In that micro-ocean, your gray eyes shut
In desperation, clinging to your only hope,
Yourself, imitating her position, her purpose,
Hugging and bowing into yourself,
Into your own stubborn strength,
Curving your feet so tightly against you
They would need casting,
The tide flowing, seeming to drain, leech you
Fair black child
You are free,
Out, I tell her, second daughter,
Dara. The Beautiful One, last
Child (before they close her)
Is free.

Gerald Barrax

THE BEST YEAR OF HER LIFE

When my two-year-old daughter
sees someone come through the door
whom she loves, and hasn't seen for a while,
and has been anticipating
she literally shrieks with joy.

I have to go into the other room
so that no one will notice the tears in my eyes.

Later, after my daughter has gone to bed,
I say to my wife,

"She will never be this happy again,"
and my wife gets angry and snaps,
"Don't you dare communicate your negativism to her!"
And, of course, I won't, if I can possibly help it,
and of course I fully expect her
to have much joy in her life,
and, of course, I hope to be able
to contribute to that joy—
I hope, in other words, that she'll always
be happy to see me come through the door—

but why kid ourselves—she, like every child,
has a life of great suffering ahead of her,
and while joy will not go out of her life,
she will one of these days cease to actually,
literally, jump and shriek for joy.

Gerald Locklin

BATHING THE GIRLS

At 2 & 4 they easily fit
in the old clawfoot tub.
I let them steep awhile,
talk and splash until the scrubbing.
With hands lathered
I start low, work upward,
loving the part of me I was
so unprepared for: female
selves that make it possible
to find the only strand
of loneliness overlooked by joy.
I wash their hair
then rinse with a dented pot.
These bodies are what the earth
tells me, but still new
to such powerful words, I listen
by kissing shoulders and necks,
bellies and backs!
Just between us, there is no past.

Barry Sternlieb

FOR KYLA, AGE 3

Tonight I read my daughter
the story of a Cree hunter

who has killed his first birds
in early spring, the Moon of Geese.

He prepares and cooks them himself,
keeping his family silent

during the meal or the bird spirits,
which are stronger than the birds,

might grow angry and change the season's
luck from good to bad.

When all have finished eating,
he collects the bones and sings them

into the fire where they are purified
and returned by way of ashes

to the heart of things: earth and water.
My daughter takes the book

she is too young to read, the wings
of its pages alive in her hands,

and wants to know what happens next.
Already, the hunger begins.

Barry Sternlieb

UNDRESSING AUNT FRIEDA

Undressing Aunt Frieda, I think of how,
undressing me, she would tilt back her head
as if listening for footsteps, the faint marching
of the S.S. men whose one great dream
was her death. They must have feared
how her young Jewish fingers unbuttoned
and buttoned, as if they had continents
to cross, as if here, in East New York,
I was already tiring, and no one at home
to put me to bed.

Undressing Aunt Frieda, I try to imagine her
healthy, undressing herself, slowly at first,
as if for the love of a man, untying
her green checkered apron with the secret pockets,
unwrapping the frail "just shy of five foot" body
whose scarred beauty Reubens would surely have missed,
but Rembrandt, in the loneliness of his dying days,
might have immortalized.

My daughter at my side grows restless.
She unties her shoes, tugs at each sock.
She has learned, recently, to undress herself,
and pausing occasionally for applause,
does so now. Naked, she shimmies up onto the bed,
curls her thin fingers around Frieda who,
as if she wished herself already dead,
doesn't coo or even smile.

"A dream of love," Frieda preached, "is not love,
but a dream." "And bad luck," I'd say, "follows
the bitter heart." But undressing her now,
I remember the lightness of her hands
and their strength, which somehow lifted me
above the nightmares she had known.
I'll care for you, she whispered once
as if you were my own. My daughter yawns.
I lift her gently, hoping she'll sleep
the hour drive home.

Richard Michelson

THE LAST DEATHS

I.

A few nights ago I was half-watching the news on television and
    half-reading to my daughter.
The book was about a boy who makes a zoo out of junk he finds in a lot—

I forget exactly; a horse-bottle, a bedspring that's a snake, things like that—
and on the news they were showing a film about the most recent bombings.
There was a woman crying, tearing at her hair and breasts, shrieking
    incomprehensibly
because her husband and all her children had been killed the night before
and just when she'd flung herself against the legs of one of the soldiers
    watching her,
Jessie looked up and said, "What's the matter with her? Why's she crying?"

2.

I haven't lived with my daughter for a year now and sometimes it still hurts
    not to be with her more,
not to have her laughter when I want it or to be able to comfort her when
    she cries out in her sleep.
I don't see her often enough to be able to know what I can say to her,
what I can solve for her without introducing more confusions than there
    were in the first place.
That's what happened with death. She was going to step on a bug and when
    I told her she'd kill it,
it turned out that no one had ever told her about death and now she had
    to know.
"It's when you don't do anything anymore," I told her. "It's like being
    asleep."
I didn't say for how long but she's still been obsessed with it since then,
wanting to know if she's going to die and when and if I am and her mother
    and grandma and do robbers do it?
Maybe I should have just given her the truth, but I didn't: now what was I
    going to say about that woman?
"Her house fell down," I said. "Who knocked down her house?" "It
    just fell."
Then I found something for us to do but last night, again, first thing,
"Tell me about that girl." "What girl?" "You know." Of course I know.
What could have gone on in my child's dreams last night so that woman was
    a girl now?
How many times must they have traded places back and forth in that
    innocent crib?
"You mean the lady whose house fell down?" "Yeah, who knocked her
    house down?"

164

3.

These times. The endless wars. The hatreds. The vengefulness.

Everyone I know getting out of their marriage. Old friends distrustful.

The politicians using us until you can't think about it anymore because you
    can't tell anymore

which reality affects which and how do you escape from it without
    everything battering you back again?

How many times will I lie to Jessie about things that have no meaning for
    either of us?

How many forgivenesses will I need from her when all I wanted was to keep
    her from suffering the same ridiculous illusions I have?

There'll be peace soon.

They'll fling it down like sick meat we're supposed to lick up and be
    thankful for and what then?

4.

Jessie, it's as though the whole race is sunk in an atmosphere of blood

and it's been clotting for so many centuries we can hardly move now.

Someday, you and I will face each other and turn away and the absence,

the dread, will flame between us like an enormous, palpable word that
    wasn't spoken.

Do we only love because we're weak and murderous?

Are we commended to each other to alleviate our terror of solitude and
    annihilation and that's all?

5.

I wish I could change dreams with you, baby. I've had the bad ones, what
    comes now is calm and abstract.

Last night, while you and that poor woman were trading deaths like
    horrible toys,

I was dreaming about the universe. The whole universe was happening in
    one day, like a blossom,

and during that day people's voices kept going out to it, crying,
    "Stop! Stop!"

The universe didn't mind, though. It knew we were only cursing love again

because we didn't know how to love, not even for a day,

but our little love days were just seeds it blew out on parachutes into the
    summer wind.

Then you and I were there. We shouted "Stop!" too. We kept wanting the
    universe to explode,
we kept wishing it would go back into its root, but the universe understood.
We were its children. It let us cry into its petals, it let its stems bend
    against us,
then it fed and covered us and we looked up sleepily—it was time
    to sleep—
and whatever our lives were, our love, this once, was enough.

C. K. Williams

SHALL I TEACH MY DAUGHTER TO FEAR THE OCEAN

To her
beauty is gentle,
the surf, the churning undertow—
all smooth forms one
with breast or hand. Her eyes
float out and she, toddling,
buoyed by wonder, would embrace
the sea. The magic stones
light up the tide,
the slow boats gliding
call Emily. I too hear
the foghorns, sirens
to the deep. My voice
is danger, a calling
to knowledge
of gasp and fall.
Though I wish to walk with you
there avid as Christ
for a surface firm
and warm beneath us,
I will show you
this life, a constant

recoil of desire.
My hand on your shoulder
is the first denial.
I am teaching my daughter
to fear the ocean.

Jim Heynen

POEM FOR NINA HELOISE

> The Shoshone, on discovering his new child
> is a daughter, walks down into the beautiful
> valley where the seeds grow

I have walked that way four times in my life.
The first time after long hours of watching
and waiting, tired and disappointed I made that journey.
Once I came back in a slow falling rain. Another time
I walked across the great desert to return to my house.
Finally, I went to that valley on a summer day
bright with sunshine and blue.

On the day my youngest daughter begins her menses
I will go to my doorway and shout the news to the village
and give away one of my horses to an old man

Carlos Reyes

DAD'S EXCUSE

Beverly explains to me
about being kicked out
at fourteen;
about leaving
the Reservation.

I tell her
of my daughter's room,
the things she left behind.

Oh! the promises
and the poems
to my daughters;
all the things I would do
when they were grown.

My middle daughter asked me
the other day
if I had given that horse away
to an old man of the village—something
in a poem I vowed to do
when she became a woman.

Our world today,
I tell her,
is no village.

There is no room in it
for horses to give away.

Everywhere are daughters gone,
old men,
taverns like the *Dad's Excuse*
and the Beverlies to remind us
of unkept promises.

Carlos Reyes

WORDS FOR MY DAUGHTER

About eight of us were nailing up forts
in the mulberry grove behind Reds' house
when his mother started screeching and
all of us froze except Reds—fourteen, huge
as a hippo—who sprang out of the tree so fast
the branch nearly bobbed me off. So fast,
he hit the ground running, hammer in hand,
and seconds after he got in the house
we heard thumps like someone beating a tire
off a rim   his dad's howls the screen door
banging open   Saw   Reds barreling out
through the tall weeds towards the highway
the father stumbling after his fat son
who never looked back across the thick swale
of teasel and black-eyed Susans until it was safe
to yell fuck you at the skinny drunk
stamping around barefoot and holding his ribs.

Another time, the Connelly kid came home to find
his alcoholic mother getting fucked by the milkman.
Bobby broke a milk bottle and jabbed the guy
humping on his mom. I think it really happened
because none of us would loosely mention that
wraith of a woman who slippered around her house
and never talked to anyone, not even her kids.

Once a girl ran past my porch
with a dart in her back, her open mouth
pumping like a guppy's, her eyes wild.
Later that summer, or maybe the next,
the kids hung her brother from an oak.
Before they hoisted him yowling and heavy
on the clothesline, they made him claw the creek bank
and eat worms. I don't know why his neck didn't snap.
Reds had another nickname you couldn't say
or he'd beat you up: "Honeybun."
His dad called him that when Reds was little.

So, these were my playmates. I love them still
for their justice and valor and desperate loves
twisted in shapes of hammer and shard.
I want you to know about their pain
and about the pain they could loose on others.
If you're reading this, I hope you will think,
Well, my dad had it rough as a kid, so what?
If you're reading this, you can read the news
and you know that children suffer worse.

Worse for me is a cloud of memories
still drifting off the South China Sea,
like the nine-year-old boy, naked and lacerated,
thrashing in his pee on a steel operating table
and yelling "Dau. Dau," while I, trying to translate
in the mayhem of Tet for surgeons who didn't know
who this boy was or what happened to him, kept asking
"Where? Where's the pain?" until a surgeon
said "Forget it. His ears are blown."

I remember your first Halloween
when I held you on my chest and rocked you,
so small your toes didn't touch my lap
as I smelled your fragrant peony head
and cried because I was so happy and because
I heard, in no metaphorical way, the awful chorus
of Soeur Anicet's orphans writhing in their cribs.
Then the doorbell rang and a tiny Green Beret
was saying trick or treat and I thought *oh oh*
but remembered it was Halloween and where I was.
I smiled at the evil midget, his map light and night
paint, his toy knife for slitting throats, said,
"How ya doin', soldier?" and, still holding you asleep
in my arms, gave him a Mars bar. To his father
waiting outside in fatigues I hissed, "You shit,"
and saw us, child, in a pose I know too well.

I want you to know the worst and be free from it.
I want you to know the worst and still find good.
Day by day, as you play nearby or laugh
with the ladies at People's Bank as we go around town
and I find myself beaming like a fool,
I suspect I am here less for your protection
than you are here for mine, as if you were sent
to call me back into our helpless tribe.

John Balaban

CONDOMS

She says the book she is reading is gross.
She says she won't tell me what "gross" is.
Hours later, at bedtime, she asks about condoms.
I don't tell her
about the first rubber I ever saw,
fished out of a St. Louis drainage ditch in 1956,
dripping with sewage and ooze,
or about how Johnny Ferretti
blew them up like balloons
for the girls at the Country Day grade school,
or how "for the prevention of disease only"
we'd buy them in the men's room
of Bob Winston's Skelley Station
and keep them like ID's in our wallets.
Instead, I slip over them
that slick word, *prophylactics*,
and tell her they are a birth control device
used by two people making love.
When I bend down to kiss her
she pulls her head under the blankets.
Okay, she grimaces. *That's* gross.

Ronald Wallace

GHOST STORY

Sometimes while passing a playground
you see a child so like my mother
you believe for the length of a pang it's me.

You can't understand I'm not a child anymore
but a young girl,
that I have, like you, grown older.

If there is joy in even the smallest secret,
then I was your greatest, never to be shared
because there was no other you loved.

But now I am asking you to acknowledge
that even the dead want to be seen
for what they've become.

There are no memories of me to forget,
only that I was the beginning of a past
you keep forcing into the future.

I am too big to be carried, even by a father,
and you were never as strong
as you pretended to be.

Mark Osaki

MY DAUGHTER AND APPLE PIE

She serves me a piece of it a few minutes
out of the oven. A little steam rises
from the slits on top. Sugar and spice—
cinnamon—burned into the crust.
But she's wearing these dark glasses
in the kitchen at ten o'clock

in the morning—everything nice—
as she watches me break off
a piece, bring it to my mouth,
and blow on it. My daughter's kitchen,
in winter. I fork the pie in
and tell myself to stay out of it.
She says she loves him. No way
could it be worse.

Raymond Carver

MEN AND WOMEN

"Stones

not even the fish

will pause to tell apart"

STONES

> A man in terror of impotence
> or infertility, not knowing the difference. . . .
> —Adrienne Rich

We live in dread of something:

Need, perhaps. Tears,
the air inside a woman's dress,
the deep breath of non-ambition.

In a valley of stone,
men had to carry stones.
In a sea of fertility,
women could drown
in the wake of conceptions.

We no longer build in stone—
houses of rice paper, beds
of feather. Manhood
is the one stone we still
insist on, lifting it

From abandoned quarries,
carrying it on our backs
even when we make love,
until the woman beneath us
calls passion a kind of

Suffocation, surfaces for air
like a young child whose head
has been pushed beneath the water,
a way to learn swimming.

Did you come? we ask,
her head bobbing above the brine
that pours from us. Applause
is what we want now,

Her wet hands
clapping in the last wind
before she sinks again,
before she holds us again
so tight we both plunge
like a cry for help
into the water,

Before we fall to the bottom—

Stones
not even the fish
will pause to tell apart.

Michael Blumenthal

MEN & WOMEN

When I was five, my mother and father,
Uncle Chris, Aunt Evelyn and I drove
to the home place near Olney. I stood
in the front seat between the shoulder
pads watching for fires and wild animals.

At Grandmother's house I played outside.
I liked to hear the Savage .22 and see
the fields of blood. I liked to pee
with the men behind the haunted barn.
Their zippers were long as train tracks
and I wanted my little thing to be big
and wrinkled and sleepy-looking like theirs.

Later riding through the dark I sat between
my mother and her sister so close that
when they talked the feathers on their
hats touched. *Well, not now* she said
he knows he said it does it hurts some
time have you you do he does he wants

I dozed there in a mist of secrets, slipping
from one fragrant lap to another, hearing
underneath the silver fox, and gabardine
the hearsay of the real silk.

At home, Daddy carried me inside and everyone
came to watch me sleep. There they stood,
there I lay, surrounded by men and women.

Ron Koertge

YOUNG WOMAN

Young woman, sensitive dark lovely angry hot cold,
old people are spending their last days
deep in your life.
You help them yet they do not trust you.
You empty their clear piss;
and joy drains from your warm cruelty.
You burn wet red roses and eat tiny sardines
from the can. You stand on the outhouse
throwing grain at dumb chickens.
What kind of lady can you become?
Whores in the Valley knew your Indian mother,
the gambling drunks in town
were cheated by your black father.
Who are you? Where can you live?
Remember your grandfather's mule?
Left it to your father. Lost in a crap game.

The young mothers on the hill whisper your name.
The word is out: you're a threat.
Husbands are wild and helpless!
Still, I love you
and want to take you with me
to Denver.

Clarence Major

WANDA PICKLES

In the talent search you sang *Smoke Gets in Your Eyes*
In such a chanteuse way that Jack Pease and I
Stopped making fun of everything and
Goosing one another and the fat girls whose butts
Stuck out of those metal folding chairs
In the cafeteria-auditorium. Wanda Pikulski,
Touched by a magic wand—I mean smoke *did*
Get in our mean eyes and every boy in the 8th
And 9th grades dropped the drawers of adolescent
Adoration down to his ankles for the cross-eyed girl
Who never said more than an averted hi. Good-goddamn!
The sweet-strings background music staticked out of
Those old bullhorn speakers, and above it and through it
And beyond it thrilled that unbelievable contralto voice,
Assured, controlled, husky in all the right places. And how
Dressed up you were in that low-cut gown, make-up and no
Glasses, and the spotlight on you like a rouged Miss America.
When you repeated "When a lovely flame dies,"
A thousand 13-year-old hearts died right there with you and ached
For you never to stop. Wanda "Pickles," the nerdy duckling,
So sophisticated she could have been a movie star. And it
Wasn't just the song but the way you hung out over the edge
Of the melody, pushing it up and over the entire Lowell
Junior High Assembly, including the teachers in the back
Row—as if you were the heroine on a precipice

And kept hanging over, teetering there to our oohs and aahs
And the prayer of Sweet Jesus don't let her fall over. We knew in our
Nasty but innocent hearts that in a being so transformed
Into sweet celebrity, there was hope for us all.

That in the agony of acne and pimples that bled
And all those hormones ballooning in our bodies,
And voices that were adenoidal and sinus-hoarse—
That never repeated anything the way it was rehearsed
In the fever of imagination, where they were always suave
As Melvyn Douglas wooing society ladies
At the Orpheum Theater on Saturday night—
Where we never suffered the nerves of bad breath
Or had our voices, strangulated, break—
You were not only speaking but singing for us all,
And you brought the song off with a high crescendo,
Leaving the last sibilant, the last liquid syllable
Like a soap bubble poised in the air,
Trembling with the promise of a rainbow life.

Lloyd Van Brunt

EACH DAY

Cynthia Matz, with my finger in your cunt
and you sliding back and forth on it,
protesting at the late hour and tiredness
and me with kidneys straining to capacity
with piss I had no chance to release
all night, we got up from the park bench
and walked you home. I left you
at the door. You said something
despairing about taking a chance
and settling on me. I had left Janette
to chase after you running out
of the ice cream parlor where

the three of us had sat—I had felt
so sorry and so guilty to have you
find me with her in the street.
You and I had gone to shows together.
You needed me to talk to and I was glad.
The talk always was about him
whom you still loved. He had jilted
you for someone else. I'm sorry, Cynthia,
that it had to end this way between us too.
I did not return the next day,
after leaving you at the door.
I did not return the following day either.
I went with Janette in whom I felt
nothing standing in the way,
while with you it would have been
each day to listen to your sadness
at having been betrayed by him.
I was not to be trusted either.
I too wanted love pure and simple.

David Ignatow

MALE SPRINGTIME RITUAL
                              for Hugh Masekela

it's hard on male eyeballs walking new york streets
in springtime, all the fine flamingo ladies
peeling off everything the hard winter forced them to put on
now, breasts shook loose from strait-jacketed, layered clothes
overcoats, tease invitations of nipples
peek-a-boo through see through, clinging blouses
reveal sweet things our imaginations need to know to fire mystery
they jelly-roll, seduce through silk, short-circuit connections
of dirty old men, mind in their you-know-what young men, too
they fog up eyeglasses, contact lenses, shades—
& most of these sho-nuff hope to die lovers

always get caught without
their portable, windex, shade-cleaner bottles
& so have to go blind through the rest of the day
contemplating what they thought they saw

eye mean, it can drive you crazy, walking behind one of those
memorable asses in springtime, when the wind gets cocky
& licks up one of those breeze-blown, slit, wraparounds, revealing
that grade A, sweet poontanged, rump of flesh & it is moving, deep
like those old black african ladies taught it to do & do
eye mean, it's maybe too much for a good old, staid, christian
chauvinist, with a bad heart & a pacer
eye mean, what can you expect him to do—
carrying all that kind of heavy baggage around—
but vote for bras to be worn everyday & abolish any cocky wind
whose breezy tongue gets completely out of hand
lifting up skirts of young, fine, sweet thangs
eye mean, "there ought to be a law against some things"
eye'm sure he would say, "reckless eyeballin' "
eye'm sure he would say

anyway, it's hard on menfolk streetwalkers in springtime
liable to find your eyeballs roaming around dazed
in some filthy new york city gutter
knocked there by some dazzling, sweet beauty, who happened along
your limited, field of vision—who knows, next thing you know
they'll be making portable pacers for eyeballs—
& who cares if you go down for the whole ten count
& never pull your act back together again
& so become a bowery street bum, a dazed babbling
idiot, going on & on about some fine, flamingo lady you thought
you saw, an invitation, perhaps
& who cares if her teasing breasts shook you
everwhichaway, but loose

it's springtime, in the old big apple
& all the fine, flamingo ladies, are peeling off
everything the hard winter forced them to put on
their breasts shake loose from overcoats
tease invitations of nipples

it's all a part of the springtime ritual

& only the strongest eyeballs, survive

Quincy Troupe

BULLFINCH KNEW

Back when I was a character in
classical mythology, I was hanging
out with this overly hyperactive
girl; I was the god of Curiosity;
she goddess of Catch-me-if-you-can.

She had dead bugs, crushed flowers,
and twigs in her knotted hair; she
was a living tribute to nature and
her navel had dirt in it.

She was elusive and thrifty with
words. She was mute ¼ of the day,
made noises another quarter,
verbose for 6 hours and the rest I
don't know, for this time I spent
eavesdropping on the other gods.

They were selfish, stupid and
egotistical; they were lusty, bawdy
and lazy. They seldom bathed they
lied, tricked and tried to take
advantage of each other,
successfully.

They raped, teaming up to create a
complicated ruse to confuse a
common enemy in ruthless tortures
they called "practical jokes."

They made me sick and so I took my
curiosity elsewhere, caught-her-as-
I-could, and dove in way past the
metaphysical; here's what happened:

Through a means not suitable for
the ears of children, we sired the
sun, five trails of liquid ran down
our thighs and became the oceans;
five tears of our ecstacy made the
Great Lakes.

The bickering of the gods was
passed on to mankind, and I stood
with her, holding hands, watching;

then we fell.

Eric Brown

WHAT HEATHENS DO DURING MIDNIGHT MASS

Fifteen years later I still give thanks
for your wise gift one Christmas Eve when
sweat bubbled on our tingling skin,
oozed into carpet that tickled and burned
as we played on the edge of passion, and sin.
We were all lips and tongues
when a tabernacled guilt unlocked in me,
Mea Culpa whispering soft and secret
from musty altared faith,
your woman smell mingling in memory with incense,
the tight-throated fumes of melting candle wax,
and the sticky sweetness of early morning wine.

Fifteen years ago, remember?
Beneath my parents' wedding picture on the mantle,
beneath Christmas cards and candles and cuckoo clock,
we squirmed sweetly together,
damp and warm in front of flames
that hissed and spit at our gleaming skin,
hellishly warm,
heavenly warm,
squirming sweetly together
when staccato cuckoos cursed above our heads,
yanked me to my feet, chilled with dread,
my nakedness a shivering shame.

The silence echoed black inside me,
contrition throbbed through every throbbing pulse,
the silence a sore and aching thing
until you nudged it with your purling giggle,
a woman's giggle, deep and gurgling,
your breasts jiggling to the sound of giggles
tumbling over giggles with glee and gladness
and something else I barely heard—
an unheavenly grace,
a gentle benediction

that drew me down next to your goodness,
drew me down, hushed and warm
inside your arms floating up and circling round,
held me safe in your giggling mirth
in communion and salvation
like a musky angel come to earth.

Michael Cleary

BLIND GIRL AT THE SINGLES BAR

I don't know what the blind girl sees
in me. She keeps staring at me as if
she can see as well as anyone else
in the place. Only her cane, propped
against the bar, gives her away.

Others in the crowd might think she's lame.

Behind her dark designer frames,
her eyes don't have that blind kind of look.
They dart about the bar in such a focused way.

Maybe a little light still gets in.

I've got my Walkman turned way up.
That puts us on an equal footing.

Occasionally, our elbows touch.

From the way she's dressed, almost
draped in a green running suit, I can tell
how much someone must love her.

When her cane falls against my leg,
she has to touch me to get my attention.

I have to turn off The Police to hear
her apology. "I didn't feel a thing,"
I lie, and offer her another Marguerita on me.

While it's mixing, she tells me
how she loves the sound of the blender,
so cheerful among the babble of voices.

To me it sounds like buzzsaws.

She goes to the restroom and comes back.
She seems to know her way around.
Now and then we sip our drinks.
It's hot in here.

The ice cubes make a reassuring sound.

I eye the three gray ceiling fans that did not wobble
when they were brand new. That's part
of the way I describe the room to her. Along
with the photos of the cowboys on the walls,
looking authentic, gunslingers quick on the draw,
the owners and the dusty ranch hands of the *Rocking R*
posed by the corral.

                    The deep gray-blue
of the walls themselves, a little barb of cactus
on each table with a little candle.

The music, mostly Steely Dan, speaks for itself.

She's buying now: "You're not trying
to get me blind drunk, are you?" she says
and grins. I laugh right back
and ask her how she lost it.

"I was working in a lab, there was a blinding

flash. That was that. The hardest part,"
she says, "was making friends with the dark."

She is surprised to hear the way blindness
runs in my family, how my father blinded himself
in one eye in a childhood accident.
Years later, the eye had to be removed
to save the sight of the other.

When I was young, I used to stare
at his glass eye in the medicine chest
at night, wondering if it could see me.
It looked as if it could, fostered
by the game we played. If he caught me
in a lie, he'd say, "Tell me that again,
and look me in the eye, *the good one,*"
which was blind. It always worked.

We decide, a little drunkenly, to take a cab.
I provide a running commentary on the view
to her place in Chelsea. It's large and bright
and airy. There's a grand piano sitting
in one room.

"I think of myself as Lady Beethoven," she says,
just as I take it in, "except I still hear
what I'm doing."

Sitting on the loveseat with a cool breeze
coming in, she squeezes both my hands
with a surprising strength. We kiss.
I let myself be led into her bedroom.
Gray walls. Pink spread. A large and original-
looking Monet above the bed.

"You're so sweet," she tells me,
"I can tell everything about you
just from the sound of your voice."

While we make love, I stare at her
and she stares back. I sing love songs
to her in my head no one will ever hear.

Her fingers read my mind. She turns on
a dim lamp on the table near the bed,
thinking it might be dark. It almost is.
I know I'm in good hands. I turn the light
back off, and when she hears the click,
she smiles her perfect smile
in the remaining light.

I tell her what I look like.
She touches me. "Your face feels attractive,
but how can I be sure?"

She has to take me at my word.

"At least you haven't let your body go
too far."

Then she walks, naked, to the piano
and plays a Chopin nocturne.
It's a calculated play. Even I know
the piece quite well. She sings "Chelsea Morning,"
rocks on to Stevie's "damn the dark,
damn the light."

My harmonies, half-hearted, soft,
inspire her to laugh. When she's done,
we sit propped up in her bed, her dark
hair against my face, her open mouth
against my chest, taking away my breath.

She explains how simple darkness is.

There is no silence after that, only
the fear of silence.

I can see the light but I can't explain it.

Our blue eyes lock. She hangs on
every word, and now we touch
with an unexpected genius of the heart,
whispering promises no one could ever keep
in the failing light.

Nick Johnson

SHE FUCKS AND I FUCK

She fucks and I fuck
and both of us are fucking
Now I'm up, I'm thinking I'm fucking
then I'm not thinking I'm fucking
I'm just fucking
Then I'm telling her how good it feels
then I'm feeling how good it feels
I want to come and I don't want to come
She wants to come and she doesn't
want to come, oh not just yet
you can't fuck and think about fucking
all at the same time, your leg is in
her cunt all of a sudden and you want
to be her cunt all of a sudden
to be fucked, not to fuck,
to include, not to penetrate,
to be killed, not the killer
Oh and it's always moving,
it's going to be over
suddenly you think and then you don't think,
A tongue licks your closed eye
and it licks your closed chest
and you lick back,
thinking of licking,

then just licking
and your heart breaks,
it breaks,
you're fucking the woman you love
and it breaks your heart.
You're deep and full
in pity and in pain,
coming up from life
for air,
and yes, I love me now,
I am plunged and raised,
set down and risen,
the inside breaks against the bone,
and God, dear God,
if You could fuck the woman You love
when You are loving her,
everything that hurts
in Your heart
would come true.

Jack Grapes

CYNTHIA

When I take off your red sweatpants,
sliding them over the ass I love,
the fat thighs, and now my hands
are trembling, my tongue is muzzy,
a fire runs under my skin.

Cynthia's red-gold muff caught
the morning light as she strode from my bed,
upright and proud. Her body was
a vehicle for pleasure. It had carried us
into sleep as if we were children,
protected forever from the void and dark.

She slept with him
if at dinner he pleased
her. If he did not, she
did not. She was free
to choose, without
the drags of love.

Every day I wonder about you—
why it is your eyes look so wild
sometimes. Other times, so naked,
so pure-blue naked. Your shields, you say,
speaking of your diaphragm, your contact lenses.
Nevertheless, you think of yourself as being at home
in this world in a way I am not.
I understand it is my myth-making intelligence
gets me in trouble, makes me want to fix you
as earth nourisher, source of comfort,
when it is what is lost and erratic in you
brings you to my bed, beatings against fate
or circumstance, stabbings toward transcendence
that leave us both bruised and happy in ourselves.

To be with her
was to be in a cloud
of sexual joy—hair, eyes,
speech. The merest
flick of her tongue
on a word set off
resonances.

I fell in love with
one of the poisonous tomatoes of America.

Mind-fucking at 3 A.M.
because where are you
and that's where you are.

At the instant of her coming, she makes a throaty sound.
It is back beyond words, low in the throat,
away from the tongue. I never try to translate it,
any more than I would translate sunlight or deep shade.

Before sleep, C in my arms, her back toward me,
puts my right hand on her left breast. If I
could make an amulet of that.

She is beautiful to me
as she wakes from sleep,
sits straight up—
force, energy, and purpose
in her straight spine.

I wonder where her cunt is tonight
and her proud head. She did
make me happy, more than once.
One Sunday morning, light everywhere
in the living room, she on the couch
facing me, garbed in my blue bathrobe,
one breast shapely through the opening
of the robe while I drink my coffee, happy.

The last time
I went down on Cynthia
was the last time
though her petals
in the rose red light

   She said she had taken on seven students the previous
night on her visit upstate, and that all had watched,
masturbating as each colleague performed. One had her
in the missionary position, one took her from behind,
one made her ride on top, one came in her mouth, one
had her lean over a table, one did her on his lap, one fucked
her up the ass. The last to have her, she said, because
he had come six times, had trouble achieving an erection.

After she had told all this to her lover, fiction or fact,
he became the eighth man.

There'll always be room for you
in my capacious vagina, she said.
At the elevator door. Some parting!
("Capacious quiff" would have been catchier.)

All the questions she asked him
he answered from another life.

He was trying to understand
the nature of the pain.
Maybe when a woman
aborts a child
it is like this: killing
something in oneself.
Someone else has already done
the killing, yet there
is more left to kill.

She was hidden in his thought
like a tick in a dog's fur.
He could feel the rise with his finger
where her mouth sucked blood.

Harvey Shapiro

A STORY ABOUT THE BODY

The young composer, working that summer at an artist's colony, had
watched her for a week. She was Japanese, a painter, almost sixty, and he
thought he was in love with her. He loved her work, and her work was like
the way she moved her body, used her hands, looked at him directly when
she made amused and considered answers to his questions. One night,
walking back from a concert, they came to her door and she turned to him

and said, "I think you would like to have me. I would like that too, but I must tell you that I have had a double mastectomy," and when he didn't understand, "I've lost both my breasts." The radiance that he had carried around in his belly and chest cavity—like music—withered, very quickly, and he made himself look at her when he said, "I'm sorry. I don't think I could." He walked back to his own cabin through the pines, and in the morning he found a small blue bowl on the porch outside his door. It looked to be full of rose petals, but he found when he picked it up that the rose petals were on top; the rest of the bowl—she must have swept them from the corners of her studio—was full of dead bees.

Robert Hass

THE NEW MOVIES

Friendship is possible.
He's studied that young woman
On the bench, her jaw and the lick
Of hair that falls over her eyes.
She is reading a book, a bitten apple
At her side, and it's his task
To greet her, to talk small talk,
Then large issues, like whales,
Until her hand is in his,
And they're off to a museum and then coffee,
A foreign movie they don't get.
There is late dinner, a flush
Of wine, and his right hand
Like a badge on her blouse.
They're on the couch, then the floor,
The tongue taking its place behind an ear.

After it's over they stare
Into the fire that's gone down,
The smoke of two drinks
Behind their eyes.

They talk about artichokes,
Then beets, cucumbers, sprouts . . .
They talk about clouds
Seen from jets, until their talk
Stalls like a cloud. It's 2 A.M.
He pats her hip, smiling.
There's little to say
Now that they've come this far.
She steps into her skirt,
He into his pants. The room fills
With the sounds of things closing,
Buckles and snaps, buttons
And earrings, zippers that yawn
On the floor but grit their teeth
When they close to say good-bye.

Gary Soto

SECTS

We were talking about tent revivals
and softshell Baptists and the one-suspender Amish
and being told whistling on Sunday made the Madonna cry.
One fellow said he was raised in a church that taught
wearing yellow and black together was an important sin.
It got me thinking of the failed denomination
I was part of: that old false dream of woman.
I believed it was a triumph to have access to their mystery.
To see the hidden hair, to feel my spirit topple over,
to lie together in the afternoon while it rained
all the way to Indonesia. I had crazy ideas of what it was.
Like being in a dark woods at night
when an invisible figure crosses the stiff snow,
making a sound like some other planet's machinery.

Jack Gilbert

PORNO LOVE
      for Darlene & Mae

You send me a photograph
of you in which your genitals
are not only exposed
but offered close-up to the lens
like a piece of good advice.
I've never met you
though you say,
"We think you're swell."
I appreciate the gesture:
I've been exposing my genitals
in poems for a long time now,
at least when they're good.
So I know you mean nothing obscene
by it. Your squat is humble,
as mine is, even now.
I am writing this poem
naked, up close.
I am writing it with my penis.
No one but you two sisters
will understand
how such a poem is innocent,
how, as with a confidence to a friend,
no shock is intended,
how what we stick in the faces of our loved ones
is our way of saying, I trust you will not
seal me shut
or cut me off, I love you that much.
Surely we will meet with our clothes on,
that is the point.
But when I say, Thanks for the picture, Girls,
it's nicely cropped,
and you say, We liked the feel of your poem,
I'll be thinking how certain private parts
made vulnerable
give greatest pleasure

in a consummation
of good will.

Philip Dacey

GLIMPSE ON OUR WEDDING DAY

Across that hotel's roof of tar
an old man sat on his bed,
his underwear yellow as bulb overhead.

He spooned beans from a can.
Someone left him, someone like you,
years ago. I touched your cold shoulder,
took breast in my hand.

David Ray

TOUCHING

Light is a distant world
though at 5 A.M. in the bedroom
window where the spider plant hovers
shining, there is a silken presence
where it traces, leaves a constellation.
I roll over and the room moves
a little closer, it is light—
like when Karen sleeps beside me
turned away but warm rubbing back
and I curve myself like hers
to hold her body for seeing
whatever is far in her.
Now I'm almost dreaming.
Words run transparent from my mouth

and almost find the edge of things.
Across the street in the park
a big hawk sails, gently flapping,
its outspread arms hugging the air
just as the sun kisses upward
to find its way through the sky.
Back here off the edge of the bed
my fingers, blind at both ends,
dangle in a void like starlight
traveled so far its source burned out.
Now a light goes off in my head as
I hold this hand that seems so far away.
I think of the monster fullback
in high school, after running over me
he dropped the ball to see was I hurt.
Where is he now, or the woman
who put the message in the bottle
I found splashing in the fouled waters
off Point Pelee. What was on her mind
writing, *kindness anywhere is still kindness,*
I'm in Cleveland, cold, alone—
wherever you are you hold this part of me.
I roll over in the glow
where sunrise goes across the bed,
knowing our age thinks light is wavelike
bundles spreading outward like ships
floating home in measured gaps toward each shore.
So part of the world waits distant.
For all I know as a man it might happen
like kelp bits drifting to no shore.
Still if there's a moment somewhere
equal to this light filling my skin,
then there is a constant I can count on
and I'll go forth and live with that.

Christopher Gilbert

QUICKIE

both kids watching morning TV
wife glistening from the bath
target of opportunity
I propose a quick hit
wife and mother she agrees
we're at it one minute
toddler blubbers at the door
a few seconds to finish
thanks honey quick kiss
ejected like a jet pilot
into empty altitudes
suspended and shaky
coming down by parachute

Paul Gianoli

THE ROSE

Home late, I eat dinner
& read the paper
without noticing
the rose in the yellow
glass on the dining room table—
not until
Mary shows it to me.
"Isn't it lovely?"
"Where'd you get it?"
"A fellow named Bill."
"Oh?"
"Just some guy who comes in
to the bar occasionally . . .
Isn't it lovely?"
"He gave it to you?"
I turn to the editorial page.

"Yes . . .
he just got out of the hospital."
She bends
& takes in its fragrance.
She is wearing that black negligee.
"The hospital?"
She straightens up & looks
at me & sighs.
"He's dying of cancer."
We stare at each other.
I want to embrace her,
tell her how much I love her,
how much I have always loved her.
But I don't.
I just sit there.
When she walks back into the bedroom
I see it at last,
glowing on the table,
leaning toward me
on its heartbroken stem.

Steve Kowit

THE GREAT HOUSE
for Suzanne

Over and over it happens, my wife and I are
Out walking, we come to a great stone house
Built into a hillside. We are young again;
All things seem possible on this perfect day.
Suddenly we know that the house is ours!
We enter in joy, exulting in what we own:
Circular staircases, niches, ballrooms,
A dozen rooms full of leatherbound books,
Lace curtains, puppet theatres, daguerreotypes,
Chests full of doilies and ancient manuscript,

Hand printing presses, bowls of potpourri;
There are antique cribs, rocking chairs,
A canopied bed. We could start our lives again!
All windows swing open to singing birds and trees
Through which we see a whitewashed, sunlit city.

At night, after a lingering dinner and wine,
Lieder and string quartets by candle glow,
We ascend the tower, open the skylight
And turn the huge reflector into position.
The shimmer that we see has traveled for eons.
Under the circling stars, the birds against
The moon, with the vast rooms breathing
Beneath us, we know that the only sadness
In the world will be to leave this house.

Paul Zimmer

THE MORTAL WIFE

The woman on fire who walks away and disappears,
down the endless walkway of the airline terminal
until only her hair is seen, a flame against the
blinding whiteness of the passage as he flies to
bathe in his birth in the queenmother of cities,
is the queen of women his mortal wife and seems,
as she disappears into the distance dearest ever
inscribed into the hindsight of his wounded eye.
Later, in the city he sleeps his way from street
to street, each one of them familiar to him even
tho, in any individual case, he may not know it:
the overlaps of forms, colors, and smells betray
the overarching city map into his mind. Her eyes
that (walking away from him) see her own purpose
restore her to her own births and float her down
quite other streets. He wants to be solo he sees

because he wants to be alone with her. He cannot
talk of their lives even to *simpatico* strangers.
In streets further away than they could dream of
marriage glows, in pride of place, assumes them.

Nathaniel Tarn

LOVE SONG

Though we have traveled far
we have not reached
the mountains.
            Mons Veneris,
the mountain of love,
is as far from us now
as when we set out fresh
in the early morning.
Now we are tired, and feel old.
The only things worth looking at
are the mountains:
            Love's
and a few others,
catching the late flame of the sun,
almost down,
            behind us.

Theodore Enslin

TAKING THE MOVIES TO THE STREETS

The French movie takes off her blouse,
Puts it back on. Nothing
For you Pierre,
This week,

204

Next week,
And if I have it my way,
As long as that thing stands up.

The movie ends.
The patrons blink when the lights come on.
I help my wife with her coat;
My friend helps his wife with her coat.
The men around us are just as helpful.
Are any of them like me,
Confused about what they just saw,
Two hours of bedroom crying?
And why did the old nun beat herself with a candle?
What was this about a saint with a flying cape?
Where did the mouse come from
When the violins started?
(Poor, brie-fed mouse, ten minutes
On camera and no credit in the end.)

Outside, the stars mingle with neon.
The faces of newspapers drink from the gutter.
We walk back to the car, the four
Of us smiling. What was it
About? I look back: the marquee glows "psycho-drama."
That's what I need in life. Lust is a slow slime
In the heart. I nudge against my friend's
Wife's tear-shaped ass. She's beautiful.
I've seen her hang laundry and board a bus
In high-heels. "Psycho-drama," I breathe
In her ear. She squeals, laughs, and tells
Her husband, "Honey, he's doing it again!"

Honey punches me in the arm,
Softly. "Psycho-drama," he says,
And places a creepy kiss on my screaming wife's mouth.

Gary Soto

You were just a med student then,
and as evenings grew dark and scattered with stars,
you'd return from the County coiled tight, straight
from the trenches, drugged by the lack of sleep:
"At ten a stab.* case came in. The woman was moaning
(she'd been found behind the Seven-Eleven).
David, half of her skull had been crushed in,
her whole left side paralyzed. She
was naked from the waist down. . . .
No, they didn't catch him. And no one knows
who she is. I just hope she wasn't conscious.
They thrust tubes down her throat, her nose,
IV's in her body, and left her stripped, exposed
on the table, while the doctors and nurses gathered
their instruments. It was like another assault.
I sat there and wrote it down, instrument by
instrument, procedure by procedure, cut by cut
. . . Now? If she's lucky, she won't wake up. . . ."

Later, down in Arkansas, they picked him up,
brought him back for trial. Barely
literate, a black ex-con. On t.v., in a brief clip,
his face looked hollowed, haggard, his teeth
gapped and twisted, his eyes dead. It was as if
he'd become a thing like stones or dust,
sand or salt, his soul a net full of shadows.
I felt unnerved, fatuous, somehow responsible. . . .

And the victim? Beneath the covers, shivering
almost unconsciously, you left her for another,
her story spilling out—

                       "That wasn't all. At two
a woman came in with her blouse torn open,
her skirt in shreds. She was in shock.
Gradually I got her story out: From the age

*Stab.: short for stabilization, pronounced with a long a.

206

of before she could remember, she had been raped
by her father. David, I couldn't believe it:
She was thirty-four. . . . Finally, she moved
across the river, came to the city only for therapy:
This time her father was waiting. He chased her down 94,
forced her to the side of the road and walked her
into the woods and tied her to a tree. . . ."

Silence. You sat up, pulled your knees to your chest.
Asked for water.
                    "He tried again and again. He kept
holding his limp penis, pressing it against her.
In rage, he began to stuff mud up her vagina,
at the same time, whipping her thighs with a pine branch.
This went on from late afternoon to long after sunset. . . .
After she finished, I didn't know what to say. I just cried.
She, she seemed startled. Relieved. . . ."

Susan, what can I say? Some part of me
knows that man? What *do* I know? Even then
I knew I'd never comprehend how the rapist,
the incestuous father, his almost inhuman rage,
that could crush so endlessly his will to love,
enters, like a messenger, a woman's existence.
And yet—God, is this why I'm telling this?—
I felt jealous. You had witnessed these stories. . . .

It's years later. A friend tells me of writing on the Holocaust,
spending night after night in the office of Himmler,
in visions of ash and the crystals of gas: how the desire arose
to rub each entrenched, lime drenched body against the reader's
psyche and skin. And then on a trip to Dachau,
she was there, shaking, holding her palm to the brick
of the ovens, feeling the weight of those voices, those faces,
those spirits push against her, enfold her, a presence
as palpable as a violent wind; and yet it was only when
she walked through those gates—"Work Sets You Free"—
    emblazoned above,
and walked down the hill to a small sapling,

surrounded by pink, blushing petunias, only then
was she able to sit and rest and let it out,
the only answer annealed to that earthly beauty—
"I knew then I couldn't write it with just Himmler, the camps,
the corpses, there had to be more, these moments of release"—
a clarity of tears, sunlight, peace: to see the aimless, unfolding
hills, a sapling, petunias, bend in the breeze.

David Mura

MOMENTS WHEN THE WORLD CONSENTS

Atlantic waves roil over reefs beyond the cut
between Tooloo and Elbow Cays, boom
and boom on jagged coral, disintegrating
skyward in repeating crystal spray.
A quarter-mile away, behind the windward cays,
Abaco Sound lies blue on gently rippling
blue, and in the islands' lees, wild peas
and bougainvillaea blossom under Caribbean pines.

You lie face down; I watch the water
in the shallow sheltered cove we've come to share.
Warm wind in coconut palms along the beach
seems to set the broad green leaves to talking
softly: "Stay awhile, you two, be still;
this hour, this afternoon, this day; be
jealous of the moments when the world
consents to give you to each other
undistracted. You may not find another place
or time to smell good air blown all the way
from Africa or Spain, or lie on sand so
smooth and white and warm and meant
for you."

I let my fingers fall across your hips.
You turn, and open like a flower.
Love, like sun-warmed swirling tiny pearl waves
on satin water, laps our naked thighs.

W. D. Ehrhart

THE FLOATING WORLD
for Anna

1
Sounds of koto and flute spool from the radio
this January morning.
Thirty years ago we were in Japan.

2
Fuji's snow-cone flushed in early light
soared above the gate at the edge of the garden,
as though we'd borrowed the holy mountain—
visible from a hundred miles away
only in clearest air of winter—for the morning.
When we rose my shirt was so cold you thawed
it at the stove. I left the house,
turned a corner
and the mountain disappeared.

3
Blowing curtains in the wine shops.
Fire in the waxed paper lanterns
red as blood.

4
Returned to our room in the 300-year-old inn,
its walls, sliding doors brown as oak leaves.
In the light of the floor lamp, our futon spread
to receive us was the color of moss in noon sunlight.

Rain brushed the city, dripped
from the evergreens, the stone lantern
in our private garden.

5
You sang lieder with our student-guide in Kyoto
eight years after Hiroshima.
Temples, a palace, a walled sand garden.
Back home, I failed to answer his letter.

6
These scenes from the beginning of our story
shine like slides on a white wall.
I reach for them, give them the permanence
of thin lines of ink on ruled paper.
They can matter only to you and me.

Mark Perlberg

DISTANCES

Though she is only in the next room
he misses his wife
the distance between his waking
and her sleep is unbridgeable
and contains everything
the world is made of
pacing the living room
he thinks how perhaps
he is also in one of her dreams
a kind of split
between his own waking and sleeping
which is also a distance
too large to be crossed
he begins to think that everything
comes down to distances
that how far one thing is from another

is what defines each of them
he begins counting the inventions
meant to defeat distance
going all the way back
past the taming of animals
and the invention of language
to the first touch
between two people on Earth
it occurs to him
that these inventions
were based on the premise
that to eliminate distance was good
and necessary at all times
when his wife emerges from the bedroom
he hugs her harder than usual
defining for himself the distance
between them even then

Michael Rattee

THE PARKING LOT

I parked, left my wife
in the car.
When I came out
there was a blue van
and 2 men smoked
and drank from a bottle
in a paper sack.
They had taken women
from parking lots
before, from liquor stores
or the market
took whatever they wanted.
I saw them
glance at my wife.

There was a fat woman
between them
in a mumu, her blond hair
like tallow. She was
moving her shoulders
keeping time with the music.
They started their van
grazed my fender,
cut me off from the street.
My hands trembled
and I measured the dark, short one
who came toward me.
My knees slightly bent
my wife calling me back.

I thought of the fifties
drive-in parking lot
where Willie broke
a collar bone, a wrist
and tore an ear
with a tire iron.
I crouched in the back seat
my breath on the glass.

This time I didn't
look away or put my
head down when the man
called for the woman
and the driver,
who giggled
and put on another tape.
He looked down
said "shit, we didn't
hurt nothing"
and the van pulled up
to let me pass.

Glover Davis

SHOPPING FOR A WOMAN

Shopping for my wife, I'm lost
To the shrug of skirts, taut calves,
The hair coming up with wind—these women
With their arms hurting for one more red gift.
OK, I admit it. I'm the Catholic
In the lingerie department
Tapping slippers against my palm
And weighing nighties that are sheer as clouds,
Upfront and eager to crumble in my hands.
I buy the cloud, and on the next floor,
A woman behind a counter with
Patou, Givenchy, L'Aire du Temps
Under my nose, splashed on my wrist.
Her throat is open, eyes arched like birds,
And the dark behind her ear is a channel
To the heart. I ask, Is this what women
Want? She lifts her eyes to me
And the birds are gone: her face is fawn-colored,
Quiet in her study of me. Sometimes,
She says, and looks aside to a tray
Of jewelry—pearl necklace,
Earrings showing light. These things too,
She says. And this chain, in gold.

Gary Soto

LOVE SONG: I AND THOU

Nothing is plumb, level or square:
    the studs are bowed, the joists
are shaky by nature, no piece fits
    any other piece without a gap
or pinch, and bent nails
    dance all over the surfacing

like maggots. By Christ
    I am no carpenter. I built
the roof for myself, the walls
    for myself, the floors
for myself, and got
    hung up in it myself. I
danced with a purple thumb
    at this house-warming, drunk
with my prime whiskey: rage.
    Oh, I spat rage's nails
into the frame-up of my work:
    it held. It settled plumb,
level, solid, square, and true
    for that great moment. Then
it screamed and went on through,
    skewing as wrong the other way.
God damned it. This is hell,
    but I planned it, I sawed it,
I nailed it, and I
    will live in it until it kills me.
I can nail my left palm
    to the left-hand crosspiece but
I can't do everything myself.
    I need a hand to nail the right,
a help, a love, a you, a wife.

Alan Dugan

LIVING WITH OTHERS
                                for Arlie

Yesterday, I discovered my wife
often climbs our stairs on all fours.

214

In my lonely beastliness,
I thought I was alone,
the only four-legged climber, the forger
of paths through thickets to Kilimanjaro's summit.

In celebration then, side by side,
we went up the stairs on all our fours,
and after a few steps
our self-consciousness slid from us
and I growled low in the throat
and bit with blunt teeth my mate's shoulder and
she laughed low
in her throat,
and rubbed her haunches on mine.

At the top of the stairs
we rose on our human feet
and it was fine and fitting somehow;
it was Adam and Eve rising
out of themselves before the Fall—
or after; it was survivors on a raft
mad-eyed with joy
rising to the hum of a distant rescue.

I live for such moments.

Al Zolynas

from COUPLETS *(#9)*

She thinks if she puts out, her sainthood will be recognized.
He figures his wit and pathos entitle him to love.

She laughs and cries, showing her small teeth;
He lifts her dress and buries his face in her bush.

She loves somebody else, who doesn't give a shit.
He does too, but that's different.

It was all good clean fun that had no future
And now it doesn't even have a past.

Neither of them is even alive at this point—
There's just me, and you, I suppose, wherever you are.

What a mess, the meat burnt, the sink overflowing,
The kid won't stop crying, he wants his milk.

Robert Mezey

NO LOVE IN THIS HOUSE

Tonight I cup your breasts.
Like September's fruit
letting go of limbs.
Your nipples eyes of fire.
I kiss you deep as ripeness;
deep as a knife will go.

I pull you out of your bluejeans.
Out of your black panties with
a red rose on the crotch.
My fingers find the center of you
where human breath begins.
Where the blues begin.

I'm in a room of you
where a white horse shockwaves
through your spine.

It's hard to break away
from this truth: flesh,
fire, song, wine, language.
We curve into dance.

There's no love in this house.
When I drive myself into you
you're singing the name
of another man in Rifle Gap
with his cowboy boots
propped upon another
woman's kitchen table.

Yusef Komunyakaa

FEELING FUCKED UP

Lord she's gone done left me done packed / up and split
and I with no way to make her
come back and everywhere the world is bare
bright bone white   crystal sand glistens
dope death dead dying and jiving drove
her away made her take her laughter and her smiles
and her softness and her midnight sighs—

Fuck Coltrane and music and clouds drifting in the sky
fuck the sea and trees and the sky and birds
and alligators and all the animals that roam the earth
fuck marx and mao fuck fidel and nkrumah and
democracy and communism fuck smack and pot
and red ripe tomatoes fuck joseph fuck mary fuck
god jesus and all the disciples fuck fanon nixon
and malcolm fuck the revolution fuck freedom fuck
the whole muthafucking thing
all i want now is my woman back
so my soul can sing

Etheridge Knight

PARTING SINCE

So I said to my girl, "Damn
I'm getting tired of pushing
Cars with no gas. . . ."

"Right,"
She said,
"Now you know
How I feel about you. . . ."

And there we were,
In the most casual parting
Since oil left water.

Jack Agueros

SPIDER PLANT

When I opened my eyes this morning,
the fact of its shooting out
long thin green runners on which miniatures
of the mother will sprout,
and that each of these offshoots
could in its own time repeat this,
terrified me. And something seemed awful
in the syllables of the word "Brenda,"
sounding inside me before they made a name,
then making a name of no one I've known.
I had been dreaming I was married to Patty
again. She kept coming on my tongue
and I knew if I put myself in
we'd have to stay together this time.
But I wanted to, and did, and as I did
the sadness and pleasure of our nine years together
washed through me as a river, yet

I knew this wasn't right, it couldn't
work, and though we were now enmeshed
forever, I began to rise from my body
making love with her on the bed and to hover
at a little distance over both of us.
That's when I awoke and saw the spider plant.

Michael Ryan

FIRST MARRIAGE

We were both twenty-three years
old. I was solitary, she was
social. I liked to get up early,
she loved to sleep late. While
I read a difficult book, she curled
up with her favorite magazine.
Once I lay down for a nap and asked
her to join me: a minute later
she was cuddling up close. She
had long brown hair, and I liked
to watch her brush it. I told
her how good it looked falling on
a white blouse. Every night
we went through the ritual among
couples: she told me about her
day, and I told her about mine.
Cheerful on the telephone, she
controlled our social life.
To the marriage she brought many
art books and a fine music collection.
She introduced me to *The Golden
Bough*, Käthe Kollwitz, *Letters to
a Young Poet*, Albrecht Dürer, *The
Journal of Delacroix*, and Erik
Satie. But she called a group

of islands an archipeglio. Grunion,
the fish we watched spawning on
California beaches, were gurion.
The exterminator was The Cockroach
Man. I loved waking up on a
winter morning when we were warm
and snug under the covers. She
was one of the great sleepers,
and my first labor of the day was
to get her out of bed. I would
snuggle up, then whisper sweet
things into her ear until she began
to murmur. One morning she awakened
angry: she had dreamed that at
dinner I ate the entire chicken,
and left her only a wing. She
was unscientific, attractive to
mosquitoes, walked gracefully, wore
cotton blouses, liked to bake,
was a good swimmer. Sometimes
she cried for no apparent reason.
After she stopped, when she was just
sniffing with tears in her eyes,
I held her and kissed her salty
cheeks. For clues to her emotional
state, I learned to keep an eye on
the barometric pressure and the phases
of the moon. I liked smelling her
after a bath, hearing her laughter
on the telephone, sitting next
to her in movies. If I asked,
on the coldest winter nights she
would take off her nightgown.
When I cut myself I let her apply
the antiseptic: it would sting
anyway, and she might as well have
fun. She dragged me to evenings of
cultural torture. Barefoot in summer,
she wore Wigwam socks in winter.

I sat beside her like a schoolboy
while she translated letters from
France. When she went to bed early
I loved to tuck her in, lifting
the covers over her shoulder,
treating her like a child. I once
saw her make a sandwich and then take
a big bite before carrying it to
the table. My ultimate threat was
that I would send her back to Cleveland.
She liked to read in bed, propped
up on the pillows in her nightgown.
I often waited at the door while
she looked for her keys. Once
when she was dieting, she moaned as
I described a cheeseburger.
We communicated across the room
at crowded parties. In restaurants
we exchanged sandwich bites and
shared desserts. In bed she usually
fell asleep first, and I lay awake
in her warmth, sleepy and content.
A faithful reporter, my second pair
of eyes and ears, she told me at
breakfast the most intimate details
of the lives of her girlfriends.
I appreciated coming home in winter
to the warm and lighted apartment.
I might smell bread baking, or onions
browning in oil, or chicken roasting
in the oven. When she was away
and I began to miss her, I nosed
around in the closet, sniffing her
blouses and sweaters. She liked
French toast, giving dinner parties,
wearing my bathrobe. The lower
the temperature, the more I loved
sleeping with her. On a cold night,
with the feel of her soft body

under a flannel nightgown, she was
a universe of warmth. For that woman
to sleep alone was a crime against
nature. Passion diminished over
the years, but attachment steadily
grew. Each of us was the most important
person in the world to the other.
We doubled ourselves, worked as
a team, were true partners, made each
other complete, were mutual assets,
needed each other more than we knew.

Kenneth Gangemi

THE BURDEN

Her vertebra I touched only once after seven
years of bad marriage, a depression, a dimpled spine,
she said it was her father hit her there
with a board once, and no, it didn't hurt,
not now. I felt it, rubbed it gently,
but in my arms she always was elsewhere,
the woman a casket in a town of too many
empty caskets, the stock-pile town waiting
for a disaster in Mexico to be of any earthly
use. I wasn't dead, so what use to me
a wife who was an empty casket with a dent
in the lid where her father struck again
each day of her life?

She would not open her lid for me at night,
I lay beside her on the narrow bed,
felt her cold steel sides next to me. I knew
she wanted to be in the ground, in a nice
concrete crypt, waterproof, quiet, and dry,
only the crickets winding and unwinding their legs

like silk ribbon rubbed on silk ribbon in her hair,
hair of the dead, hair of the woman in the casket,
hair that grew, long after her death, grew out
through spaces between the lid and the box, hair
growing through screw holes, around screws, pushing
them out, pushing the screws, spiraling around
the screws, then in their animal cuticle way
twisting the screws of her casket, backing
them out, loosening the hinges and joints
of the casket.
        I could hear the dead
woman's hair growing at night, I could hear it
beside me, growing, like insect breathing,
a tiny panting sound, just for seconds,
then silent. Her hair knew I was listening
and waited. After I fell asleep her hair
twisted the screws and the squeaking would wake me.
My eyes shot wide open and I discovered
myself, there in my body, holding my breath,
beside my wife who was a steel casket
the color of dark wine in the midnight room,
slowly coming apart as the hair pushed out
through every opening she couldn't stop up,
no matter how hard she shut the lid. It would out!

I waited to see the woman inside. I imagined
a black dessicated head resting upon
a silk pillow dreaming of a dry crypt
as her hair and nails grew; hating all water,
dreading moisture's corrupting effects, her black,
retreating nose not daring to move because
she might smell the decay, smell the hand of her father
the butcher, smell the butcher's block she washed
with bleach every week, retreat from the smell of blood,
pork fat, bleach, retreat from the blades
her father swung, the board he banged on her casket
to make that dent I felt only once in the seventh
year of a bad marriage on the night I learned

my wife was a casket in a casket town
just waiting for a disaster.

So I bought her a crypt, a sarcophagus,
really. I knew of a place in Evanston
that made monuments, beside the elevated
railway embankment I used to pass every day
riding my bicycle to school. Ellis Monuments.
The cemetery across the road was their best
advertising. Angels of stone, sweet darlings
like frozen flames, rippling upward like spires,
wings of stone fire, on pedestals, like trophies;
that's what I wanted for my wife, and though
I had to pay dearly, I convinced Mr. Ellis to carve
an upright crypt, a hollow sarcophagus
for my wife.
          I placed her inside and sealed
her in. She was happy, dry at last, and if
she fell apart, no one would be the wiser.

A lovely pedestal! Stone scrolls hugged
the base, the column fluted at the edges rose
eight feet, topped by a little girl in a gown,
with angel's wings. I wanted limestone, so lovely
as it decays, as rain washes it down; after
a hundred years, not even the inscription
could be deciphered, that look of melted tallow
I treasured in old stones, old graveyards;
the nameless dead. But limestone was out of the question
Ellis said, for a crypt, a sarcophagus
under the stars, absorbing lunar cold
and stellar inertia, soaking up all that stillness;
no, I needed stone that would outlast the moon
and pinpricks of the stars, the arctic shudder
in the vacuum, dessicating space,
the earth a droplet spinning, hard and jewel-like,
creamy swirls on its tiny self-sustaining
skin. I wanted limestone that would melt,
but she wanted granite that would stay hard,

would not even crack under glaciers but would roll
smaller and smaller until it was only a pebble,
and inside safe still a tiny casket,
all fallen to pieces by then but dry, still dry,
by then a tight ball of hair.
                              So I asked old Ellis
to do it in granite, which he did, delivered it
on a flatbed truck to the cemetery plot
I purchased for this purpose of enthroning
my casket under the moon, and on cold nights
kissed by the moon I came to the graveyard
and laced my fingers through the chain link fence,
I pressed my face against the chain, so like
her touch, the feel of her, I watched the moon
cold kissing her polished granite pedestal.

One night, the moon full, I made my way down
brain-gray streets to my place at the fence
to my cemetery; she was gone,
and in her place only a hole where she sunk
of her own weight to the center of the earth;
I didn't follow her down. Instead I shivered,
went home cold and pleased to be alone and
slept alone at last.

Christopher Sweet

ADULTERY

We have all been in rooms
We cannot die in, and they are odd places, and sad.
Often Indians are standing eagle-armed on hills

In the sunrise   open wide to the Great Spirit
Or gliding in canoes   or cattle are browsing on the walls
Far away   gazing down with the eyes of our children

Not far away   or there are men driving
The last railspike, which has turned
Gold in their hands. Gigantic forepleasure lives

Among such scenes, and we are alone with it
At last. There is always some weeping
Between us   and someone is always checking

A wrist watch by the bed to see how much
Longer we have left. Nothing can come
Of this   nothing can come

Of us: of me with my grim techniques
Or you who have sealed your womb
With a ring of convulsive rubber:

Although we come together,
Nothing will come of us. But we would not give
It up, for death is beaten

By praying Indians   by distant cows   historical
Hammers   by hazardous meetings that bridge
A continent. One could never die here

Never die   never die
While crying. My lover, my dear one
I will see you next week

When I'm in town. I will call you
If I can. Please get hold of   please don't
Oh God, Please don't any more I can't bear . . . Listen:

We have done it again   we are
Still living. Sit up and smile,
God bless you. Guilt is magical.

James Dickey

IRRECONCILABLE DIFFERENCES

From the top of either of the New York Trade Towers
you feel the sway   of the wind
and the towers   seem to reach
towards one an-   other hoping to
connect. As one   leans the other
draws away and   you become aware
with each up-   rising of breeze
of the space   between them that
seems made for   daring high wire
performers who   toss a cable from
one to the other   and try to walk
across, balancing   rod in hand,
a body framed by   nothing but the dark
night air and   the wind whistling
its oblivious   accompaniment to
this crazed attempt   to prove a man can
traverse the most   unnatural spaces
that anyone anywhere   has ever created.
The glassed surfaces   of the twin towers
reflect one another   and seem to want to
be one but that   wasn't the plan and
so they reach upward   separately as two
long married people   discovering at last
their irreconcilable   differences but being
unable in their sturdy   implantation in the
earth far below   to accept the gap
between them.   The high wire man
desperately seeks   to prove the space
can be humanly   bridged as he puts
one foot in front   of the other and
tilts his rod   from left to right
while the wind's howl   grows louder, stronger
and the crowd below   holds its collective
breath, some praying   he'll make it across
others harboring   darkest wishes.

Fred Moramarco

I walk into your house, a friend.
Your kids swarm up my steep hillsides
Or swing in my branches. Your boy rides
Me for his horsie; we pretend
Some troll threatens our lady fair.
I swing him squealing through the air
And down. Just what could I defend?

I tuck them in, sometimes, at night.
That's one secret we never tell.
Giggling in their dark room, they yell
They love me. Their father, home tonight,
Sees your girl curled up on my knee
And tells her "git"—she's bothering me.
I nod; she'd better think he's right.

Once they're in bed, he calls you "dear."
The boob-tube shows some hokum on
Adultery and loss; we yawn
Over a stale joke book and beer
Till it's your bedtime. I must leave.
I watch that squat toad pluck your sleeve.
As always, you stand shining near

Your window. I stand, Prince of Lies
Who's seen bliss; now I can drive back
Home past wreck and car lot, past shack
Slum and steelmill reddening the skies,
Past drive-ins, the hot pits where our teens
Fingerfuck and that huge screen's
Images fill their vacant eyes.

W. D. Snodgrass

A MAN AND A WOMAN SIT NEAR EACH OTHER

A man and a woman sit near each other, and they do not long
at this moment to be older, or younger, nor born
in any other nation, or time, or place.
They are content to be where they are, talking or not-talking.
Their breaths together feed someone whom we do not know.
The man sees the way his fingers move;
he sees her hands close around a book she hands to him.
They obey a third body that they share in common.
They have made a promise to love that body.
Age may come, parting may come, death will come.
A man and a woman sit near each other;
as they breathe they feed someone we do not know,
someone we know of, whom we have never seen.

Robert Bly

TALKING WITH HER

Talking with her, going to the movies and talking with her,
being proud of her son with her, wishing that I could
make a son with her too, as good as the one she has,
watching the cat with her, watching the two cats put up their fur
and stalk each other under the table and between the chair legs,
shrieking at each other, the one placing its head under the paw
of the other, and then, as we sit holding hands together, the fierce
tempers subsided, the two cats, like us on the couch after,
lie together in a soft corner or on the girls' bed
curled around each other with their pointed chins up smiling
and their amused eyes shut.

                            And the rain is coming down outside
and I stand with her under the porch roof and smell the dank
almost manure smell of the first rain on the grass,
and feel the fresh wave of thunder rippling through the branches,

and she wears a hat with a wide soft brim
and goes down on her knees in the soil and arranges
the chrysanthemums hopefully and pushes away the dead leaves
from last year respectfully, pushes them aside
where the cats are out cautious at first and then suddenly
as if with a bolt of command from heaven are scrabbling
together in the loose soil by the wall where I saw snakes
last year.

And we are talking about zoos we have known,
she and I, about the Paris Zoo, where there are fabulous
creatures, and suddenly I know again that I want to take her
to stand by the river before Notre-Dame, even now as she
has soil on her hands and adjusts her brim to take a smoke
and watches the black cat sitting with his back to us ignoring
the gray cat stalking him along the concrete wall, and in this
spring garden, where the birds have lost their hesitation
and confidently zip from twig to soil and back about their tasks,
I know she will come back as the birds do and look at me
with her blue-eyed head on one side in her hat and sandy hair
and whisper again and again that she will grow old with me.

Antony Oldknow

WALKING HOME ACROSS THE ISLAND

Walking home across the plain in the dark.
And Linda crying. Again we have come
to a place where I rail and she suffers and the moon
does not rise. We have only each other,
but I am shouting inside the rain
and she is crying like a wounded animal,
knowing there is no place to turn. It is hard
to understand how we could be brought here by love.

Jack Gilbert

. o 5

If i had a nickel
For all the women who've
Rejected me in my life
I would be the head of the
World Bank with a flunkie
To hold my derby as i
Prepared to fly chartered
Jet to sign a check
Giving India a new lease
On life

If i had a nickel for
All the women who've loved
Me in my life i would be
The World Bank's assistant
Janitor and wouldn't need
To wear a derby
All i'd think about would
Be going home

Ishmael Reed

WHERE YOU GO WHEN SHE SLEEPS

What is it when a woman sleeps, her head
In your lap, in your hands, her breath easy now as though it had never been
Anything else, and you know she is dreaming, her eyelids
Jerk, but she is not troubled, it is a dream
That does not include you, but you are not troubled either,
It is too good to hold her while she sleeps, her hair falling
Richly on your hands, shining like metal, a color
That when you think of it you cannot name, as though it has just
Come into existence, dragging you into the world in the wake
Of its creation, out of whatever vacuum you were in before,

And you are like the boy you heard of once who fell
Into a silo full of oats, the silo emptying from below, oats
At the top swirling in a gold whirlpool, a bright eddy of grain, the boy,
You imagine, leaning over the edge to see it, the noon sun breaking
Into the center of the circle he watches, hot on his back, burning
And he forgets his father's warning, stands on the edge, looks down,
The grain spinning, dizzy, and when he falls his arms go out, too thin
For wings, and he hears his father's cry somewhere, but is gone
Already, down in a gold sea, spun deep in the heart of the silo,
And when they find him, his mouth, his throat, his lungs
Full of the gold that took him, he lies still, not seeing the world
Through his body but through the deep rush of the grain
Where he has gone and can never come back, though they drag him
Out, his father's tears bright on both their faces, the farmhands
Standing by blank and amazed—you touch the unnamable
Color in her hair and you are gone into what is not fear or joy
But a whirling of sunlight and water and air full of shining dust
That takes you, a dream that is not of you but will let you
Into itself if you love enough, and will not, will never let you go.

T. R. Hummer

DISCOVERY

We lay together, darkness all around,
I listen to her constant breath,
and when I thought she slept,
I too fell asleep.
But something stirred me, why I . . .
she was staring at me with her eyes,
her breasts still sturdy,
her thigh warming mine.
And I, a little shaken as she stroked
my skin and kissed my brow,
reached for the light turned on,
feeling for the heat which would

reveal how long she had looked
and cared.
The bulb was hot.   It burned my hand.

Michael S. Harper

THE MAN AND THE GOSHAWK

For two straight days
around the clock, dust
has settled on their backs
and they have shared the attic,
hollow-cheeked as lovers
who can't call it off—
the man grown stiff
in some old crushed
velvet chair his mother
left behind, the hawk
in jesses, clinging to his arm.
You'd think an artist
with a taste for veiny eyes
sat them there and bellowed:
Do not move, you're beautiful!
—and mainly they behave.
When the man's wife
hands up live blue mice
trembling in a shoe box,
she, the hawk, barely pecks at them—
you can see
her heart's not in it.
But the man does not
lose faith; he chews
another No-Doz and goes over,
once again, the book
of kings at falconry.
The thing is: he must win

the goshawk's confidence,
must wait for her to feel
free enough to fall asleep.
By tomorrow that will happen.
Then the next day
feed her beef heart, raw
—just enough
to make her hungry;
then he'll give her twenty
feet or so of line
and let her go
and pull her in,
and let her go
and pull her in again to meat.
Let her go, he thinks,
and pull her in;
let her go
and pull her in again to meat;
let her go
and pull her in,
let her go
and pull her in
until she loves me.

Gary Gildner

ASYLUM DAYS

She has a way of declaring undying love
So that you wish you were dead. The good news,
That is, was not unmixed with the bad
When she called the other night, only recently. You were perfectly happy
Not to hear from her, what a pleasure
With a few old friends, visitors, trying to recover
From prior news of her dying love; and somehow managing.
Then she spoke, like a well-oiled coin-machine:

"Love me so much that you can show restraint
In not loving me too much." Words like such.
That's about it for your choice of tone. Before she hung up the phone,
By about two seconds, she added: "As for me,
Know that I shall continue to love you
In My Own Way." No time to reply. No point of origin
To have the call traced. You drew up ten paperless telegrams,
Took twenty-two libriums, and fell on your face.
This morning, as you are cutting the carpet
Into paper dolls, with your teeth, perhaps you'll get a letter:
"I could love you much better if you'd only relax."
Attendants take your razor; they give you beltless slacks.
So many fair exchanges, blessed by selfless love. You wonder from behind
   these parted bars
Sometimes, what hate would feel like.

Michael Benedikt

ON THE RACK

i know she is hypersensitive
about her athletic stature,
her pretty smile,
her general wholesomeness,
which everyone except her considers attractive,

so i never miss a chance to allude to
farmers' daughters, sturdiness,
good breeders, and germanic stock;

and since i know she is insanely jealous,
i seldom let an evening go by
without a mention of some beautiful
and temporarily available woman
that i've run into earlier in the day;

and because she's needlessly self-conscious
about her weight,
i wouldn't think of letting a day go by
without suggesting that i run out for
a matterhorn pizza
lest she collapse within the hour
of malnutrition.

if she were a puritan,
i'd ridicule her for that,
but since she loves sex
and has few inhibitions,
i do my best to make her feel
like a nymphomaniac.

these are the ways in which i keep her
anxious, humble, and dependent.
these are the ways
in which i punish her.

and what was her offense:

that she restored my confidence
when i was nearly broken
on the rack.

Gerald Locklin

ALLA PETRARCA

Downtown
Madison, Wisconsin at night
is pretty quiet. Returning

from the dinner for scholars of Finnish
in black plastic boots that seem to be shrinking
I listen to their heels on the sidewalk and feel like

a German Romantic
a hundred and fifty years younger, enveloped
in my sense of missing you, oh fairest of ladies!

back home in Boulder,
Colorado. It is storybook time, as when we saw
that gown in the window in Stockholm Old Town

yesterday? Or the day before?
We who are of this gender, what can we do—
we know it must be a burden to you

to appear in our visions as the *summum bonum*
the great female sun our souls do yearn for
but at least you don't have to do it in person

every time. My feet hurt but I am so glad

      (receding footsteps)

Anselm Hollo

STICKS AND STONES . . .

complaint is often the result of an insufficient
ability
to live within
the obvious restrictions of this
god damned cage.
complaint is a common deficiency
more prevalent than
hemorrhoids
and as these lady writers hurl their spiked shoes
at me
wailing that
their poems will never be
promulgated

all that I can say to them
is
show me more leg
show me more ass—
that's all you (or I) have
while
it lasts

and for this common and obvious truth
they screech at me:
MOTHERFUCKER SEXIST PIG!

as if that would stop the way fruit trees
drop their fruit
or the ocean brings in the coni and
the dead spores of the Grecian
Empire

but I feel no grief for being called something
which
I am not;
in fact, it's enthralling, somehow, like a good
back rub
on a frozen night
behind the ski lift at
Aspen.

Charles Bukowski

CRIME

She lies at the side of the road, naked,
having been raped, beaten, tossed from a car.
You made her up. She is your soul's image.
Who are the men speeding away? You are.

Philip Dacey

BROTHERS, FRIENDS,

LOVERS, AND OTHERS

"Give me back my young brother, hard

and furious"

YOU CAN HAVE IT

My brother comes home from work
and climbs the stairs to our room.
I can hear the bed groan and his shoes drop
one by one. You can have it, he says.

The moonlight streams in the window
and his unshaven face is whitened
like the face of the moon. He will sleep
long after noon and waken to find me gone.

Thirty years will pass before I remember
that moment when suddenly I knew each man
has one brother who dies when he sleeps
and sleeps when he rises to face this life,

and that together they are only one man
sharing a heart that always labors, hands
yellowed and cracked, a mouth that gasps
for breath and asks, Am I gonna make it?

All night at the ice plant he had fed
the chute its silvery blocks, and then I
stacked cases of orange soda for the children
of Kentucky, one gray boxcar at a time

with always two more waiting. We were twenty
for such a short time and always in
the wrong clothes, crusted with dirt
and sweat. I think now we were never twenty.

In 1948 in the city of Detroit, founded
by de la Mothe Cadillac for the distant purposes
of Henry Ford, no one wakened or died,
no one walked the streets or stoked a furnace,

for there was no such year, and now
that year has fallen off all the old newspapers,
calendars, doctors' appointments, bonds,
wedding certificates, drivers licenses.

The city slept. The snow turned to ice.
The ice to standing pools or rivers
racing in the gutters. Then bright grass rose
between the thousands of cracked squares,

and that grass died. I give you back 1948.
I give you all the years from then
to the coming one. Give me back the moon
with its frail light falling across a face.

Give me back my young brother, hard
and furious, with wide shoulders and a curse
for God and burning eyes that look upon
all creation and say, You can have it.

Philip Levine

TRYING TO GAIN FOLDS

Sitting at last
in the solitude,
watching the hazy twilight

drip through the window
shade's holes.
Feeling my skin

grow hard around me
like a shield.
I hear the dogs bark in the alley

and like a silver bullet
through my brain
I see a sliver of truth

shining like a midday sun: Callousness.
My bones begin to bend
and twist then fold

like thick basalt.
Streams of magma cool
where blood once flowed.

I am soft rock
waiting to be stone.
And as I close my

granite gray eyes
waiting for the process
to complete, my brother

enters the room drenched
with the moist welts
of the strap, whispering

into his pillow, "Nobody
loves me." And slowly
as I watch his neck muscles

quiver, my bedrock
starts to unfold in reply
answering, "I do."

Peter Spiro

LONG FINGERS

My brother's piano was a dream of long fingers
Each night placing his hands under his pillow
He would wake from nightmares
More afraid of the dark than before

After a dream of his love dying in Guatemala
He gave up painting
And his desire for music became immense
His stubby fingers moved along the table edge
In the pattern of some breakfast concerto
Walking to class his hands conducted
A symphony among birds and weather

He believes he's outgrown the impulse
That pulling the hearts from automobiles
Has tamed his hands
But his wife knows when he strokes her breasts
They're the first two notes of a chorale
And his son's hair is an opera
That he's filled with a desire for music and long fingers

Michael Rattee

JUST CRAZY THINKING

He didn't like being caged up.

       went into the bedroom, put a .30-caliber

He had a real deep-down-inside
meanness, just like my dad.

       boilermaker's helper, his emotions

I think it was just his coming up
through all those years, not having
any real person you could look up to
and trust and talk to and respect
what they say to you.

      his emotions in tatters, went into the bedroom

He was impulsive.

      Winchester rifle against his chest

He told me he was a burden
to me and my wife. I told him
that was just crazy thinking, you know,
my brother's keeper and that kind of thing.
He thought, with people having
to take care of him like that,
he was a bum, living with us.
Really, he wasn't.

      "Goodbye, trouble," said the note

I just laughed it off, you know.
      Someone has hurt me

I told him that was just crazy thinking.

      A few days before, in a fit

He had a real deep-down-inside
meanness, just like my dad.

      in a fit of apparent rage he drew
      a hunting knife across the girlfriend's

I just laughed it off, you know.

the girlfriend's name on his arm,
cutting the flesh so deeply
that he destroyed the letters of the tattoo

"I love you both very much
"so don't forget about me OK.

and pulled the trigger

"I'm sorry if I scratched your gun
"and I'm sorry I had to use it

put a .30-caliber Winchester rifle

"but it was all I could find for a week.

against his chest and pulled the trigger

"I would like you to do me
"a favor I know you don't like her
"but for me. Tell her I love her
"very much. I love you all.

When his brother

"Goodbye trouble."

When his brother and sister-in-law
returned, the television set
and the lights were on

I don't think he understood what
he was doing, that it would be permanent.

I have a personal need in my life

lying on the edge of the bed
with both feet on the floor
the rifle between his legs

He was impulsive.

bullet hole in his chest

Reginald Gibbons

W H I S K E Y T R E E

Tree on the mountainside, hickory
or ash, the bottle bush, oak
sapling stronger than a man and
high above the valley road, back
above the branchhead at the end
of the haulroad where the boys
come to loaf on Fridays after
quitting time, away from children,
disapproving wives. They sit on
the high ground under the protecting
limbs and watch the stars appear through
the washy lens of liquor, yell
and laugh and sing to the radio
in someone's truck, or look into
the dark and end up weeping.
But always tying, fixing with
a string or wire, lace or Band-Aid
their empties to the limbs above,
climbing into the forks to stick
a pint or jug on the end of
a twig, until the sapling seems
some Christmas tree in sunlight,
or starlight, bearing its yield of
bulbs that pull like enormous tears

as the tree is stunted, bent and
burdened under its cold harvest,
a tree of the knowledge of
forgetfulness, radiant with
memory on a winter morning,
as crows avoid the shining bush.

Robert Morgan

POISON LIGHT
                        for J. Overstreet

Last night
I played Kirk Douglas to
Your Burt Lancaster. Reflecting
20 years of tough guys I
Saw at the Plaza Theatre in
Buffalo, New York. I can
Roll an L like Bogart
You swagger like Wayne

Ours was a bad performance
The audience, our friends
Panned it. The box office
Hocked the producers

We must stop behaving like
The poison light we grew on

Ancient loas are stranded
They want artfare home
Our friends watch us. They
Want to hear what we say

Let's face it
My eye has come a long way
So has your tongue
They belong on a pyramid wall
Not in a slum
("Dead End"; 1937)

Ishmael Reed

MEN TALK

It was the winter I had to get away.
Though I didn't know it then,
I needed the kind of solace
you get at depressing movies
if they're good, all those others
just like you. In Orlando,
biding time, I watched peacocks
among people in a wooded preserve,
then drove further inland past cattle
to where my friend lived.

I was glad the peacocks made awful
sounds, and I was glad—
after we jogged his circular path
through the orange groves—
that our polite, complete sentences
broke down into talk
of his empty house, the woman who left,
and then my house far away.
I told him what staying meant, as if
I knew, the precipice in every room.
Friendship: someone leaning
to your side of the truth.

Next day was beautiful,
seventy-five degrees, and each of us
silent, back in control.
We walked into the countryside,
pointed away from ourselves
toward the landscape,
took possession of it for a while.
Kumquats were growing next to lemons
and white birds rode the backs of cows.
Though it wasn't, it seemed enough,
seemed we'd never have to speak again.

Stephen Dunn

GIRL TALK

During "The Desires of Monique"
my friend and I were chatting
about the alarming number of men
who tore off Monique's flimsy panties
with their teeth.

The theatre was shrine-like—
vast, smoky, and dim—so we confessed
that neither of us had ever
chewed away any underwear.

We agreed, though, that perhaps age
and experience could explain that.
In the 50's there was something
called a panty girdle and, believe me,
after gnawing on a panty girdle
for a while, a person gets full
and has to ask for a doggy bag
to take home the rest for later.

On the screen, Monique dreamed
of her voracious lovers. There they
were—laughing, waving, flossing.
This is where we came in, but leaving
we vow that the first one to devour
an entire pair will call the other
immediately.

That is the kind of friends we are.
We talk on the phone for hours
and we tell each other everything.

Ron Koertge

A   YEAR   HAS   PASSED   ALREADY,   SO
for Tim Riley

Sidestepping the amenities, we leave our wives
awkward with each other in the house,
and balancing our glasses of bright wine,
settle as if forever into a frail pair of lawnchairs
that creak and lean and threaten to collapse.
The yard in back—tall with dandelions tilting
in a shimmer of warm wind—hums with bees
that bumble on dull pollen-fluffy thighs
and blurring wings back and forth
to a hive hung like the moon in woods behind us.

Higher on the hill, the steady sound of traffic,
and below, the bursting of waves white against black rocks
rises muffled through wild vines and roses
blossoming between us and a sheer fall to the sea,
the two sounds, at that distance, hard to distinguish.

Watching from the windows, our wives,
still strangers, crowd words about the children
into the hopeless silence of neat rooms
where they are trapped and helpless. Our daughters
trade their toys and blows, shyly, with clumsy hands.

We drink and talk as drunken bees
stumble among the yellow sunlit crowns of wild flowers
sprung up in your absence, all but hidden
by June grass I haven't cut yet in July.

By dusk we are quiet, easy with each other,
still among the drowsy pollenated blossoms
abandoned by the bees at last, moonlit, slowly
closing in the dim light at our feet.

William Pitt Root

CLEANING THE CHIMNEY

The peak of the old roof
slants forty feet up,
there my grandfather walked,
even when he was 80.
I follow his footsteps
with a rope and a feedsack
holding bricks to drop in
and clean out the flue.

Placing my hands
on each side of the chimney
I remember again Jim Bradshaw,
Sigma Nu and the autumn of '62
when we did handstands
on the metal rail
above deep Cascadilla Gorge.

His legs were always
straighter than mine,
his back better arched—
like a question mark—
a diver held in stop action.

That year neither of us fell,
even though we looked down
as they said we should not,
the quicksilver thread
of stream far below,
lovely in those
sweet seconds of risk.

The creosote shines
like a grackle's wing.
Half-filling the chimney,
charcoal fists clench tight.
Hot air from the woodstove
lifts dust past my face.

In 1963 Jim Bradshaw
left school for Nam
in an officer's green.
His last moment of balance
was held over Phu Bai
before Charley's rockets
ripped through his copter.

Twenty years later,
there's strength in my arms
to do one more handstand

where no one would see
except birds and the trees,
for neighbors and drivers
keep eyes straight ahead.

Instead I just stand,
finish cleaning the chimney,
give one more moment
to memory and height,
then, holding that balance,
go back down the ladder.

Joseph Bruchac

TO A COLLEAGUE. FROM THE COUNTRY

I'm jealous of your life. What
are you doing out there. You're
probably having a drink at that
bar and trying to get into you-
know-whose panties and joking with
those friends of yours I don't
even know while I am sitting here
all alone in the snow having no
fun. Man, man to man, I hardly know
you so why are you doing this to me.

Alan Dugan

LETTER TO DONALD FALL

I walked a hangover like my death down
the stairs from the shop and opened the door
to a spring snow sticking only to the tops
of air-conditioners and convertibles, and thought
of my friend Donald Fall in San Francisco.
Toothless in spring! old friend, I count
my other blessings after friendship
unencumbered by communion: I have:

a money-making job, time off it, a wife
I still love sometimes unapproachably
hammering on picture frames, my own
city that I wake to, that the snow
has come to noiselessly at night, it's there
by morning, swallowing the sounds of spring
and traffic, and my new false teeth,
shining and raw in the technician's lab
like Grails, saying, "We are the resurrection
and the life: tear out the green stumps
of your aching and put plastic on instead:
immortality is in science and machines."
I, as an aging phony, stale, woozy, and corrupt
from unattempted dreams and bad health habits,
am comforted: the skunk cabbage generates its
frost-thawing fart-gas in New Jersey and the first
crocuses appear in Rockefeller Center's Channel Gardens:
Fall, it is not so bad at Dugan's Edge.

Alan Dugan

BOB SUMMERS' BODY

I never told this—I saw Bob Summers' body
one last time when they dropped him down the chute
at the crematorium. He turned over twice
and seemed to hang with one hand to the railing
as if he had to sit up once and scream
before he reached the flames. I was half terrified
and half ashamed to see him collapse like that
just two minutes after we had sung for him
and said our pieces. It was impossible
for me to see him starting another destiny
piled up like that, or see him in that furnace
as one who was being consoled or purified.
If only we had wrapped him in his sheet

so he could be prepared; there is such horror
standing before Persephone with a suit on,
the name of the manufacturer in the lining,
the pants too short, or too long. How hard it was
for poor Bob Summers in this life, how he struggled
to be another person. I hope his voice,
which he lost through a stroke in 1971,
was given back to him, wherever he strayed,
the smell of smoke still on him, the fire lighting up
his wonderful eyes again, his hands explaining,
anyone, god or man, moved by his logic,
spirits in particular, saved by the fire and clasping
their hands around their knees, some still worm-bound,
their noses eaten away, their mouths only dust,
nodding and smiling in the plush darkness.

Gerald Stern

HOT SUMMERNIGHT CLOUDBURST RENDEZVOUS

The two boys embracing in the thunderstorm
Don't care if they get drenched,
Don't care if as they strip each other
     their clothes drop in lightninglight
         into puddles
     and are kicked laughingly into the mud.
It's the first time they've kissed each other,
The first time either of them ever kissed
     a boy
And neither has ever kissed
     a girl
And neither ever kissed before
     with his tongue.
They had no idea
     how passionate

passion could be—
        they can hardly believe it,
That merely putting their lips together
        could be so . . .
                ah.
For a moment they stand apart
        silently gazing at each other
                in the flashes and thunder,
Centuries of Boyhood, Aeons of BoyLove
        proud in their playful smiles,
Knowing just what they're going to do,
        even though they never did it before,
Knowing that before long
        each of them is going to jack off
                the first boy they ever jacked off
        beside themself,
Knowing both of them can come
        and giving in, giving themselves
        to boyfriendship's ultimate gesture,
Knowing they both know
        how to jack off real good
        and aren't going to stop frenching
                while they whimper toward the brink.
Sure, it's beautiful
        to see a boy you love
                ejaculate in the lightning in the rain,
Crying with pleasure while the thunder thunders
        and the sky ejaculates millions of raindrops
As you squirm in rapture
        on the muddy grass
                under the tossing trees.

Antler

Once, depressed and drunk on the worst wine, Christopher N. and I sat out on the fire escape. That was before he got weird, before I moved back to L.A.: we shared a second-floor single apartment in the Tenderloin. Christopher N. (an alias): seventeen, innocent-looking, runaway from the complacent suburbs across the bay, smiling defiler of the scriptures of his strict father, a Baptist minister. That night on the fire escape: genesis of intense gestalt friendship. Ritual of confession. We hugged each other and cried. That night I told him someday I'd write about us sitting on the fire escape. Somewhere a phone was ringing. He finished the last glass of Ripple (Pagan Pink) and pitched it at the brick wall of the opposite building. It shattered and we laughed.

Later, back inside: steam heat, *Discreet Music*, stamping on cockroaches on red carpet cigarette scars. The walls cracked like in *Repulsion*. Lavender and green lanterned light bulb of Blanche DuBois. Initiation rite: I gave him my junior high school St. Christopher (with a surfer on the other side).

Things he did I thought delightful: took taxis, wore suspenders, spit on silver cars, drew dark circles around his eyes with shoe polish for poetic effect, cut pictures out of library books and taped them to the apartment walls, insisted upon passion, allowed himself spontaneous spasms of unlimited excess, praised Tim Curry, praised Bryan Ferry, praised the gospel according to Pasolini, named his cat Icarus, created his own art form (shock), hocked records he tired of listening to to buy used books, which he read and then hocked to buy our booze, spray painted "D" in front of Ada Street, cried when I told him he was my Holly Golightly, cursed money for its ability to corrupt purity.

But then he got weird. St. Christopher of the Club Baths. St. Christopher of the trench coat and collect calls. His Philip Marlowe hat. St. Christopher of the transfer ticket. Turned eighteen. Moved into a condemned flat below Market. Folsom: factories murmuring all night, leather bars. St. Christopher of the postfascist lost degeneration. Devout disciple of Peter Berlin. St. Christopher of the punk rock safety pin. Pierced his nipples. Placed explicit *Advocate* ad. St. Christopher of the forbidden fetish. The decidedly strange attraction to rubber. St. Christopher of the cock ring and handcuffs. Spiked dildo. Branded asses. Undressing in the balcony of the

Strand during *Maitresse*. Blond boy snorting Rush stroking himself
underneath smooth leather sucked off behind bushes in Lafayette Park after
dark. St. Christopher with superclap. St. Christopher of the 120 days of the
Baptist apocalypse. Sexual dementor. Collector of dentures and dead rats,
bloodletters. St. Christopher of the Castro hard hat and jockstrap. St.
Christopher kicking pigeons and poodles in Union Square. St. Christopher
picked-up on Polk and Pine: twenty-five dollars for shitting on his trick.

My last visit to San Francisco: saw vomit on the sidewalks, saw piss
streaming down steep streets. Bandaged panhandler. Black kid lifting the
crutches of a fallen drunkard. Transvestite prostitute throwing beer bottles
at a passing bus. Old women with shopping bag suitcases picking in trash
bins as if testing produce. At the airport terminal, before he turned to go,
Christopher N. said: "You're so prissy I can't see how we could ever have
been friends." I flew home. *Angels of the complacent suburbs! of discotheques! of
hostile police!* Got drunk.

Jeannette MacDonald, there's a dark alley for every perversion in your
sickening city (water sports, B & D, fist fucking). No one is ever innocent.

David Trinidad

THE POET AS ACTOR, YOU AS DIRECTOR

The huge king fatigued
leans against the bulbous garish tin
side of his Moorish kiosk.
He has sapped himself here
groping soldiers he's commanded
to dance naked together for his pleasure.

He observes the soiled depressions
made by his body in the obese Turkish pillows
and dismayed tries to wrench off a handful
of his left breast. He repels the men he loves!
Once his mustache brushes a svelte buttock

or his jewelled fingers heft a scrotum
the men swirl away as if his sucking them
would be a lie, the aftertaste of their
privates on his tongue would be a lie—
how can they love him?
The long ago abandoned its swaddling clothes.

Below, in the upscale coffee house
where the espresso steams and the sprout salads
wait garnished with tomato chips
the red knobs of the sound system glow.
You look up, script in hand, directing me
so that I don't fumble.
I am at the point, after the death-songs of swans
where I yank off my wig and scream
I am *King of the Night,* am *King of Ice!*

My lips are the mad king's.
And I fear death's slippery stench,
as does the author, as does the king.

Robert Peters

PETER

1. Tattoos

Right arm: a many-splendored
Korean dagger-and-heart
Wound in a scroll, or banner—
DEATH BEFORE DISHONOR.

(Between the H and O
One barely audible
Stammer of skin,
DISH ONOR—so.)

Then left: italic *Lillia,* herself
Far out in Venice West
With the car and the children, sinking
Painlessly in

Under a BB shot
Probed to this white star
Through deepening north woods where "Spring was best"
And "never human foot . . ."

But your chest, a boy's no longer,
Paler, leaner
From night shifts at the Mill:
Across it still, over your real heart—rainbow

Fixes of plumage all that while postponed—
The USA's storm-blue
Project of an eagle
Glides, with nothing in its claws but you.

2. Bad Trip

Gray light. A cautious tread.
Your weight
On the bedside, shuddering—
Eighty million comets in your head!

Walking all night
Beach after beach, surfstrafe,
Starknout, clockwise flailings of the dark . . .
I want to think we're safe,

Each of us, in each day's golden scales.
From your unwinking stare
A juice of pain
Trickles between knuckles. There,

The tranquilizer's working. There, lie back,
Hush. Tears
Wetting the pillow touch
Its featherbrain

And soon enough a suite for solo pharynx
Clumsily bowed and scraped will find me bent,
A room away, on putting words
Into an angel's mouth. Thirty-eight years

No less the waif
Afraid of dark? Sunshine
Spread over hurt feet, snore to your heart's content
And mine.

3. Future Apples Inc.

You've fallen on work.
Luck smiles her little smile, by legerdemain
Those knuckles turn to outcrop,
Those tricklings to a wind-creased pool,

And here's your form
Reflected in a farm!—
Gaunt, lightly, chronically stoned
Latterday Eden with its absentee

Landlord, its wary creatures. The mud-caked brush-hog
Loves no man yet, neither (to judge by scratches
On wrists and calves)
Do the blackberry patches.

Some trees then, old as wives,
But bearing. And uphill, a beard
Of second growth, fruitless perplexities,
Dead roots, bygone

Entanglements *away* from light
Beg to be cleared.
It's winter wheat, clover, and timothy,
Seasons of sweetening

If young limbs are to climb
Where a brow's furrowed, and the first-born so deftly
Hefts his bushel that you blink astonished
From time to time.

4. The First-Born

—Of *this* union.
Fact is, you've children everywhere,
Vermont, Korea, some
Grown-up enough to have kids of their own,

For misspelt pleas to come—
Illness, abortion, welfare, and parole.
They all need help.
You're sorry and would like to help

But figure you help them more in the long run
By not helping now.
And so you grin and shrug
As at the mention of vasectomy—

Genetic litterbug!
This latest batch is "different"—still unscarred
By life, you mean?
In drifts the six-year-old

Wearing his mother's blouse (where's she?
oh, "off on a rampage"),
Red polish on the fingernails
Of one hand. Drawn to me,

He lolls between my knees, asks *why* and *why*,
But listens also, much as if the die
Hadn't been cast. Will he have you—will I—
When all else fails?

5. "Fidelio" from the Met

Upon a certain rock
—Glacial warden over "dreams come true"—
You kept on building castles, no,
Dungeons in air,

Unspeakable, unvisitable glooms
Whose guiltless prisoner,
Wasted beyond recognition, was alive
Just barely, just because you were.

(How often in the city
I'd see you—boots, jeans, glasses, hair—
And shout. As if you could do better than
To look like everyman.)

Yet when that boulder you'd go sit on,
Peter, come night,
To smoke and watch the constellations
For its dislodging needed dynamite

And like the heaviest heart at freedom's trumpet
Leapt awkwardly an inch, and broke,
There was no question whose
Whole life, starwise along its faults, had started

To set the musical
Crystals, feldspar and quartz,
Aglow down pristine faces only now
Seeing the light.

James Merrill

THE MAGIC CAT BONE (*from* A Childhood)

Grandaddy,
since your death I have been engaged
in rewriting
the family history:
When an English exiled Jew
married an African princess
all hell broke loose. . . .
If I could feel your laugh again—

Always you sit on the porch,
with your Don Quixote slimness and griot's gift
for charming a child;
even death can't stop
your storytelling:
I'm hearing Tar Baby, Br'er Rabbit again,
the woman who was slapped
by a ghost, and my favorite,
the magic cat bone:
"Boil a black cat," you say, "on the night
of the full moon, then slip the bones
gently through your lips;
the one that slides smoothest
is the magic bone. . . ."

Grandaddy, in the world I live in now
we say we have no need
of tales or talismans. But tell me,
can the magic cat bone
give me back the soul
I had as a child?
Yes, of course, you nod, waving the bone
like a wand.

And here I am again,
small, eternally
starting at strange sounds:
"Grandaddy, who's there?"

"*Haints* of slaves snowblind from the cotton."

Cyrus Cassells

NEGURA DE TIMP

In Grandfather's poetry we feel the wind
filling the world

        sun   stars   birds
              fires   mountains

all
at the service of love
an invisible woman
who breathes at the center

"Come to me, oh, you, my sweet star
To show me the stars in heaven
Light me aflame in the night
Hard sadness in my breast"

he prays to his queen
passionate naive young man

and I
an idolator, too,
hunker before his hunkering

these silent
dangling
symbols of heaven

mumbling
rocking
for the lightning

from my grandfather
who died before I was born

Half my age
at the fin de siecle
he writes in the Romanian language
a soulful measured script

negura de timp   the mist of time

sweet flowing stone

Richard Silberg

GRANDFATHER-IN-LAW

It's nothing really, and really, it could have been worse, and of course, he's
     now several years dead,
and his widow, well, if oftentimes she's somewhat distracted, overly
     cautious when we visit—
after all, Boston isn't New York—she seems, for some reason, enormously
     proud that there's now a writer in the family,
and periodically, sends me clippings about the poet laureate, Thoreau,
     Anne Sexton's daughter, Lowell, New England literary lore—
in which I fit, if I fit at all, simply because I write in English—as if color of
     skin didn't matter anymore.
Still, years ago, during my first visit to Boston, when we were all asleep,
he, who used to require that my wife memorize lines of Longfellow or Poe
     and recite them on the phone,
so that, every time he called, she ran outdoors and had to be coaxed back,
     sometimes with threats, to talk to Pops
(though she remembers too his sly imitations of Lincoln, ice cream at
     Brighams, burgers and fries, all the usual grandfatherly treats),

he, who for some reason was prejudiced against Albanians—where on earth
  did he find them I wondered—
who, in the thirties, would vanish to New York, catch a show, buy a suit,
  while up north,
the gas and water bills pounded the front door (his spendthrift ways startled
  me with my grandfather's resemblance, familial inheritance),
who for over forty years came down each morning, "How's the old goat?"
  with a tie only his wife could knot circling his neck,
he slipped into my wife's room—we were unmarried at the time—and
  whispered so softly she thought
he almost believed she was really asleep, and was saying this like a wish or
  spell, some bohunk miscalculated Boston sense of duty:
"Don't make a mistake with your life, Susie. Don't make a mistake. . . ."
Well. The thing that gets me now, despite the dangling rantings I've let go,
  is that, at least at that time,
he was right: There was, inside me, some pressing, raw, unpeeled
  persistance, some libidinous desire for dominance
that, in the scribbled first-drafts of my life, seemed to mark me as wastrel
  and rageful, bound to be unfaithful,
to destroy, in some powerful, nuclear need, fissioned both by childhood and
  racism, whatever came near—
And I can't help but feel, forgiving him now, that if she had listened, if she
  had been awake,
if this flourishing solace, this muscled-for happiness, shared by us now, had
  never awakened,
he would have become for me a symbol of my rage and self-destruction,
  another raw, never healing wound,
and not this silenced grandfatherly presence, a crank and scoundrel, red-
  necked Yankee who created the delicate seed of my wife, my child.

David Mura

DREAM LADDERS

When grandfather went to the dances
he'd wrap in a blanket like a woman
and sit all day beside a handmade

wooden ladder he'd carry there himself.
As he got older, he made it lighter and
lighter but never let us help:
"It's for the dreams, the little stray dreams
kicked up in the dust."

Last night, lying beside my woman,
I dreamed of two trains crashing,
turning over and over in the snow,
cars and rails twisted around each other
until I couldn't tell which was which
and I lay awake and afraid staring
into the dark corners of the room.

I thought I heard grandfather saying
those trains were like ladders:
walk away and don't look back.
What about your dream ladders?
"Dreams, shit, just like people:
mostly a waste of goddamn time."

George Perreault

NO PALOOKA

A frown gathers behind my wife's smile
as I open another bottle of wine
and pour out the story of my Uncle Jack
to my wife's friends, sidestepping
vacations and mortgages and children's braces,
wanting them to meet me through a memory.
>   *My penance for being a child*
>   *involved the ritual of Saturday visits,*
>   *the tedious drive to Schenectady*
>   *where hunched in the kitchen corner,*
>   *Uncle Jack drank beer from a pewter mug,*
>   *horseshoe scar hung on the bridge of his nose,*

squashed ears as large as saucers.
My father let me join them there
as Uncle Jack rambled through the afternoon
recalling his days as a club boxer
when he was "Killer Cain" in an emerald robe
and he dazzled them with footwork.
Once he sparred with Willie Pep,
said he never saw the jabs, a hundred, maybe more,
but could hear the dull popping of leather,
feel them banging inside his head,
could taste them when he swallowed blood.

Sometimes between rounds he'd notice me,
crouch forward in his chair, roll his shoulders
and tuck his chin, throw a playful punch,
ask, "How much you weigh, kid?"
I'd duck down into my Coke, redfaced and grinning,
hide under their haze of cigarettes and beer
as Uncle Jack saw Willie Pep through the years,
remembered popping leather and the taste of blood.
And always the groggy refrain,
"How much you weigh, kid?"
even to my mother, looking girlish and flustered,
trying to catch my father with a glance.

"How much you weigh, kid?"
That slurred riddle rang
like a bully's jeering taunt
even after I'd taken my father's chair
until once in mid-week I discovered him—
the soft voice, the easy smile.
He told me the time he was fifteen
and he'd sneak into the fights at St. Stephen's
to watch the Pollacks and Micks
pound faith into the Protestants and Jews.
He remembered the ringed fingers of the Monsignor
squeezing his shoulder, still heard the question,
"How much you weigh, kid?"
the question leading him down to the locker room

into the sick kid's trunks and heavy gloves,
into spending money and club fights and emerald robe
as he dazzled them with footwork, toughing it out
through the Depression with sixty fights,
sparring with Willie Pep and learning
the manly art and the thick taste of blood.

My wife's friends struggle into smiles
as I rub red wine beads against my glass
into squeaking sounds, wanting these strangers
to see how that square ring shaped my uncle's life,
but when all was said and done, he was no palooka.

The silence rises between us, swollen and awkward.

Later, in a sort of apology,
I fix coffee in the kitchen,
resigned to acquaintanceship
but angry for squandering the memory.
So I tuck my chin and roll my shoulders,
shuffle footwork into a dazzling dance,
whisper pop, pop, pop-pop
to the beat of bloodsoaked gloves
drumming into the bobbing faces of my guests,
my uncle hunched and rambling at his table,
and the redfaced boy who won't be talked away.

Michael Cleary

FOR   WCW

Now they are trying to make you
The genital thug, leader
Of the new black shirts—
Masculinity over all!
I remember you after the stroke

(Which stroke? I don't remember which stroke.)
Afraid to be left by Flossie
In a hotel lobby, crying out
To her not to leave you
For a minute. Cracked open
And nothing but womanish milk
In the hole. Only a year
Before that we were banging
On the door for a girl to open,
To both of us. Cracked,
Broken. Fear
Slaughtering the brightness
Of your face, stroke and
Counterstroke, repeated and
Repeated, for anyone to see.
And now, grandmotherly,
You stare from the cover
Of your selected poems—
The only face you could compose
In the end. As if having
Written of love better than any poet
Of our time, you stepped over
To that side for peace.
What valleys, William, to retrace
In memory, after the masculine mountains,
What long and splendid valleys.

Harvey Shapiro

HIS GRAVITY WAS A BELL THAT SHALL BE RUNG

> in memory of Tony Wilkins, 27, former chairman of Black
> Studies, California State College, Long Beach, who was
> shot to death by Long Beach police 3 August 1974

His gravity was a bell that shall be rung,
    that shall be rung,
his gravity was an undeciphered book:
and every coffin-face who strove to hang
    his manhood on a hook
shall be remembered with a shovelful of dirt
    on freedom's night,
shall be remembered with a shovelful of dirt.

His love was a bell that shall be rung,
    that shall be rung,
his delicacy was a bell that shall be rung:
and every tear his sisters drop upon the cushion
    of his cheek
shall be remembered when the scythers cut the corn
    on freedom's night,
shall be remembered when the scythers cut the corn.

His anguish was a bell that shall be rung,
    that shall be rung,
and his manhood was a bell that shall be rung:
his rage will scuttle sharks and shuttle centuries into quays,
sever continents to let the peoples through
    on freedom's night,
sever continents to let the peoples through.

Lance Jeffers

BABY VILLON

He tells me in Bangkok he's robbed
Because he's white; in London because he's black;
In Barcelona, Jew; in Paris, Arab:
Everywhere and at all times, and he fights back.

He holds up seven thick little fingers
To show me he's rated seventh in the world,
And there's no passion in his voice, no anger
In the flat brown eyes flecked with blood.

He asks me to tell all I can remember
Of my father, his uncle; he talks of the war
In North Africa and what came after,
The loss of his father, the loss of his brother,

The windows of the bakery smashed and the fresh bread
Dusted with glass, the warm smell of rye
So strong he ate till his mouth filled with blood.
"Here they live, here they live and not die,"

And he points down at his black head ridged
With black kinks of hair. He touches my hair,
Tells me I should never disparage
The stiff bristles that guard the head of the fighter.

Sadly his fingers wander over my face,
And he says how fair I am, how smooth.
We stand to end this first and last visit.
Stiff, 116 pounds, five feet two,

No bigger than a girl, he holds my shoulders,
Kisses my lips, his eyes still open,
My imaginary brother, my cousin,
Myself made otherwise by all his pain.

Philip Levine

A STEPFATHER, A CHILD

Forgiveness is a key
I found. This newsphoto of you
begs for it: restrained

after taking some scissors
to a pair of drivers
at the ambulance wheel

mid-transfer from one hospital
to another.
All I can think of is twenty

years ago and how I prayed
the trick of our sex together
wouldn't sicken me,

like a secret. I wondered how you
made it, in total power
those nights

we brewed alone, relentless
in a two-family house—I wondered
how you magically reduced

to a passive boy my age
so I could get away with seducing you
as my mother walked a thinning dog named Star,

knowing nothing, and kept walking
to her death: a skilled wish,
rising out of Brooklyn.

And I wondered how
wanting your love,
however strangely unwilling,

got to something like this:
hand coming down
on a crotch

the way the passenger's arm
will strike the driver just before
the steering column snaps

or how we never kissed
because it would have given
violation an intimacy to

diminish its force.
But let's face it—the picture
isn't about that, really. It's about

how you're not
making it. It's about scars
that never finish healing

because the mind
secures them from the body.
And because I could never

understand male affection
without a trail of
quixotic acts,

I stand a life of not getting it
fully. So how you are
of dry-mouthed patients that wait

for a door to open out
from Rockland State, is how still I am
in searches for men to love:

whole and rushing
tantalizing schools
of them.

Michael Klein

SAILORS

When the ship gets into port the sailors all go nuts. They get drunk and
dance and wake up the next afternoon in the whorehouse. And if a sailor
gets thrown in jail he doesn't care because he just got paid and has enough
money to get out. None of the sailors wants to go back to the ship. One thing
sailors can't stand is the sight of water. One sailor hides out in a laundromat.
One makes plans to marry. Another is still drunk. The sailors hate this lousy
port. The ship sails at dawn with all hands, but someone has sneaked whiskey
aboard. By midnight the crew is drunk and the ship is dead in the water. The
captain is furious and shouts over the intercom to the engine room. But they
are all asleep, rocked in their little cradle on the sea.

Louis Jenkins

TATTOOS

after our first
liberty half of the
sailors came back with
tattoos. I had never
seen such a use
of skin. a heart
hopped when a muscle
flexed   a tiger bled
a forearm   and then
the scabs puffed like
cotton. everyone

was sorry. I almost
had a scarab inscribed
on the web of my thumb
in honor of my uncle
who had one there.
I could see my hand
red or blue
like a lip   and thought
of the gold stuck
on the collars of officers.
we'd wear animals
forever. we'd be
like pets.
                    my skin
breathes   tans
lightly or fades
mottled by leaves or
water marks when light
bounces from waves.
I knew the day was
coming when I'd strip
jumper, white hat,
bell bottoms, bundle
them into an incinerator.
no birds on my arms
reminding me of the
ensign smelling undershirts
for sweat   the smudge
on shoes polished
like mirrors where
his face comes back
from my foot.

Glover Davis

FROM AN INMATE RULE BOOK

Know your number
and cell location
if you forget
look in the mirror
and read them
in your eyes

when you have eaten
drop your spoon
into the bucket
beside the door
there are no knives
allowed in here
aside from those
in the Captain's smile

walk near the walls
they are the only
friends you can
always depend upon
to guard your back

wash as often
as they allow
try to convince
yourself the water
which falls
from the showerhead
is not some
invisible indelible paint
to mark you for
the rest of your life

Joseph Bruchac

Hard Rock / was / "known not to take no shit
From nobody," and he had the scars to prove it:
Split purple lips, lumbed ears, welts above
His yellow eyes, and one long scar that cut
Across his temple and plowed through a thick
Canopy of kinky hair.

The WORD / was / that Hard Rock wasn't a mean nigger
Anymore, that the doctors had bored a hole in his head,
Cut out part of his brain, and shot electricity
Through the rest. When they brought Hard Rock back,
Handcuffed and chained, he was turned loose,
Like a freshly gelded stallion, to try his new status.
And we all waited and watched, like a herd of sheep,
To see if the WORD was true.

As we waited we wrapped ourselves in the cloak
Of his exploits: "Man, the last time, it took eight
Screws to put him in the Hole." "Yeah, remember when he
Smacked the captain with his dinner tray?" "He set
The record for time in the Hole—67 straight days!"
"Ol Hard Rock! man, that's one crazy nigger."
And then the jewel of a myth that Hard Rock had once bit
A screw on the thumb and poisoned him with syphilitic spit.

The testing came, to see if Hard Rock was really tame.
A hillbilly called him a black son of a bitch
And didn't lose his teeth, a screw who knew Hard Rock
From before shook him down and barked in his face.
And Hard Rock did *nothing*. Just grinned and looked silly,
His eyes empty like knot holes in a fence.

And even after we discovered that it took Hard Rock
Exactly 3 minutes to tell you his first name,
We told ourselves that he had just wised up,
Was being cool; but we could not fool ourselves for long,

And we turned away, our eyes on the ground. Crushed.
He had been our Destroyer, the doer of things
We dreamed of doing but could not bring ourselves to do,
The fears of years, like a biting whip,
Had cut deep bloody grooves
Across our backs.

Etheridge Knight

AMERIKI: BOOK I, PART VIII

Well, once dawn fooled me
the stars & moon helped
so I went up the mountain in the night
yeah, it was still nighttime
when I got to the top.
I could hear the evergreens
groan & the beeches creak
& a partridge singing.

. . . by the dawn's early light

                              the coastline
                              of greater Vin-

land—

         whether for grapes, cranberries,
         meadows or all—

but especially

             great timbered forests

of Cape Cod,

             dunes now
             on which
                         A man
may stand . . . and put all America
behind him,

             working on the discovery

of his mind.

                    Let him
in his sunwatch
                         warn against
                         that morning light
by which a story is heard
to flow divinely divinely,
                              to thank providence for corn
                              others starved for lack of
(yet the rites of survival
become religion)
                         as we take our pleasure
                         in a perfect gem of a story:
the young son
John Billington, Jr.
lost in the woods
                         found by Nauset Indians
& returned at First Encounter Beach
where an Indian woman wept
to see his mother rejoice
because she recalled her own 3 sons
some years before abducted by Capt. Hunt
                                        & some years after
the lost son was found
the father—
                    John Billington, Sr.
                    took his gun
                                   & killed
John Newcommin.
                    With his execution
                    the first blow of justice
in Plimoth Plantation.
                         It dawns on us ♂
we are the story—
the outworking light
& blossoming release
of our fathers' findings.
                              if) with curses on our breaths
                              lightly lightly, nothing to live by

however great a curse
they might have been to us.

                        if) with reverence & thanks
                        let it be un-stammeringly
& not just
for momentous flowers
pressed in books.
                   Our seedings have come from the ships
                   & wrecks of every continent . . .

George Economou

PASSING THE ORANGE

On Halloween night
the new teacher gave a party
for the parents.
She lined up the women
on one side of the schoolroom,
the men on the other,
and they had a race,
passing an orange
under their chins along each line.
The women giggled like girls
and dropped their orange
before it got halfway,
but it was the men's line
that we watched.
Who would have thought
that anyone could get them
to do such a thing?
Farmers in flannel shirts,
in blue overalls and striped overalls.
Stout men embracing one another.
Our fathers passing the orange,
passing the embrace—the kiss

of peace—complaining
about each other's whiskers,
becoming a team, winning the race.

Leo Dangel

BASEBALL
for Walt Dusza

Maybe it was the salmon cakes
He damn near inhaled for breakfast,
Or the hundredweights of cabbage. By Jesus
He was a ballplayer. A hitter, he could go
To either field or behind a runner. He always batted
Second. Played every position but catch
(We couldn't risk his fingers.)
Home though was second base where he pulled
Out hot grounders
And double played all but the fastest clubs
To death. His pitchers loved him.
In '62 when we took it all
He hit .600 in the play-offs and saved
The final game in the eighth
With his glove.
The scout from Boston nodded.

He had to be big.
A couple of years in the farm system
To develop, put on a few pounds,
A season in Triple A ball,
Then into the "Fens" with its friendly
Left fence and water-green infield. Ads
For Gillette.
But something screwed up. He stopped,
Married a big babushka headed girl,
Bought an 18 wheeler

And hauled produce and Christmas trees out of Boston
Going right past Fenway Park.

I reject this. Walter
You were born for ball, not Peterbilts. When you
Went to your right
Your arm moving across your body,
Or rippled a high hard one into the corner
I could feel the lyricism and sex
Inherent in great baseball.
Watching you read hitters, work the infield
In the hot summer leagues
(If the wind was right I could smell
cabbage from the dugout.)
Making bozos out of the best men.
You robbed me. You should've been at second
Against Cincinnati, faced Guidry in '78,
You would have made it good,
Two Series for the Sox,
My dream intact,
And I could have shown you to my boy.

Norman Hindley

COACH ON VACATION

Swathed in Number 4 Coppertone, Coach
sits in his beach chair, watching
the Atlantic roll itself toward his toes,
his belly white as a gull's,
the sun playing him tight.
He listens to the waves, the children squealing,
the stockbrokers still talking big bucks
as their wives try to coax them offshore,
and the teenagers laughing as they roll
under the cool water or whispering

as they bake next to each other, fingers
laced. Suddenly he wants to buy
some jeans, open his shirt, take
his wife across state lines.
But his brain's a gym.
Every move he makes draws jeers.
Even here, dreaming himself a surfer,
builder of sandcastles, a stud
who strolls the shoreline, or just
leaning back into the sand to feel
the salt air sift across his body,
he can hear the catcalls—"You're
a bum, Coach. You're a lousy bum."

Jack Ridl

PHONE CALL

Hello.

Hello, Mr. Williamson? This is David Lee, I live in Paragonah. During my
morning run I passed by your stockpens west of Paragonah and I saw that
one of your cows, the black white-face, I think, seems to have calved during
the night. I think around sunrise, the calf was still steaming, at least I think
so. But the cow seems to be in some trouble, I think her uterus has prolapsed
and she probably needs some help. I was running and I didn't stop and walk
over to see, instead I turned around and came back to call and let you know
so you can go out and see if she needs help.

Who's this? Is this church business?

No, no. Wallace, I'm the guy who runs out by your stockpens every morning.
You wave at me. Today I ran early and saw that you've got a cow in trouble.
She's an angus-hereford cross. She's calved and her vagina has protruded.
You ought to go out and check on her as soon as you can.

Is this about selling Amway?

286

Listen
:goddammit, this morning
in your west pen
the black balley dropped her calf
and her ass is out
down to her knees.
She needs help.

Oh goddam
it's that two year old heifer
I didn't know she was that close
I gotta go.
Look mister whoever you are
you call back
take and give my wife your name
I owe you
but I cain't talk now
I gotta go
but I sure thank you
I'll make it up to you
someday somehow
      Bye

David Lee

CROSSING THE DESERT

Finally I got up & walked over
to the couple at the next fire ring.
Look, I said quietly,
I'm trying to sleep.
Pal, the guy looked up,
this here is our campsite & we'll
talk as long as we goddam feel like it.
He had on a blue Padres cap
& was sprawled out in the tent
on his belly with a sixpack of Coors,

& she was outside on a folding chair
by the fishing rods,
swinging a leg
that was marble in the moonlight.
The last thing I needed was trouble,
but I took a step toward him
anyhow. It's midnight, I said,
hunkering down. I don't
think you have any idea how—
Buddy, he raised himself on one elbow,
I'll tell you this one last fucking time—
But I turned around & walked off.
In the dark, among strangers,
you never know what can happen.
He must have thought I was going back
for a pipe-wrench or my .22,
because there wasn't a sound after that.
I dragged my sleeping bag out of the tent
& as I lay there in the stillness,
circled by the silhouettes of camper-
shells & winnebagos,
everything grew strange—
as if, unmoored from time, I'd stumbled
on the ruins of some ancient caravan:
a savage & nomadic people
is how they'll remember us
a thousand years from now when we're
not even dust anymore,
is what I was thinking,
lying there under those billion stars,
the silence broken only by the thin,
electric buzz of the cicadas; wind
rasping in the chaparral; & what
must have been the canopy of someone's tent
out in the darkness, flapping.

Steve Kowit

MEN AT WAR

"I have become Death's own mouth

eating myself elbow to asshole.

Some night, I'll swallow everything."

Scorch of flanged wheels,
train brakes' moan:
a dog being eaten by bees.
By half moon, conifers
whirlpool over valleys.
I point them with a hungry eye.
The night is fat with stories.
In the washroom,
a drunk's is a hard mumble,
hissing how the fire ate everything,
a throat peristaltic with his house,
family.
A passenger's nodding head
cautions me back to these reports:
Near the crest of a bald-headed hill,
we found a clearing encased by jungle.
Conners lay in a shallow square pit,
his limbs staked five-point,
arms and chest exfoliated
into bloody feathers, mouth stuffed
with his giblet testicles.
The conductor dims the car.
In front of me two voices accelerate
toward sleep:
we will pass Mt. Shasta, but never see it,
a spirit place, Indians said,
creation's hub.
My stomach slops with lounge car beer.
Along the aisle I find the place where I
loose with time, but never distance:
"Do you always dream in color?" the shrink smiled.
I do, I said,
in red and black most often.
Waist high, I wade a sea of blood,
waves undulating along
a dark shoreless expanse.
Heads bob against me, soggy cabbages I gather,

never waking
till I recognize my parents', childrens',
wife's.
The sun is an ambush, a bullet shattering
glass from a hazy horizon.
Bodies stretch, yawn myopic smiles,
like figures I once saw
in a painting reaching
awkwardly toward their god.
I edge to the bathroom.
There he sits, the old man,
a tangle of gray roots on the blue
vinyl couch.
In the night it was bourbon,
now a belch of apple wine
surfaces him to speech.
"Accident this morning, car
ran into the train."
Trees scuttle across the window;
he rocks in sun, his face a dry eggshell.
"Some migrant goin' to the fields.
Police had him stretched out by the siding."
"Does it surprise you?" I murmur.
I wash my eyes. Here is what I saw:
The Cong fixed bombs to whatever floated;
where the river wound through the city,
there were explosions anytime.
The people ate the sharks that came up
with the tide,
trained them to strike whatever
broke the surface. On board the LT,
you'd free fire anything in the water.
In my seat again,
a burlesque of apples over my tongue:
outside, the brown hills roll fields
into the sun.
There is my family
walking away from me again.
Am I comfortable, the conductor asks.

What do I know?
I have become Death's own mouth
eating myself elbow to asshole.
Some night, I'll swallow everything.

Robert Ward

BURNING SHIT AT AN KHE

Into that pit
    I had to climb down
With a rake and matches; eventually,
    You had to do something
Because it just kept piling up
    And it wasn't our country, it wasn't
Our air thick with the sick smoke
    So another soldier and I
Lifted the shelter off its blocks
    To expose the homemade toilets:
Fifty-five gallon drums cut in half
    With crude wood seats that splintered.
We soaked the piles in fuel oil
    And lit the stuff
And tried to keep the fire burning.
    To take my first turn
I paid some kid
    A care package of booze from home.
I'd walked past the burning once
    And gagged the whole heart of myself—
It smelled like the world
    Was on fire,
But when my turn came again
    There was no one
So I stuffed cotton up my nose
    And marched up that hill. We poured
And poured until it burned and black
    Smoke curdled

But the fire went out.
	Heavy artillery
Hammered the evening away in the distance,
	Vietnamese laundry women watched
From a safe place, laughing.
	I'd grunted out eight months
Of jungle and thought I had a grip on things
	But we flipped the coin and I lost
And climbed down into my fellow soldiers'
	Shit and began to sink and didn't stop
Until I was deep to my knees. Liftships
	Cut the air above me, the hacking
Blast of their blades
	Ripped dust in swirls so every time
I tried to light a match
	It died
And it all came down on me, the stink
	And the heat and the worthlessness
Until I slipped and climbed
	Out of that hole and ran
Past the olive drab
	Tents and trucks and clothes and everything
Green as far from the shit
	As the fading light allowed.
Only now I can't fly.
	I lie down in it
And finger paint the words of who I am
	Across my chest
Until I'm covered and there's only one smell,
	One word.

Bruce Weigl

C O U S I N
for John H. Kent, Jr., 1919–1982

I grew up staring at the picture of him:
oak leaves on his shoulders, crossed rifles
on his lapels, and down his chest so many medals
the camera lost them. He wore gold-rimmed
glasses, smiled, had jokes to tell. World War II
exploded for me summers on the front porch
when he'd visit and talk. Wounded twice, he knew
he'd almost died. Courage rang in his voice.

Ten years from my war, thirty from his, we
hit a summer visit together; again
the stories came. He remembered names of men,
weapons, tactics, places, and I could see
his better than mine. He'd known Hemingway!
I tried hard couldn't find a thing to say.

David Huddle

H U N T I N G

Sighting down the long black barrel,
I wait till front and rear sights
form a perfect line on his body,
then slowly squeeze the trigger.

The thought occurs
that I have never hunted anything in my whole life
except other men.

But I have learned by now
where such thoughts lead,
and soon pass on
to chow, and sleep,
and how much longer till I change my socks.

W. D. Ehrhart

NOON

I'm digging holes for three wilted saplings—
pin oak, mulberry, flowering crab—
behind a tract house reeking freshly sawn
boards in the heat of a July afternoon.
After 22 years in dorm rooms, the Air Force,
a string of roach-filled apartments, and rent
houses, I am a home owner. Transparencies
swarming from my hat, I squat on my heels
among clods of red clay and green shoots of grass
then let myself unroll. I am forty.
In ten years I will be fifty and
this yard will be shaded. Now, the heat
is excruciating. The rumble of trucks
and cars floats over across rooftops
from the throughway. It is the Delta and I
am sprawling on my back in copper-colored
dirt after filling sandbags. Through the earth
I feel the kicks of an airstrike that goes on
a klick away. Choppers are wheeling
overhead like hornets. But this
is not a poem about the war.
I'm tired of it always being the war.
This is a poem about how, if I place
my head, that stick of a mulberry tree
in the shape of a Y shades my eyes from the sun.

Perry Oldham

STARLIGHT SCOPE MYOPIA

Gray-blue shadows lift
shadows onto an ox cart.

Making night work for us,
the starlight scope brings
men into killing range.

The river under Vi Bridge
takes the heart away

like the Water God
riding his dragon.
Smoke-colored

Viet Cong
move under our eyelids,

lords over loneliness
winding like coralvine through
sandalwood & lotus,

inside our skulls years
after this scene ends.

The brain closes down
to get the job done. What
looks like one step into the trees,

they're lifting crates of ammo
& sacks of rice, swaying

under their shared weight.
Caught in the infrared,
what are they saying?

Are they talking about women
or calling the Americans

beaucoup dien cai dau?
One of them is laughing.
You want to place a finger

to his lips & say "shhhh."
You try reading ghost-talk

on their lips. They say
"up-up we go," lifting as one.
This one, old, bowlegged,

you feel you could reach out
& take him into your arms. You

peer down the sights of your M-16,
seeing the full moon
loaded on an ox cart.

Yusef Komunyakaa

WE NEVER KNOW

He danced with tall grass
for a moment, like he was swaying
with a woman. Our gun barrels
glowed white-hot.
When I got to him,
a blue halo
of flies had already claimed him.
I pulled the crumbled photograph
from his fingers.
There's no other way
to say this: I fell in love.
The morning cleared again,
except for a distant mortar
& somewhere choppers taking off.

I slid the wallet into his pocket
& turned him over, so he wouldn't be
kissing the ground.

Yusef Komunyakaa

OK CORRAL EAST BROTHERS IN THE NAM

Sergeant Christopher and I are
in Khanh Hoi down by the docks
in the Blues Bar where the women
are brown and there is no Saigon Tea
making our nightly HIT—'Hore Inspection Tour
watching the black   digging night sights
     soul sounds   getting tight

the grunts in the corner raise undisturbed hell
the timid white MP has his freckles pale
as he walks past the high dude
in the doorway in his lavender jump-suit
to remind the mama-san quietly of curfew
        he chokes on the weed smoke
        he sees nothing his color here
and he fingers his army rosary   his .45

but this is not Cleveland or Chicago
he can't cringe any one here and our
gazes like brown punji stakes impale him

we have all killed something recently
we know who owns the night
and carry darkness with us

Horace Coleman

A BLACK SOLDIER REMEMBERS

My Saigon daughter I saw only once
standing in the dusty square
across from the Brink's BOQ/PX
in back of the National Assembly
next to the ugly statue of
the crouching marines facing
the fish pond the VC blew up
during Tet.

The amputee beggars watch us.
The same color and the same eyes.
She does not offer me one of the
silly hats she sells Americans and
I have nothing she needs but
the sad smile she already has.

Horace Coleman

BASKET CASE

I waited eighteen years to become a man.
My first woman was a whore off Tu Do street,
But I wish I never felt the first wild
Gliding lust, because the rage and thrust
Of a mine caught me hip high.
I felt the rip at the walls of my thighs,
A thousand metal scythes cut me open,
My little fish shot twenty yards
Into a swamp canal.
I fathered only this—the genderless bitterness
Of two stumps, and an unwanted pity
That births the faces of all

Who will see me till I die deliriously
From the spreading sepsis that was once my balls.

Basil T. Paquet

BECAUSE THE SNOW WHICH FALLS

Because the snow which falls
north of the 38th parallel

must be the same snow which
falls south of the 38th

parallel—Christ-
mas white, intricate parallax,

peace-all-at-once—
once, half-drunk on OB's

on a country bus snaking
to Ilyong, a student

soldier proclaimed to the
sleeping citizens, *No more*

38th parallel, just snow . . .
just snow falling over fences,

tunnels, trenches, filling
the ricefields north of Seoul.

Night and the peace of

snow. Yet parallel lines
never touch, the badges

will come out, will glare
their red-and-blue differences,

until another shot
rings out upon the snow

as it falls upon the snow
which falling for another

thousand years cannot
rinse the blood of Korean

brothers, which flows over
the 38th parallel,

which does not exist.

Rob Wilson

PLAYING   DEAD   LOVE

How many of us have forgotten
How we loved pretending to die,
How we spent afternoons ecstatic
Being killed by make-believe bullets
Or in a duel of invisible swords
                stabbed in the heart.
No one could make the sounds of guns and bombs
                better than us.
We were virtuosos of richochet sounds.
Slave, Guard, Spy, Explorer, Pirate, King—
We were them all in our secret games.
Each of us knew in his own best way
When the imagined foe dealt the mortal blow
                just how to topple
                down snowy hills

Rolling every posture into a tumbled sprawl
                    and there, at the bottom
                    in that breathless Wow
We'd lay, playing dead the way we loved,
Motionless, watching the drifting sky,
Or eyes closed, feeling the earth spin
Letting ourselves be buried
By softly falling snow
                    till we heard our mother
                    in the growing dark
                    calling us home.

Antler

TO A FRIEND KILLED IN
DRAGON VALLEY, VIETNAM

Under other circumstances—you didn't
know me then—I sat with such a blistering
lamp as this beside my face and wrote
those letters that you've found. The full moon,
like a white, disembodied ear, would leap up
above the city, like this one, and hang listening
to the pencil scratch. A chill on the glass.

August. October. You lie there, second wife,
and fall asleep in the white debris reading
the ones returned, all from a friend
who wrote about the moon on a southern ocean,
falling in love in foreign bars, the roar
of a thousand trees snapping at once,
and how it rained on certain sweet autumn
nights something like grease and vinegar.

That's all. Or maybe that time deceives.
I copied out the weather in return, my loss of heart,
friends, and wife, how it ages me, but that I wouldn't die.
The sky's small as a lamp now. The window intimate
as a cheek. A table, a pool of light to extinguish.
When I lie down next to you the pages crackle
like little fires in an enormous field surrounding
us, that makes a mystery out of space, out of
closeness, and who is listening and who is burning.

Frank Stewart

VIETNAM INCIDENTS

I
Intelligence had heard for several days
that we would be hit any night
and Steele shows up that day
somehow without an M-16
and that night the perimeter guards
fired a few rounds, nothing else
Steele pleading hysterically for a razor
just a straight razor as if
this was a rumble with the VC back in Philly

II
Bates was sent out as FO that night
Then his begging

The VC waiting, his screams tempting
Until at last first light

when the company swept the area
His skin beside him like a twin brother

III

Somehow Jimmy was always alone since that day
the VC surrounded his recon team
and he was the one the chopper brought back alive
His eyes. Those so green, so weary such
inexplicably shattered eyes
His life awarded him posthumously
He would haunt himself forever

Leroy V. Quintana

VIETNAM MEMORIAL

We who didn't go to Vietnam
Planned our lives around it just the same.
The first thing we said to each other was,
How are *you* going to get out of the army?
It was the year of the lottery:
Each birthday was tagged with a number
And if yours was low enough, you went
For a physical at draft headquarters
Where you saw boys you hadn't seen
Since you were in kindergarten together.
It was the year of the psychiatrist:
I said I was living in despair
And he replied, "Hah! What do *you* know
About despair?" Then we were thrust
Into a locked room, blindfolded,
And after the eye test, when we could see again,
A man in a military uniform
Who might have been a doctor or a priest
Dealt us tarot cards. I drew
The two of cups and the seven of wands.
The doctor went to the sink to wash his hands
And said, "See you in Vietnam."
The priest blessed us. It was the year

Of tear gas dispersing the protesters at Fort Dix,
Students in denim on one side of the fence
Saying "We're on your side," to the raw
Recruits on the other side of the fence,
Who jeered. We were lucky. We didn't go.
Everyone had a different method for staying out.
Chuck said you could pack peanut butter
Up your ass and then, when you had to drop
Your trousers at draft headquarters,
You reached down and tasted it. It was the year
Robert Kennedy was killed and we
At Columbia went on strike. A bearded boy
Threw a brick through a library window
And called it a critique of pure tolerance.
Herbert Marcuse came to the campus
As did the Grateful Dead. But even when I read
Plato, I couldn't get my mind off Vietnam.
Some of the guys got their 4-Fs with ease.
Art had track marks on his arms and Stuart
Had been seeing a shrink since he was twelve.
Robbie said he was going to go to Canada,
And did. Some numbers never came up.
We were the lucky ones. The ones who went
Were forgotten. And I am thinking of them today,
Thinking of death in Vietnam, and the dead bodies
That might have been ours, bodies
Tagged and bagged and stacked, before the last
Helicopter lifted off the embassy roof
And the war, *our* war, was over.

David Lehman

ALL THE DEAD SOLDIERS

In the chill rains of the early winter I hear something—
A puling anger, a cold wind stiffened by flying bone—
Out of the north . . .

                and remember, then, what's up there:
That ghost-bank: home: Amchitka: boot hill. . . .

They must be very tired, those ghosts; no flesh sustains them
And the bones rust in the rain.
                         Reluctant to go into the earth
The skulls gleam: wet; the dog-tag forgets the name;
The statistics (wherein they were young) like their crosses, are
    weathering out.

They must be very tired.
                But I see them riding home,
Nightly: crying weak lust and rage: to stand in the dark,
Forlorn in known rooms, unheard near familiar beds:
Where lie the aging women: who were so lovely: once.

Thomas McGrath

THE HEARTS OF MEN

"he

didn't live here any longer. He was

settled in a suburb, north of himself."

DOWN HOME

Those sudden weathers, those awkward
encounters! He kept meeting feelings like
old schoolmates, faces whose names he'd
forgot. He came on feelings he could
enter again only as a stranger might
a house he'd once lived in; feelings like
places changed almost beyond recognition: a
once-green pasture field grown up in
pines too thick ever to enter again. Oh,
some of them he picked up as easily as gripping
this ax by its smooth helve, or the handles
of that plow leaning unused a long time
in the toolshed. But what about those
feelings he came on like graves of
childhood pets—a dog, a brindled cat, a bird—
their little bones in hidden graves
marked only in memory? He had to admit it: he
didn't live here any longer. He was
settled in a suburb, north of himself.

Jim Wayne Miller

INVENTING A FAMILY

You can have daughters, sons.
Parents, if you like. An uncle or aunt.
All the relations, all in your home.

Point, and your knee is a son,
white, knobby.
He'll follow you. You'll name him.
Just reach down. He's there.
You can hug him. Never be alone.

Across the room imagine a wife.
Stretch her out on the couch.
Put her there, on the couch, like a friend.

Have as many daughters
as you can. Delight in them.
See them as women, grown.
See them as nothing like your knee.
They are your stomach, or your hands.

Have a father, have a mother.
Have anniversaries.
Trouble yourself remembering birthdays,
the seasons moving through your rooms.

Soon you'll never be alone.
Imagine that.
Sitting together. Eating. Talk
in the dark.
Whole rooms full.
Arrange whole nights up.
Everyone talking to everyone.
Father to Mother. Brother to Sister.

Your knees. Your stomach.
Feel so much stirring. Feel yourself.
Never be alone. Never be alone.
Turn over in the dark. Careful.
There's Mother. There's Sister.

Dennis Saleh

THE FATHER

When I am walking with the children, and a girl
still hard in the buttocks bends to them with a laugh,
my heart bangs where it hangs in my empty carcass.

But you knew that. It has already passed
the stage of neighbor's gossip and attained
the clarity of a historical fact.
A myth comes down your street: here on my right
toddles my twinkling daughter, who loves me, while
on my left marches my son, who does not.

It's all true, but it does not matter;
in twenty years my son and I will have reached
a silent understanding, whereas (poor fool,
already growing hollow) some pimply bastard
will have made off with my blessings and my daughter.

Donald Finkel

MY PARENTS BOUGHT ME COMIC BOOKS

In those days there were dimestores, and I supported them
Myself. I have no doubt that many of the deepest wrinkles in my brain
Were cut by Superman and Donald Duck, G.I. Joe and Goofy.
In time I graduated to the skinny but sophisticated classics:
Swiss Family Robinson, The Pathfinder, Treasure Island, Robin Hood.
William Tell could raise the hair on any crewcut head.
Archie and the Gang instructed me about the agonies of sex
And the pleasures of the drugstore, but I am married now,
And there are no drugstores anymore.

I am very famous in my family
For the way I wallow in nostalgia,
But I didn't save my comic books
Or baseball cards or any of the relics of my youth
That now might be quite valuable. Besides,
My boyhood's not for sale, though I am always eager
To swap with anyone who knows enough
To keep some favorite memories
Reserved like silver bullets, the super special ammo
We fire when surrounded by depression and fatigue.

I am proud of my nostalgia, and who wouldn't be today,
But I'm not simple-minded. The past was painful, too,
And the low-brow literature I read was packed
With vivid illustrations. Even then I knew
The loneliness of Crusoe, the problems Robin had with Marian.
My childhood was not protected. I read everything
At once, like Superboy, so it was simple to predict
The booby-trap and ambush, villains everywhere,
And I was not surprised in later years
By my exposure to the Krypton of despair.

The present isn't bad, but the past is more believable,
And when I read the papers now and find a friend has died
Or visit certain scenes of youth and childhood
And see the bridge demolished, the church and schoolhouse gone,
Or I go home and find my father not himself
But someone else, some stranger, bald and thin,
And my mother dead and gone, a ghost, and the ghost gone, too,
And this other woman living with him over twenty years,
And my brothers and my sisters, gone, left the country,
And I see my father nodding, dreaming so agreeably
Beside the fireplace, who once was wide awake,
What I feel is not some gooey kind of grief,
Sticky with self-pity or bittersweet affection,
But utter disbelief. Or, rather, the stupid kind of wonder
Baby Huey must have felt when that dumbbunny stood
Bewildered, with his finger in his mouth,
And the big cartoon balloon above his head said: "Duh!"
Or as Lash Larue would say whenever he was bushwhacked:
    "What the—!?"

Barton Sutter

August lightning opens the afternoon sky
As one might open an egg.
Opens, or breaks, the same way
Those album photographs get ripped
Then Scotch-taped back together.
The pictures we look at today
They are like that, angry and then soothed,
Good to look at again and nod,
Worth having kept track of.
    Thunder too is there, a man's voice,
His roll of words, twisting
Fingers in a fist, the moment
Tearing apart more than the photographs.
    Rain too in the open hand of the sky,
    The work of rain and sparrows and wind.
These are better photographs
Of what is not there in them:
All the times we cried at having wanted
Something, a father maybe,
To come home, wanted him there
Enough to rip apart.

Alberto Rios

HOME

Take this kid, for example,
walking with his father
across the Harlem River.
The bridge, narrow and high, shivers in the wind.
He holds to the railing, holds
his daddy's hand, afraid
of the water below,
the hulking shapes of buildings

on the far side.
When he's older
the soot in the air's so thick
he washes his father's car
and an hour later the paint's
got a gritty film on it;
everyone he meets wants something fast—
the time, directions to the Stadium,
a dime, a fight, a fix.
At night his mother and father sulk
and listen to the Yankees.

Returning from the Service
he sees from the bus the boarded hulks,
cardboard inserts with painted curtains
where windows used to be,
and knows no matter how far he's traveled
he's addicted to decay—
this road, his memory, the main line.
Under the El on Jerome
cars belly in the gutter,
their trunk lids sprung.
Graffiti bruises the walls
of the Stadium.

Living in the suburbs now—
a young woman is murdered in Sycamore Park,
kids shoot up in the alleys
of shopping malls.
At night he stands on his back porch
and smells the air fouling out
from the city, from the factories
at the edge of town.
He tells himself he doesn't want
to have children.
He watches the Yankees on TV
and does not marry.

Philip Cioffari

FAMILY TIES

Mountain barbecue.
They arrive, young cousins singly,
older aunts and uncle in twos and threes,
like trees. I play with a new generation
of children, my hands in streambed silt
of their lives, a scuba diver's hands, dusting
surface sand for buried treasure.
Freshly shaved and powdered faces
of uncles and aunts surround taco
and tamale tables. Mounted elk head on wall,
brass rearing horse cowboy clock
on fireplace mantle. Sons and daughters
converse round beer and whiskey table.
Tempers ignite on land grant issues.
Children scurry round my legs.
Old bow-legged men toss horseshoes on lawn,
other farmhands from Mexico sit on a bench,
broken lives repaired for this occasion.
I feel no love or family tie here. I rise
to go hiking, to find abandoned rock cabins
in the mountains. We come to a grass clearing,
my wife rolls her jeans up past ankles,
wades ice cold stream, and I barefooted,
carry a son in each arm and follow.
We cannot afford a place like this.
At the party again, I eat bean and chile
burrito, and after my third glass of rum,
we climb in the car and my wife drives
us home. My sons sleep in the back,
dream of the open clearing,
they are chasing each other with cattails
in the sunlit pasture, giggling,
as I stare out the window
at no trespassing signs white flashing past.

Jimmy Santiago Baca

A man's family leaves on a trip to Idaho.
He drives them out to the station
at Columbus, Wisconsin, where the train
barely stops, just slows down and lets them on
and then speeds up again and is gone
before he's even noticed. He had planned
to get on that train and examine
the seats, take care of the luggage, fluff
the pillows, with hugs and kisses around.
He would have given his two children
spending money to remember him by,
and told his wife he loved her, after all.
But they're gone.
The tracks are gray and filled with rain,
and he's a stranger in this small town.

Later, on the ridge behind his house,
looking at the oak tree he built steps onto
for the children, he imagines he is
the director of a film about loss,
and the lead character, and the audience sitting down.
He looks at the tree and sees through a mist
the superimposed ghost figures of his children,
the sound of their echoing laughter,
and then there is only the sound of the wind,
and the trees, and the rain, and the tears on his face
streaming down. Did the train crash in the night?
Was no one heard from again? Did the man grow
old in his young family's dying?
No. It was only a movie.
His family comes back as if nothing
has happened, right on schedule,
the day bright and slow and immortal.
But no matter how hard he tries not to
he goes through his life
thinking somehow they're all still in Idaho.
Somehow they're no more than a flat flicker of light,

a half-finished reel that will end, as it must,
in some theater of loss, with its own train of thought,
in the rain, in the dark, without any of them.

Ronald Wallace

A DEAR GERALD NOTE

i awake today to a note from my wife:
"i'll be taking the kids to my mother's
after work today
to celebrate valentine's day."

it is february 17.
valentine's day was 3 days ago.
we've been celebrating valentine's day
for about ten days. i tried to keep up
with the celebration,
but i dropped out about february 13.

today, february 17, is not valentine's day,
but it *is* my birthday.

no matter.
my wife will remember within a week
and rush me something i like
from the liquor store.
and, in the meantime, not all the money
in the world could purchase a gift
as exquisite as this finely nurtured hurt.

Gerald Locklin

WALKING HOME FROM WORK

Asphalt and gravel flex with my shoes as the heel
hits and pulls the rest of my body forward.
Ahead of me, twilight is ending
and the ragged outline of the mountain
is glazed with iridescence, each tree
singular and sure.
Each night the same. Or if not
the same, then part of one long night
that leads me to my house, there
on the high ground of the foothills.
A thin streak of gray smoke
rises from the chimney,
a string from which the house
is suspended in the darkness.
I am a block away before shadows appear
moving against the fogged
windows in the kitchen.
My wife is baking bread. A hand
reaches up and wipes away the steam.
Light spills out of the kitchen
and begins to fill the world.

Gary Young

TOAST

There was a woman in Ithaca
who cried softly all night
in the next room and helpless
I fell in love with her under the blanket
of snow that settled on all the roofs
of the town, filling up
every dark depression.

Next morning
in the motel coffee shop
I studied the made-up faces
of women. Was it the middle-aged blonde
who kidded the waitress
or the young brunette lifting
her cup like a toast?

Love, whoever you are,
your courage was my companion
for many cold towns
after the betrayal of Ithaca,
and when I order coffee
in a strange place, still
I say, lifting, this is for you.

Leonard Nathan

CHANGE OF ADDRESS

"It doesn't get much light," the real
estate agent allowed, and didn't say,
as Nora Joyce did of a flat James let,
"It's not a fit place to wash a rat in."

Figure a 50% divorce rate,
you've got one chance in two a sale
provokes another sale and maybe
two transactions after that,

a pyramid scheme for grief. The agent didn't
smirk, I'll hand her that. When I'm asleep
and my navel is like the calm bubble
in a carpenter's level, rage is safe,

the way animals in a zoo are safe,
a little skittish and depressed but safe,
and yes, a little off their feed but safe.
And the rat? The rat looks radiant.

William Matthews

STANDING IN THE RECEPTION LINE AT THE WEDDING OF MY EX-WIFE

I remember last week in a warehouse
style department store—the one
where shoppers squeeze through
jean-tight aisles and clerks
seem always on coffee
breaks—a woman turned to me
smoothing a half-buttoned designer
blouse that was tagged *slightly irregular*

"Does my bra show through?"
                                        she asked

And without hesitation *I told her*

"Yes"

As though we had once made love
in the back of her father's immaculate
Buick, as though I had grown quite used to
shaving in the shadows of her drying
nylons, and chatting like ten-year
pinochle partners we could leave the
lingerie behind us, stroll down the aisle
lined with panty shields, deodorant pads
and colored mouthwash.

I turned away. In the record department
a couple was locked in a Ken and Barbie
embrace, the two of them spinning, oblivious
to the prerecorded cordial voice that
abruptly invited all shoppers to gather
in the garden section for a special on
pink plastic flamingos.

She decided not to take the blouse
and together we walked toward the smell
of peat moss, hearts pumping like blue strobes.
For fifteen minutes we shifted the weight
from foot to foot in a line where, somehow,
total strangers had managed to
speak.

Certainly something will come to mind.

James Plath

MON SEMBLABLE

No man has ever dared to describe
himself as he truly is
—Camus

I like things my way
every chance I get.
A limit doesn't exist

when it comes to that.
But please, don't confuse
what I say with honesty.

Isn't honesty the open yawn
the unimaginative love
more than truth?

Anonymous among strangers
I look for those
with hidden wings,

and for scars
that those who once had wings
can't hide.

Though I know it's unfair,
I reveal myself
one mask at a time.

Does this appeal to you,
such slow disclosures,
a lifetime perhaps

of almost knowing one another?
I would hope you, too,
would hold something back,

and that you'd always want
whatever unequal share
you had style enough to get.

Altruism is for those
who can't endure their desires.
There's a world

as ambiguous as a moan,
a pleasure moan
our earnest neighbors

might think a crime.
It's where we could live
I'll say I love you,

which will lead, of course,
to disappointment,
but those words unsaid

poison every next moment
I will try to disappoint you
better than anyone ever has.

Stephen Dunn

WIND CHIMES

Begin with a Victorian cottage in a Rhode Island
resort town—a two-story house of yellow shingles
a block from the ocean with a roof like a Chinese
pagoda and a screened-in porch on three sides.
A wooden croquet set lies scattered on the lawn
which is surrounded by a chest-high privet hedge.
Hanging from the porch ceiling, a wind chimes
with eight glass bars swings gently in a breeze
smelling of salt and fried food from hot dog stands
along the beach. In the middle of the living room,
a boy lies on his stomach reading a Batman comic.
Around him are wicker chairs with white cushions.
The boy's knees are bent and the soles of his tattered
gym shoes point toward the ceiling. As he reads,
he slowly bumps his heels together as if in time
to the sound of the surf he hears in the distance.
A collie dog lies panting at the foot of the stairs,
while in a bedroom at the top of the stairs
a man lies naked on white sheets smoking a cigarette.
His wife, also naked, sleeps with her head on his chest.
As he smokes, the man carelessly strokes her back and
stares up at the lines and angles of the white ceiling
until it seems he's looking down from some high place,
a plane or hilltop. From where he lies, he can just see
the roofs of other houses and he imagines his neighbors
drowsing their way through the August afternoon.
White curtains sway in the breeze from the open window,
while the smoke from his cigarette seems to turn blue
as it rises through bars of sunlight to the ceiling.

From nearby, the man hears the sound of people
playing tennis—an occasional shout and the plonk
of the ball against the webbing of the racket;
from the porch, he hears the tinkling of wind chimes
like a miniature orchestra forever warming up.

Years later the same man is lying fully clothed
on his bed in a city hotel. It is evening and
the only light comes from the street and a blinking
red sign outside his window. He's waiting for a friend
and soon they will go to dinner, but as he waits
he watches the shadows on the ceiling and either that
reminds him of the wind chimes or perhaps
it is some combination of sounds from the street.
His son is grown up; his wife has remarried.
He himself has a new wife in another city
and he's away from home only because of his work
in which he thinks himself happy and successful.
But for a moment, he clearly hears the wind chimes,
sees the swaying curtains in that summer bedroom,
even feels the faint pressure of his ex-wife's
sleeping head upon his chest. But then
it slips by and in its place he has an awareness
of all the complicated turnings of his life,
and he wonders if what he had seen as progress
was only a scrambling after circumstance, like a boy
trying to scramble into the back of a moving truck;
and while he doesn't regret his life, he grieves
for all that was lost, all that he had to let go.
He thinks of that ocean house and wishes he were back
in his former life or that one could take one moment
and remain inside it like an egg inside its shell,
instead of constantly being hurried into the future
by good luck or bad. Again he hears the wind chimes,
even sees them hanging in the dark with their
eight glass bars and red oriental designs, but then
they begin to get smaller as if quickly receding,
until they are no more than a speck of bright light

which at last blinks out as his friend starts hammering
at the door and his whole busy life rushes forward.

Stephen Dobyns

B R E A S T S

I love breasts, hard
Full breasts, guarded
By a button.

They come in the night.
The bestiaries of the ancients
Which include the unicorn
Have kept them out.

Pearly, like the east
An hour before sunrise,
Two ovens of the only
Philosopher's stone
Worth bothering about.

They bring on their nipples
Beads of inaudible sighs,
Vowels of delicious clarity
For the little red schoolhouse of our mouths.

Elsewhere, solitude
Makes another gloomy entry
In its ledger, misery
Borrows another cup of rice.

They draw nearer: Animal
Presence. In the barn
The milk shivers in the pail.

I like to come up to them
From underneath, like a kid
Who climbs on a chair
To reach a jar of forbidden jam.

Gently, with my lips,
Loosen the button.
Have them slip into my hands
Like two freshly poured beer mugs.

I spit on fools who fail to include
Breasts in their metaphysics,
Star-gazers who have not enumerated them
Among the moons of the earth . . .

They give each finger
Its true shape, its joy:
Virgin soap, foam
On which our hands are cleansed.

And how the tongue honors
These two sour buns,
For the tongue is a feather
Dipped in egg-yolk.

I insist that a girl
Stripped to the waist
Is the first and last miracle,

That the old janitor on his deathbed
Who demands to see the breasts of his wife
For one last time
Is the greatest poet who ever lived.

O my sweet yes, my sweet no,
Look, everyone is asleep on the earth.

Now, in the absolute immobility
Of time, drawing the waist
Of the one I love to mine,

I will tip each breast
Like a dark heavy grape
Into the hive
Of my drowsy mouth.

Charles Simic

TURNING FORTY IN DENVER

I wonder what they think, women, of men's
obsession with breasts, our tendency
to touch and wonder, to watch and wait

while they dress for work, hurried
in the morning, and lean into their clothes
as if it were merely biology bulging there.

I dream of such shapes while walking,
geometer of desire, desultory to work.
Churlish child of my own passion,

I watch the arc of mountains through mist
above the bundle of the city and think
of textures, a torrent of tactile fallings

down curved edges from eloquent tips
of rock and ice. The happy husband
has an indifferent wife amused

by his furious fondling, tolerant
of touch; meanwhile mothers mumble
into the nestled heads of small sons.

Bin Ramke

GIANT RED WOMAN

I have a delicious problem:
a huge woman I do not know,
lives and grows fast in my tiny office.
A quaint office in a purple cottage,
her presence is an unfair delight.
When she speaks
her voice causes my entire body to vibrate.
Her woman smell consumes me.
Her breasts push their way out the two tiny windows
toward the apple orchard. She is too much:
thighs, hips, arms, hands, face, feet, neck, ass,
too much. She continues to expand—my desk is crushed,
the chairs are inaccessible, the bookshelves are smashed,
the walls are cracking. The people who come to see me
say they cannot see her, that she is in my head.
Yet they remain unable to enter the space.
It is full of my own struggle to live.
I slide around the edges of her, trying both to
live with her and to escape.
Soon, movement will be impossible.
She also refuses to stop growing.
And, I cannot enter her openings nor leave the office.
The pressure is liquid. I wait here, against the wall.
This cannot go on.

Clarence Major

LATE SPRING

Sitting up ahead of me on someone's doorstep,
a fat woman in a housedress stamped with faded purple
blotches of flowers juts her legs apart,
the thigh closest to me

blocking the other leg, her skirt hiding the near leg down to the ankle,
angled across her lap to the hip, apparently accidental
—like those times at a play
waiting for it to begin when you watch the middle

of the curtain where it isn't quite closed and catch
flashes of hands, secret preparations through the black crack.
I'm half a block away. Then I'm in front of her and look.
No underpants, no awareness on her face—of her, of me—

no change of her large, wet, doll eyes,
and I can gaze directly at it:
delicately hairy, bearded, Mandarin-like, innocent,
the lips that could have been unbearable to see

not there—thank God, not in sight.
In Logan Square halfway to the center of town
child-sized copper frogs squirt water, three giant
nude female and male bronze gods, in the immune, aloof postures of sheer
    pleasure,

relax beneath sheets of water gushing from nozzles behind their heads.
Stripped tulips circle the pool, nothing but stalks;
a few stray bits of paper, cellophane;
sprawled, rain-flattened leaves, clipped hedges;

weeds up in ragged clumps; a chaos of red petals
stuck to the dirt and grass.
Her casual, idiot presence made it all ordinary,
she oozed indifference like a goddess, like this May morning,

the glistening frogs and gods joyous in a heaven of static, self-contained
    passion,
whiffs of old age blowing from houses, potatoes boiling,
the irises (that's what they were) adrift on her sleazy rayon frock,
replicas of death.

Stephen Berg

O TEMPORA! O MORES!

I get these girly magazines in the mail because
I'm writing short stories for them again
and here in these pages are these ladies
exposing their jewel boxes—
it looks more like a gynecologist's
journal—
everything boldly and clinically
exposed
beneath bland and bored physiognomies.
it's a turn-off of gigantic
proportions:
the secret is in the
imagination—
take that away and you have dead
meat.

a century back
a man could be driven mad
by a well-turned
ankle, and
why not?
one could imagine
that the rest
would be
magical
indeed!

now they shove it at us like a
McDonald's hamburger
on a platter.

there is hardly anything as beautiful as
a woman in a long dress
not even the sunrise
not even the geese flying south
in the long V formation
in the bright freshness
of early morning.

Charles Bukowski

A S W E L L I D E A

One of these days
while demonstrating the use
of the possessive pronoun
preceding the gerund
I'll tell her a little joke,
grow playful,
stroke the soft hairs
on the back of Melanie's neck
then slip my hand
over her breast.
Just as I've dreamed!
She'll groan.
She'll giggle & put
her hand over mine.
She'll love it!
If not, what have I lost?
If she screams
& the others rush in
I'll deny everything.
I'll stand there

shaking my head,
"She's crazy she's
making it up she
practically forced me
for chrissake I'm
sick I'm a sick man
I need help
Help me!"
I'll cry out
in a hoarse,
broken voice
& slip to my knees
& bury my face in my hands.

Steve Kowit

MY PENIS

Ordinarily I call it "my cock," but
often there is a strange formality about it,
this rocket with wattles.
"Penis" and "Vagina," a dignified couple
immobile on a Grecian urn
or at times engaged in elegant ballet and
desiring frequent medical checkups.
"Cock" and "Twat," two funloving kids
traveling from Pittsburgh to Tangiers
with a hundred bucks in their pockets,
laughing at Baptists but loving God.

Alone, it's
crazy and laughable, like the man
who stands up at every Quaker meeting,
testifying to his version of the Truth—
a drag to others but a private solace,
refusing to sit down when others whisper

"shush," "shame," "time and place for everything"—
a dotty old turkey continually rising in wonder,
even on lonely winter evenings refusing
not to point to the stars.

Ed Ochester

VASECTOMY: A POEM IN TWO PARTS

I.
I know many men who wouldn't
couldn't bring themselves to lay
beneath the sharpest blade
& I can't blame them, knowing
what I know, I feel, I felt.
It seemed appropriate that
my doctor was Swedish.
But was it me or was there really
a faint Aryan swagger on his lips
as he confessed he'd gotten
into this for "variety"?
& why was he trying
to talk me out of it?
Was I "serious"?
Had I considered
"The Matter"?
Especially the cough cough
"irreversible nature of
The Matter"?
Why did it sound
like a prenuptial interview
with a priest?
The legal briefs came next:
waivers, fine print disclaimers
that had to be signed
& swallowed like gum.

What a strange linking
of reassurance & abdication!
I was not to worry, but
I was to understand
that medicine was an inexact science;
operations involve risks.
There was always the exception
the outside chance that
the very thing I desired
would not for all their efforts
be dismantled.
It occurred to me:
He could have been describing
The Rhythm Method.
I told myself
he was merely being modest.

Then came V-Day
& the first surprise:
the orderly & his shaving kit:
a jocular Chicano
who did not have to tell me
to lie still.
(All the men in the audience
have my permission
to make noises.)
Then the doctor & the nurse
& theneedleinthecrotch.
The apron/tent for modesty,
the glorious I.V.
that felt like 3 martinis—
we were pals after that.
Then he made the cuts
& Juan held the mirror
so I could watch
& this black nurse smiled
& passed instruments of steel.
Did I hear snips?
I think I heard snips.

& after I was turkey-sewed
she said "Well! Now you're a Freedom Rider!"

It was by then
a wonderful experience.
I mean, *There We Were,*
three total strangers
in the same room
talking about my balls.
It was a vision of utopia,
a glimpse of a better world
where Swedes & Chicanos,
men & women,
the thin & the overweight,
the hardy & the lame
could gather under one
fluorescent lamp
united in one purpose:
to rid the world of my descendants,
to render sex stressless.
Actually that's *two* purposes, isn't it?
No matter!
One stroke!
One painless stroke
had undone the Catholic
chains of probability.
My God, My God,
what a world!

Of course my wife drove me home.
I felt too wonderful
to take the wheel
& I didn't want to miss
the pageantry of houses,
cars & concrete.
I had never seen
such vivid colors;
I had never noticed
the genius, the design

of, say, a freeway exit ramp.
It was a humbling journey
& I felt the privilege
of being born.

II.
It is a matter of hours
before you understand
what all the legalese was for.
Before you experience
what they call "Discomfort."
Hours. You start counting
the hours between dosages
of codeine capsules
that rattle in your pocket
like maracas.
Because, men—
there is no pretty way to say it
—your balls begin to swell.
They get very big.
Bigger than you ever
dreamed/imagined/hoped.
They get as big as
your scrotum will allow.
& then
they get a little bigger.
As important as they are now
they become more so.
They become the hub
of your existence.
They rule your every move,
roost upon your every thought,
assert themselves like
whining twins.
Never your most attractive feature
they now resemble
plucked chickens,
rotting cacti,
or newborn butch marines.

They itch but can you scratch them?
Noooo!
They gripe but can you quiet them?
Noooo!
They bleed & you must wrap them
like mummies
oh so tenderly in gauze
& you must bath them
in iodine which makes the gauze
sticky, purple & disgusting.

Now you women in the audience,
you're used to bleeding
Down There.
You regularly flow
& cope with blood
Down There.
But this is NEWS for men.
It is particularly distressing
to be bleeding
Down There.
But the bleeding
is a picnic
to the pain. The Pain. THE PAIN.
A pain so fierce
it can only be compared
to childbirth.
(A metaphor
which my wife
insists is offensive.)
O.K. Then.
Remember when you had
your wisdom teeth out
& they left holes
in your mouth
& the local wore off?
Multiply that.
You will be out of pain
only when you are drunk.

You'll walk like a cowboy.
It won't help.
You'll pray like a martyr.
It won't help.
You'll live with this
hanging bruise
for 2 gulag weeks
before anything approaching
relief comes.

& six weeks later
you must endure
the further indignity
of carting your
unspiked semen
around a hospital
of total strangers
in a transparent dish
that is the spittin' image
of those tartar sauce containers
they give you at
Long John Silver's.

All this
for the privilege
of being neutered,
mortal,
a missing link,
a Freedom Rider.

Patrick O'Leary

THE BALD SPOT

It nods
behind me
as I speak
at the meeting.

All night
while I sleep
it stares
into the dark.

The bald spot
is bored.
Tired of waiting
in the office

sick of following me
into sex.
It traces
and retraces

itself,
dreaming
the shape
of worlds

beyond its world.
Far away
it hears the laughter
of my colleagues,

the swift sure
sound of my voice.
The bald spot
says nothing.

It peers
out from hair
like the face
of a doomed man

going blanker
and blanker,
walking backwards
into my life.

Wesley McNair

HEART

He tells me I'm a risk:
he is small, blond, Mississippian. I trust him.
I am fighting my genes, he says, fighting
my father at fifty-two pulling off the highway
that had become a gray blur
trying to call to anyone from a phone booth
while it broke in his chest, calcified, knobby
like an ankle bone
and then again, over and over
in the hospital while doctors
ran up and down the halls trying to stop
that sequence of explosions,
that string of firecrackers.

You see yourself as glass
for the first time, transparent,
shaken and fizzing, a bottle
of soda, and start watching
for potholes.
Or maybe you just learn to live
with a cart with square wheels
thudding in your breast

trying to carry whatever it is
there,
before it's too late.

This is how to become
old—worry only
about yourself.
So that if there come
bombs out of clouds
or lovers into rooms, saying
goodbyes, learn
how to cup your hand around it, as if
in a world of wind
there is this one candle
that must be saved.

William Greenway

JUST LOOKING, THANK YOU

And when suddenly it hit me
that I would never get taller
or wiser or learn Greek
or interpret birds for humans
or humans for humans, never
get the first prize or be kissed
for courage, never be more
than the third (if that) person
to be contacted in case
of an emergency or love,
only a guilty bystander
who didn't get the facts straight
and who envied the truly good
and the lucky,
      I was not sad,
merely a little relieved,

feeling the spirit warmly
dissolve in my flesh like soap
in bathwater, and the food
placed before me then,
even the mashed potatoes,
became intensely personal,
and the stars over my head
unimportant except
as somehow necessary
to the local situation,
and the wars abroad something
to measure indifference by,
and you, the same as always—
turned sidewise with your own
occult obsession, and I felt
like a man in a hiding place
from the wind, or like a shadow
of a rock in a weary land,
secure in the dry lull
or depression between cause
and effect, for whom eating
mashed potatoes was OK,
and OK also allowing
the birds to mean nothing,
the humans to mean whatever
they mean, or so I believe
I believe—and just looking,
thank you, just looking.

Leonard Nathan

THE DAY I WAS OLDER

The Clock
The clock on the parlor wall, stout as a mariner's clock,
disperses the day. All night it tolls the half-hour
and the hour's number with resolute measure,

approaching the poles and crossing the equator
over fathoms of sleep. Warm
in the dark next to your breathing,
below the thousand favored stars, I feel
horns of gray water heave
underneath us, and the ship's pistons
pound as the voyage continues over the limited sea.

The News

After tending the fire, making coffee, and pouring milk
for cats, I sit in a blue chair each morning,
reading obituaries in the *Boston Globe*
for the mean age; today there is MANUFACTURER CONCORD 53,
EX-CONGRESSMAN SAUGUS 80—and I read
that Emily Farr is dead after a long illness in Oregon.
Once in an old house we talked for an hour, while a coal fire
brightened in November twilight and wavered
our shadows high on the wall
until our eyes fixed on each other. Thirty years ago.

The Pond

We lie by the pond on a late August afternoon
as a breeze from low hills in the west stiffens water
and agitates birch leaves yellowing above us.
You set down your book
and lift your eyes to white trunks tilting from shore.
A mink scuds through ferns; an acorn tumbles.
Soon we will turn to our daily business.
You do not know that I am watching, taking pleasure
in your breasts that rise and fall as you breathe.
Then I see mourners gathered by an open grave.

The Day

Last night at suppertime I outlived my father, enduring
the year, month, day, and hour
when he lay back on a hospital bed in the guest room
among cylinders of oxygen—mouth open, nostrils and lips
fixed unquivering, pale blue. Now I have wakened
more mornings to frost whitening the grass,

read the newspaper more times, and stood more times,
my hand on a doorknob without opening the door.
Father of my name, father of long fingers, I remember
your dark hair, and your face almost unwrinkled.

The Cup

From the Studebaker's backseat, on our Sunday drives,
I watched her earrings sway. Then I walked uphill
beside an old man carrying buckets
under birches on an August day. Striding at noontime,
I looked at wheat and at river cities. In the crib
my daughter sighed opening her eyes. I kissed the cheek
of my father dying. By the pond an acorn fell.
You listening here, you reading these words as I write them,
I offer this cup to you: Though we drink
from this cup every day, we will never drink it dry.

Donald Hall

LATE NIGHT ODE (Horace IV.i)

It's over, love. Look at me pushing fifty now,
    Hair like grave-grass growing in both ears,
The piles and boggy prostate, the hanged man's penis,
    The sour taste of each day's first lie,

And that recurrent dream of years ago pulling
    A swaying bead chain of moonlight,
Of slipping between the cool sheets of dark
    Along a body like my own, but blameless.

What good's my cut-glass conversation now,
    Now I'm so effortlessly vulgar and sad?
You get from life what you can shake from it?
    For me, it's g.-and-t.s all day and CNN.

Try the blond boychick lawyer, entry level
    At eighty grand, who pouts about the overtime,
Keeps Evian and a beeper in his locker at the gym,
    And hash in tinfoil under the office fern.

There's your hound from heaven, with buccaneer
    Curls and perfumed war paint on his nipples.
His answering machine always has room for one more
    Slurred, embarrassed call from you-know-who.

Some nights I've laughed so hard the tears
    Won't stop. Look at me now. Why *now*?
I long ago gave up pretending to believe
    Anyone's memory will give as good as it gets.

So why these stubborn tears? And why do I dream
    Almost every night of holding you again,
Or at least of diving after you, my long-gone,
    Through the bruised unbalanced waves?

J. D. McClatchy

THE AGING PROFESSOR CONSIDERS HIS RECTITUDE

There was something he had it on his mind to say
in class, a handsome catch of words that might have gone some way
toward explaining why, when he stood close to them,
he watched them surreptitiously, and waited for a hem
to rise. He pondered, too, the complex social laws
that he had wished to break, break like those men bred on applause
who drink their way from one small college to the next,
whose reputations burgeon as their eyes stray from the text
out to the breasts and suntanned knees in the third row.
Shopping the other day, he thought of it. He turned to go,
took up his groceries with a vague sweep of his arm,

and walked into the brilliant parking lot, his mind a swarm
of words and bits of words that winked out—like the stars?
No. More like blinding sunlight on the windows of parked cars. . . .
He would behave himself. He would not sidle up
to them before the weekly cinema, prepared to cup
a hand around a breast after the lights went down,
or else to take the attitude of a lascivious clown
whose very clownishness might let him get away
with saying, "How's about a little roll in yonder hay,
baby?" Somehow, he thought, he could explain all this
so they might feel how much he missed the things he chose to miss,
and think how noble his choice was. And then, they might . . .
too bad. Across the street, as he sat waiting for the light
to change, a boy was standing under the marquee
at the Home of the Whopper, catching a six-inch plastic E
at one end of a long aluminum shepherd's crook.
He watched the boy lift up the letter to its place, unhook
the pole, and slowly let it down to snag an A.
He almost had the hang of it. There went the final K.
The light turned green, and he turned right. The thought of STEAK,
as he drove home, gave way in time to how the rules might break
his way for once, if once the words would go his way.
His shepherd's crook somehow might catch a dream of making hay
long after sundown. In his narrow room, he changed
his shoes, unpacked his shopping bag. Slowly letters arranged
on cans of corn began to circle in his head
like some right words at some right time. They might somehow be said.

Henry Taylor

AT SIXTY

I have pried up, brushed off the self in me
that hugged secrets—the griever, the night walker,
the peeping-tom who promised to reform,
thumbing through porn all day. Acknowledge all

his lapses, his intensity. Never fault him for feeling:
fault him for what he endangered: creeping into
beds so sweet that he could not recall the breathing.
He bubbled promises to keep his lovers
deaf to the lofty inflections of a desire
that had no mind to remember what it had sworn,
or whom it had been sworn to, or when. Could he expect
to anticipate the lurches of his guilt?

Well, things have changed for the good. The world looks clear.
That self has bleached: his harshest needs are gone.
Yet sometimes at the drawing in of day
when I am too beaten down to lift a spoon
I taste the sharp pepper of his cruelty.

Peter Davison

IN THE SENEX CRIB

Having entered
my elderly babyhood
I gurgle and giggle
stare at the ceiling
wait to be hugged
fall asleep easily

I mutter gibberish
to sound interesting
or say nothing at all
because I no longer know
what my elders
are talking about

I live for my meals
and my defecations
I peepee and poopoo often
Having no diapers handy
I wear jockey shorts
under my pajamas

Once I preferred to make
cleverer things than turds
but now it doesn't matter
I have abandoned
ambition and boredom
for metaphysical questions

While I lie wiggly here
preparing for
my next incarnation
do I smell like
a babe about to be born
or an old man rotting?

James Broughton

DEFECTIVE WIRING

I labored to embrace light
in as many encounters
as I could turn on.

Have you ever tried to
take the world in your arms?
It resists being fondled.

Out all day setting fires
under crotches
that refuse to burn.

Now that it's dark I
stay close to my hearth
and leave the porch light on.

I want Death to feel welcome.
I look forward to
dazzling dawns at his house.

James Broughton

A MAN WRITES TO A PART OF HIMSELF

What cave are you in, hiding, rained on?
Like a wife, starving, without care,
Water dripping from your head, bent
Over ground corn . . .

You raise your face into the rain
That drives over the valley—
Forgive me, your husband,
On the streets of a distant city, laughing,
With many appointments,
Though at night going also
To a bare room, a room of poverty,
To sleep beside a bare pitcher and basin
In a room with no heat—

Which of us two then is the worse off?
And how did this separation come about?

Robert Bly

THE HEARTS OF MEN
for Karen Allen

Swing
like pendulums
from rage to remorse,
from anger to shame.
They do not know
The smaller increments
of a gradual birth,
the gentler shocks
of a congruent light.
All eruption, they pour
their grief like tide
into the air
and move out again,
like Odysseus,
into the deep sea
of disconnectedness,
the wide berth
of their denials. Once,
loved for their weeping,
they were coddled like yolks
in some womanly forgiveness.
Then, they became
what all men become
to earn their one stifled syllable—
an instrument
so hampered in its range
it becomes a bellows,
so shortened in its stops
it resembles a trumpet.
What will they do now
who have gone so long
without weeping,
who seem to have lost forever
the gradual repertoire,
the harp and the flute,
the piccolo and pizzicato?

In whose name,
impoverished ones,
will they learn to love? Who
will embrace them once more
for the shaken trill
of their weeping—
their cleft, broken hearts?

Michael Blumenthal

HISTORY OF MY HEART

I

One Christmastime Fats Waller in a fur coat
Rolled beaming from a taxicab with two pretty girls
Each at an arm as he led them in a thick downy snowfall

Across Thirty-Fourth Street into the busy crowd
Shopping at Macy's: perfume, holly, snowflake displays.
Chimes rang for change. In Toys, where my mother worked

Over her school vacation, the crowd swelled and stood
Filling the aisles, whispered at the fringes, listening
To the sounds of the large, gorgeously dressed man,

His smile bemused and exalted, lips boom-booming a bold
Bass line as he improvised on an expensive, tinkly
Piano the size of a lady's jewel box or a wedding cake.

She put into my heart this scene from the romance of Joy,
Co-authored by her and the movies, like her others—
My father making the winning basket at the buzzer

And punching the enraged gambler who came onto the court—
The brilliant black and white of the movies, texture
Of wet snowy fur, the taxi's windshield, piano keys,

Reflections that slid over the thick brass baton
That worked the elevator. Happiness needs a setting:
Shepherds and shepherdesses in the grass, kids in a store,

The back room of Carly's parents' shop, record-player
And paper streamers twisted in two colors: what I felt
Dancing close one afternoon with a thin blonde girl

Was my amazing good luck, the pleased erection
Stretching and stretching at the idea *She likes me,*
She likes it, the thought of legs under a woolen skirt,

To see eyes "melting" so I could think *This is it,*
They're melting! Mutual arousal of suddenly feeling
Desired: *This is it: "desire"!* When we came out

Into the street we saw it had begun, the firm flakes
Sticking, coating the tops of cars, melting on the wet
Black street that reflected storelights, soft

Separate crystals clinging intact on the nap of collar
And cuff, swarms of them stalling in the wind to plunge
Sideways and cluster in spangles on our hair and lashes,

Melting to a fresh glaze on the blood-warm porcelain
Of our faces, Hey nonny-nonny boom-boom, the cold graceful
Manna, heartfelt, falling and gathering copious

As the air itself in the small-town main street
As it fell over my mother's imaginary and remembered
Macy's in New York years before I was even born,

II

And the little white piano, tinkling away like crazy—
My unconceived heart in a way waiting somewhere like
Wherever it goes in sleep. Later, my eyes opened

And I woke up glad to feel the sunlight warm
High up in the window, a brighter blue striping
Blue folds of curtain, and glad to hear the house

Was still sleeping. I didn't call, but climbed up
To balance my chest on the top rail, cheek
Pressed close where I had grooved the rail's varnish

With sets of double tooth-lines. Clinging
With both arms, I grunted, pulled one leg over
And stretched it as my weight started to slip down

With some panic till my toes found the bottom rail,
Then let my weight slide more till I was over—
Thrilled, half-scared, still hanging high up

With both hands from the spindles. Then lower
Slipping down until I could fall to the floor
With a thud but not hurt, and out, free in the house.

Then softly down the hall to the other bedroom
To push against the door; and when it came open
More light came in, opening out like a fan

So they woke up and laughed, as she lifted me
Up in between them under the dark red blanket,
We all three laughing there because I climbed out myself.

Earlier still, she held me curled in close
With everyone around saying my name, and hovering,
After my grandpa's cigarette burned me on the neck

As he held me up for the camera, and the pain buzzed
Scaring me because it twisted right inside me;
So when she took me and held me and I curled up, sucking,

It was as if she had put me back together again
So sweetly I was glad the hurt had torn me.
She wanted to have made the whole world up,

So that it could be hers to give. So she opened
A letter I wrote my sister, who was having trouble
Getting on with her, and read some things about herself

That made her go to the telephone and call me up:
"You shouldn't open other people's letters," I said
And she said "Yes—*who taught you that?*"

—As if she owned the copyright on good and bad,
Or having followed pain inside she owned her children
From the inside out, or made us when she named us,

III

Made me Robert. She took me with her to a print-shop
Where the man struck a slug: a five-inch strip of lead
With the twelve letters of my name, reversed,

Raised along one edge, that for her sake he made
For me, so I could take it home with me to keep
And hold the letters up close to a mirror

Or press their shapes into clay, or inked from a pad
Onto all kinds of paper surfaces, onto walls and shirts,
Lengthwise on a Band-Aid, or even on my own skin—

The little characters fading from my arm, the gift
Always ready to be used again. Gifts from the heart:
Her giving me her breast milk or my name, Waller

Showing off in a store, for free, giving them
A thrill as someone might give someone an erection,
For the thrill of it—or you come back salty from a swim:

Eighteen shucked fresh oysters and the cold bottle
Sweating in its ribbon, surprise, happy birthday!
So what if the giver also takes, is after something?

So what if with guile she strove to color
Everything she gave with herself, the lady's favor
A scarf or bit of sleeve of her favorite color

Fluttering on the horseman's bloodflecked armor
Just over the heart—how presume to forgive the breast
Or sudden jazz for becoming what we want? I want

Presents I can't picture until they come,
The generator flashlight Italo gave me one Christmas:
One squeeze and the gears visibly churning in the amber

Pistol-shaped handle hummed for half a minute
In my palm, the spare bulb in its chamber under my thumb,
Secret; or, the knife and basswood Ellen gave me to whittle.

And until the gift of desire, the heart is a titular,
Insane king who stares emptily at his counselors
For weeks, drools or babbles a little, as word spreads

In the taverns that he is dead, or an impostor. One day
A light concentrates in his eyes, he scowls, alert, and points
Without a word to one pass in the cold, grape-colored peaks—

Generals and courtiers groan, falling to work
With a frantic movement of farriers, cooks, builders,
The city thrown willing or unwilling like seed

(While the brain at the same time may be settling
Into the morning *Chronicle*, humming to itself,
Like a fat person eating M&Ms in the bathtub)

I V

Toward war, new forms of worship or migration.
I went out from my mother's kitchen, across the yard
Of the little two-family house, and into the Woods:

Guns, chevrons, swordplay, a scarf of sooty smoke
Rolled upwards from a little cratewood fire
Under the low tent of a Winesap fallen

With fingers rooting in the dirt, the old orchard
Smothered among the brush of wild cherry, sumac,
Sassafras and the stifling shade of oak

In the strip of overgrown terrain running
East from the train tracks to the ocean, woods
Of demarcation, where boys went like newly converted

Christian kings with angels on helmet and breastplate,
Bent on blood or poaching. *There are a mountain and a woods*
Between us—a male covenant, longbows, headlocks. A pack

Of four stayed half-aware it was past dark
In a crude hut roasting meat stolen from the A&P
Until someone's annoyed father hailed us from the tracks

And scared us home to catch hell: We were worried,
Where have you been? In the Woods. With snakes and tramps.
An actual hobo knocked at our back door

One morning, declining food, to get hot water.
He shaved on our steps from an enamel basin with brush
And cut-throat razor, the gray hair on his chest

Armorial in the sunlight—then back to the woods,
And the otherlife of snakes, poison oak, boxcars.
Were the trees cleared first for the trains or the orchard?

Walking home by the street because it was dark,
That night, the smoke smell in my clothes was like a bearskin.
Where the lone hunter and late bird have seen us

Pass and repass, the mountain and the woods seem
To stand darker than before—words of sexual nostalgia
In a song or poem seemed cloaked laments

For the woods when Indians made lodges from the skin
Of birch or deer. When the mysterious lighted room
Of a bus glided past in the mist, the faces

Passing me in the yellow light inside
Were a half-heard story or a song. And my heart
Moved, restless and empty as a scrap of something

Blowing in wide spirals on the wind carrying
The sound of breakers clearly to me through the pass
Between the blocks of houses. The horn of Roland

V

But what was it I was too young for? On moonless
Nights, water and sand are one shade of black,
And the creamy foam rising with moaning noises

Charges like a spectral army in a poem toward the bluffs
Before it subsides dreamily to gather again.
I thought of going down there to watch it a while,

Feeling as though it could turn me into fog,
Or that the wind would start to speak a language
And change me—as if I knocked where I saw a light

Burning in some certain misted window I passed,
A house or store or tap-room where the strangers inside
Would recognize me, locus of a new life like a woods

Or orchard that waxed and vanished into cloud
Like the moon, under a spell. Shrill flutes,
Oboes and cymbals of doom. My poor mother fell,

And after the accident loud noises and bright lights
Hurt her. And heights. She went down stairs backwards,
Sometimes with one arm on my small brother's shoulder.

Over the years, she got better. But I was lost in music;
The cold brazen bow of the saxophone, its weight
At thumb, neck and lip, came to a bloodwarm life

Like Italo's flashlight in the hand. In a white
Jacket and pants with a satin stripe I aspired
To the roughneck elegance of my Grandfather Dave.

Sometimes, playing in a bar or at a high school dance, I felt
My heart following after a capacious form,
Sexual and abstract, in the thunk, thrum,

Thrum, come-wallow and then a little screen
Of quicker notes goosing to a fifth higher, winging
To clang-whomp of a major seventh: listen to *me*

Listen to *me*, the heart says in reprise until sometimes
In the course of giving itself it flows out of itself
All the way across the air, in a music piercing

As the kids at the beach calling from the water *Look,*
Look at me, to their mothers, but out of itself, into
The listener the way feeling pretty or full of erotic revery

Makes the one who feels seem beautiful to the beholder
Witnessing the idea of the giving of desire—nothing more wanted
Than the little singing notes of wanting—the heart

Yearning further into giving itself into the air, breath
Strained into song emptying the golden bell it comes from,
The pure source poured altogether out and away.

Robert Pinsky

THE ICE FISHERMAN

From here he appears as a black spot, one of the shadows that today has found it necessary to assume solid form. Along with the black jut of shoreline far to the left, he is the only break in the undifferentiated gray of ice and overcast sky. Here is a man going jiggidy-jig-jig in a black hole. Depth and the current are of only incidental interest to him. He's after something big, something down there that is pure need, something that, had it the wherewithal, would swallow him whole. Right now nothing is happening. The fisherman stands and straightens, back to the wind. He stays out on the ice all day.

Louis Jenkins

THE MAN WHO NEEDED NO ONE

He wanted to need no one, not
love or thirst, not even sunrise
and the sweet amulets of water
that fall from the heavens.

No, he wanted to be an island
of self-sufficiency, to sleep
with his arms around the pillow,
a jack-in-the-pulpit alone on his throne
in the damp woods, singing to himself
beneath his curled umbrella.

And this is how he lived for many years—
a solitary song, a soliloquy
spoken into the small mirror
that hung above the wash basin,
with its blue towel and basket of dead flowers.

But something remained wrong—
a dull ache whispered from below his voice
where his heart should have been, a seed
rumbled in the pit of his stomach as if to suggest
a tree that had never grown, a stone skimming
the surface of water once and then sinking.

He grew old this way, never knowing
it had been need he had needed all along—
the sound of his own small voice
asking for a light to see by, a match
to retrieve his heart with from the widening dark.

Michael Blumenthal

STEPS TO BREAK THE CIRCLE

I was standing on a corner
On that cold, cold rainy day
When they blew Malcolm away.
Will the circle be unbroken
Bye and bye, yall, bye and bye . . .

The Black Man's days are epic chains
Superbad links wandering in cisterns
Dry and narrow with the unending
Echoes just jazzing nights
Riffing right through wooden walls.
These trips I takes is waking breaths
Life cycles my fathers left me pedaling.
My Mississippi manning is a message
Kilos of soul cider sipped by the music
Of a song sailed over sage oceans . . .
I wears the rapping ring of seasons
Ebony circles of blues with the road
Long and my tired strides short.

Mocking birds' mimics are mentors
I hears my soul striding down gravel
Years and the dust is dancing . . .

Undertaker he took Brother King
Laid him out in a shroud
As the troubled cloud
Gave birth to my agony,
Now will the circle be unbroken
Bye and bye, yall, bye and bye . . .

The Black Man's days are epics changing
Bigfeet to break the circle
Break the breast of beaded crises
Ships stinking with Black flesh
Cottonfields colorful with open locks
Muddy roads with stubborn mules tugging

Rivers coughing up African bodies
Fathers never seeing their chilluns mature
Chilluns never knowing their fathers,
Steps to break the circle, I takes
When I lets the leaves become
Victims of crazy winds
And I wanders on, on blacktop hunches
Trying to make a straight bound train
A train to train all my brothers
Travel with all the sisters
And trample, trample my enemy,
This train this train this train
I rides is a hundred cars long. . . .

Sterling D. Plumpp

THE FACTS

Looking down the empty Mason jars
in the cupboard, I forget myself.
I forget my name and its belongings.
I forget my plastic ID card
for the "Y," my Exxon credit card
and the square feeling it leaves in my hand.
I forget passing thirty and feeling nothing—
but dreaming blue tears that night all the same.
I forget wanting money, no, wanting
to be like the men who have money,
who piss against the wall of good fortune.
I forget wanting the honest work
that poor people do, the necessary
work a man will do despite his fortunes,
the unsour laboring for the next life's wealth.
I forget the violinist 10 years ago
playing scales, narrowing her long attention
almost Buddha-like to one fluid note.
I forget the days in the auto plant
doing seventy bodies per minute—
the tools continuous in one loud scream,
the pinch, punch, press, and pounding of steel—
a gray space inside myself driven
like a car to the next stop down the line.
I forget all the textbook recipes
and all the facts I never lived in school.
I forget the facts I lived: the wet kiss
in the heart of all events drying out.
I forget Worcester, Mass.; Oakland;
Lansing, Michigan; and Birmingham;
their industrial dream frozen in mid-air,
a black wind crying over this lost scene,
and my white words unable to call it in.
I forget Birmingham again and being born
in that foundry town, feeling 1950's
no-english baby except to act, "fuck you,"
fat newborn feet remembering an old dance,

364

kicking at the balls of the steelman's statue
that hovered over town like a speechless god.
I forget further back the rocking in water;
the water always becoming 2 kinds—
the mother water and the nightmare water
where a man will drift from home in chains.
I forget the magic gourd that fit my hands,
its shake my feeling of having a heart.
My face is a mask. Everyone wears it.
When I take it off there's another face.
I turn around to you, you this moment
I have come to empty-handed and not myself.

I am between things—what's going on?
I'm stuck. You stare with expectation.
You want a sacrifice. You take my breath.
My arm drifts off to light the stove.
The walls heave and blacken with body salt.
The cupboards fireball toward some purpose.
You want my green tomatoes stored to ripen?
Why you gaze outward, brother?
You look off like a wanderer. You mad.
You the air and there's nothing set to fill.
You making a stew. You demand something read.
I put a record on. One saxophone
and the room remembers, Bird lives!
This is my body, the horn-words say.
Bird's forwards music a feeling which is:

> *Start with another man's line.*
> *Stamp it with your point of view.*
> *Space is terms; meaning is glue,*
> *and each step you take is time.*
> *You write your self with what you do—*
> *dazzling being the world's mind.*

You stop the record, you demand something read.
It's *your* story you say, fuck Bird, the way
Bird would have put it nicely through his sax.

Listen, Chris, the mask is artifact.
There's no substitute to live for you.
Life is here; for you to be it live
without a charm to cleanse its chances.
There's no getting past its confrontations.
There just ain't. You stand atop tradition
practicing whatever is your music, lip torn
on false starts, out of breath and no one else
to play your part, your million facts—
but when your number's flashed you play.

Suppose I were to say:
Simmer soul from African water
4 centuries on disintegrating train,
no stops. No mule no 40 acres.
Remove the umbilical tongue.
Add salt to wounds repetitively.
Let stand in cold.
Remove the perfect laughing.
Look out for small movements.
Cover and boil.
Remove vestiges of celestial knowledge.
Omit a dream opened out on the world.
Forget the oblique signifying.
Sprinkle maleficence and malfeasance.
When gall arises, keep bottled. 32 years.
Remove the bits of tenderness.
Bring yourself from nothingness.
Suppose I were to say:

   I leave myself for the future of the spinach seed flying away in the sudden
breeze. A breeze goes all the way in the contours of things.

   I have decided to land someday when you know me better. Right inside
your ear. I'll grow inward there. The dark questions inside you will align
themselves along me and feel my boundaries as intimate as answers.

   I leave myself with the speechlessness of the poor woman widowed from
her old neighborhood by the shining buildings and the mayor's new plans.

   I have decided to shake the backyard pear tree and to throw its hard young
fruit. If there is any timing they'll shatter glass and burst in justice in a litany
of flame.

I leave myself and become the black body in a southern town. I am a citizen so I have this hope. One of my arms moves north to Chicago and sings the blues. One of my arms moves west to Texas and sings the blues.

I have decided to be the long black language that reaches all the way back. When I get there I keep on reaching. I write this off as jazz. Part of me is laughing at my situation. That part is the old griot walking the world, learning the zen of laughter.

I leave myself for the many versions of light as the sun comes across the rippled spit of the Atlantic.

I have decided to be the boat's prow while you're the pier. I'm tied to you. When the tide comes in I rock forward and kiss the wet black splinter on your forehead just above the water's level. There is sweat in both our mouths. You change into Yeats's glimmering girl. Your tongue speaks sunlight rising up your throat.

I have decided my joy is the rising surface of rain water in a bucket during a midwest storm. Suddenly the sky is Canadian cold clear. I give off speckles of light and am the dark patina that gathers it. I'll set myself beside the trail where you walk by. I wish you luck, you this world's blue thirst. You might be Malcolm X with one of Roethke's roses in your vest. You know the arithmetic of a double thirst. It's the same old loneliness that made Coltrane disappear. This time I'll be of use.

I have decided to be background vocal in a 60's Motown song. A grown-up adolescent love song I can leave myself in my hips to. Maybe the Temptations singing. Get ready.

I have decided to become one of Mary Driscoll's kids if she'll have me— one semester. She'll read Vallejo, and I'll be Lorca listening. Her furious Celt films are in the cupboard at her house. She keeps a projector handy. It's pure voodoo when her thing's cranked up.

I have decided to be American again, sitting naked at night on a rock in the low waters of West River, Brattleboro, 1981. Knowing poetry alone won't save us from the Russian nukes or the big Yankee Nuke and James Watt for that matter, drinking lite beer and eating corn buttered from absurdly poisoned cows. When a small fish veers too close I see its nightmare flash in its one glowing eye. It darts away renouncing our kind, and I want to be with it. Choose a far-off object and cast my spirit to it. American willing too much and too little, I cannot shed myself. I can't feel my spirit as it already swims among these circumstances till I swim my seasons of fault and loss, till I swim the recesses of the people and things I love and am connected to.

I have decided to be myself again. Thank you fahlet'n me be myself again.

Thank you fahlet'n me be myself again. Thank you fahlet'n me be my-self again.

Suppose I were to say:
I know my birth because I pronounce myself transformed.
I know my age 'cause any age will do. Age is trite because each year the
    wars go on and on, continuous and eternal.
I know my country because while I travel I meet the cowboys who own it.
    We are all of one tongue, we say every word but *friend*.
    This is their custom, this absent speech.
I know not what is lost, but I know grief is not.
I know my pride because I don't look back.
I know my shame because across the world there are people dying I pretend
    I don't know. This is that shame of looking in a mirror at a face
    pretending it knows nothing of the dying even as its honesty is killed.
I know my rage because I burn. Mortal and sacrificial, I become united with
    what is lost. Now I know that I am real.
I know my language as these words I have to say. Saying, *this*, is not an
    excuse for this.
I know my self speaking my voice. When it is wholly exact it matters, and I
    am proof the things it will come to touch talk back.
I know this is a journey, and I have gone this far. I make use of where I am.

Suppose I were to say:
The self grows, the self goes forward,
the self goes forward out of its presentness,
a batch of moments where what is being is
the meeting in each moment, the breath where it is.

Age 5, near drowning in the Red Cedar; the excited
boy holding on to the water which rocked, brown-black
and summer warm; lungs unable to fill with air, wanting
then to swallow the whole of water; thrashing for some
last breath while listening to the river in his head;
the absolute music of the water too holy to stand
apart from; yes, to go fully forward is to lose the self;
yes, I wanted to merge with the water music, be fluid in it
to make the world be dream again, whole and oncoming.
For a flash this moment mattered, not: the shore; the others

ahead swimming, their black inner tubes standing out atop
the surface; the dry midwest republican morals half-accepted
like the insufferable air—till I gave myself over to a wave
and came up convinced of swimming in the waters
on the shore.
You find the self at these moments:
the collection of possible completions and real dreams
converging like streams into one mellifluous river
rushing forward toward itself.

The live moment, a wave
comes and I am one with water,
and when I stand outside the moment
thinking my loss, the self comes forward—
like fishermen dropping anchor
this mark, this reference against chaos.
A moment lost wandering
where no one was waiting to hear
has come home to papa.
Its flesh flashing full like jars
on a shelf—YES, LORD, YES
I'VE FOUND THE STEWED TOMATOES.
While the chili is cooking
I am writing something—
for now, I've decided
let this writing be my name.
When the recipe is done
(if it's good, if it's me)
I'll be the person eating.
And the self grows,
the self grows forward,
the self grows forward
out of its reference.

Christopher Gilbert

MY ENEMY

His face is hidden in the closet
where for years he has stored
the bodies of women.

When the sun goes down
I hear him in his cellar
sharpening knives.

Now he invites me to dinner
saying blood is thicker than water,
saying that he is my brother.

Victor Contoski

DEAR TEACHER

One of my students sends me
a postcard from St. Paul's.
It features the standard
martyr and she says,
"He looks like you."

There is the bare, narrow
skull, a beard, the deep eyes
with their fashionable
dark luggage.

Lord, it's true.

In museums I am never
in The Jolly Wing with my
mistresses, my dogs
and a flagon of ale.

But alone in the study.
Or outdoors in the rain
looking chilled despite
the hair shirt.

Ron Koertge

ZIMMER IMAGINES HEAVEN
for Merrill Leffler

I sit with Joseph Conrad in Monet's garden.
We are listening to Yeats chant his poems,
A breeze stirs through Thomas Hardy's moustache,
John Skelton has gone to the house for beer,
Wanda Landowska lightly fingers a clavichord,
Along the spruce tree walk Roberto Clemente and
Thurman Munson whistle a baseball back and forth.
Mozart chats with Ellington in the roses.

Monet smokes and dabs his canvas in the sun,
Brueghel and Turner set easels behind the wisteria.
The band is warming up in the Big Studio:
Bean, Brute, Bird, and Serge on saxes,
Kai, Bill Harris, Lawrence Brown, trombones,
Little Jazz, Clifford, Fats on trumpets,
Klook plays drums, Mingus bass, Bud the piano.
Later Madam Schumann-Heink will sing Schubert,
The monks of Benedictine Abbey will chant.
There will be more poems from Emily Dickinson,
James Wright, John Clare, Walt Whitman.
Shakespeare rehearses players for *King Lear*.

At dusk Alice Toklas brings out platters
Of Sweetbreads à la Napolitaine, Salad Livonière,
And a tureen of Gaspacho of Malaga.
After the meal Brahms passes fine cigars.

God comes then, radiant with a bottle of cognac,
She pours generously into the snifters,
I tell Her I have begun to learn what
Heaven is about. She wants to hear.
It is, I say, being thankful for eternity.
Her smile is the best part of the day.

Paul Zimmer

WALKING AROUND THE FARM

This is where I shot the rabbit
from the back porch
when we first moved in
but found it inedible,
covered with fleas. This
is where we made love
in the woods, surrounded by ferns,
our asses bitten by mosquitoes.
This is where our daughter, age six,
was tossed like a tenpin
by a running bulldog.
This is the black walnut tree
beneath which we drank beer
the morning Nixon resigned.
This is where years ago
I grew reefer among the corn.
This is the gravestone
so weathered we can't read the name.
This is where Roger parked
his Volkswagen the night he came back
from Vietnam and we listened
to Van Morrison in the rain
all night delicately sipping Jim Beam.
This is where the crabapple tree fell
during the great wind of '79.

This is the mailbox
where the postman, Mr. John,
picks up his two dozen eggs a week.
This is where we picked the lambsquarters
that sustained us in our first year.
That's where I sit in good weather
when I'm thinking a poem.
That is the road that runs
into the black woods
where my daughter, age 12,
saw something running through the brush
that she said seemed almost human, but huge,
naked and terrified.

Ed Ochester

MAGRITTE DANCING

Every night I have to go to bed twice,
once by myself, suddenly tired and angry,
and once when my wife turns the weak light on
and stumbles over my shoes into the bathroom.
Some nights there is a third time—the phone
is ringing and I rush out into the hall;
my heart is pounding but nobody is there
and I have to go back to bed empty-handed
just as my brain was beginning to pick up signals.
This time it takes me all night to get back to sleep.
I don't sink again into the heavy pillow
but lie there breathing, trying to push
everything back into its own channel.
For hours I watch the dark and then gradually
I begin watching the light; by that time
I am thinking again about snow tires and I am thinking
about downtown Pittsburgh and I am thinking
about the turtles swimming inside their brown willows.

I look at the morning with relief, with something close
to pleasure that I still have one more day,
and I dance the dance of brotherliness and courtliness
as first my neighbor the postman, pocked and pitted,
goes crawling off in his early morning bitterness
and then my neighbor the body man goes bouncing away,
his own car rusty and chromeless, his T-shirt torn,
his eyes already happy from his first soothing beer.
   The dance I dance is to the tune of Magritte
banging his bedposts on a square mountain,
and Oskar Schlemmer floating up a stairway,
and Pablo Picasso looking inside a woman's head.
I dance on the road and on the river and
in the wet garden, all the time living in Crete
and prewar Poland and outer Zimbabwe,
as through my fingers and my sparkling hair
the morning passes, first the three loud calls
of the bluejay, then the white door slamming,
then the voices rising and falling in sudden harmony.

Gerald Stern

SAILING

After years by the ocean
a man finds he learns to sail
in the middle of the country,
on the surface of a small lake with a woman's name
in a small boat with one sail.

All summer he skims back and forth
across the open, blue eye of the midwest.
The wind comes in from the northeast
most days and the man learns
how to seem to go against it, learns
of the natural always crouched
in the shadow of the unnatural.

Sometimes the wind stops
and the man is becalmed—
just like the old traders who sat for days
in the doldrums on the thin skin of the ocean,
nursing their scurvys
and grumbling over short grog rations.

And the man learns a certain language:
he watches the luff, beats windward, comes
hard-about, finally gets
port and starboard straight.

All summer, between the soft, silt bottom
and the blue sheath of the sky, he glides
back and forth across the modest lake
with the woman's name.

And at night
he dreams of infinite flat surfaces,
of flying at incredible speed,
one hand on the tiller, one on the mainsheet, leaning
far out over the sparkling surface, the sail
a transparent membrane, the wind
with its silent howl, a force
moving him from his own heart.

Al Zolynas

MAKING THINGS RIGHT

He's there when I get home: white beard, Charles Atlas muscles—just like in the Sistine Chapel. I feel like Adam when he offers to shake hands.

"God," I start, "You haven't aged a day . . ."

He wastes no time. "You know that test you bombed in tenth grade? The one that kept you out of Honors Math?"

I nod.

"Misgraded; you deserved an A. Remember not making the track team?"

I nod.

"They meant to cut *Jim* Webb. Damn fool coach mixed up the names."

"What about Yale?" I prompt. "Why didn't I get in?"

"Politics." He spits. "One spot was left. You had it. Then the Dean's grandson applied."

I shake my head. "I thought I was a total zilch."

He smiles. "That's over now. I'm here to make things right." He nudges me. "Remember Jo Ann?"

How could I forget? I agonized for weeks before I asked her out. She looked me up and down, and said "I *couldn't* come between you and your zits."

Suddenly she's there.

"I was wild for you," she whispers, unzipping her dress.

I look around. God has discreetly vanished.

"I was scared of sex," she pants. "You were *so sexy*. All the girls were wild for you."

"Thank God," I wake up sobbing happily. "Thank God."

Charles Harper Webb

MY RODEO

I'm ashamed of my cheap rodeo,
so I keep it secret from my friends.
It's not even as big as theirs
and needs constant repair.
"How's your rodeo?" someone asks at a party.
"Fine!" they chirp up.
They jump at the chance
to extol the virtues of their rodeo.
Pretty soon a circle gathers
and everyone's discussing its size,
weather control, the acoustics, the peanuts.
If I stay in my corner someone will notice and ask about mine.
I don't want to talk about it.
So I join in, chirping up with *you-don't-says*,
and *isn't-that-amazings* and

what-about-the-functional-glitter?
By the time I get home
I'm exhausted from avoiding the subject of my rodeo.
I get home and there it is,
not much on weather control, lousy acoustics,
styrofoam peanuts.
There's no subculture, no glitz-trimming,
no contour illuminations, not even jacket hitch
where the top bolt exceeds the maintenance quota lining.
I'm embarrassed and ashamed of the damn thing,
give it a kick and stub my toe, then cover it with a sheet.
Maybe smother it.
I am a man who comes home depressed, lonely,
frustrated, who tries to smother his rodeo,
his cheap rodeo.
And I haven't even the courage to do that.
Imagine smothering one's rodeo.
The shame would haunt me the rest of my life.
So after a while I take the sheet off and go to bed,
hearing its slight breathing throughout the night,
its occasional cough, the short low moan
just before daybreak. My cheap rodeo.

Jack Grapes

CONTRIBUTORS

Jack Agueros, poet, playwright, and fiction writer, was born in East Harlem. His first book of poems is *Correspondence Between the Stonehaulers*. He has received many writing awards, including first prize in the 1989 McDonald's Latino Dramatists' Competition. For eight years, he was the director of the Museo del Barrio in East Harlem, the only Puerto Rican museum in the United States.

Antler, who is the author of two books of poetry—*Factory* (1980) and *Last Words*—lives in Milwaukee and spends two months of the year alone in the wilderness. He has won the Walt Whitman Award and makes a living reading his poems around America, "trying to live up to Whitman's invocation of the poet as 'itinerant gladness scatterer.'"

Charles Atkinson teaches at the University of California, Santa Cruz. His book *The Only Cure I Know* won the San Diego Poets Press Prize as well as the American Book Series Award.

Jimmy Santiago Baca is the author of *Black Mesa Poems* (1989) and *Martin* (1987). He has been a recipient of a grant from the National Endowment for the Arts.

John Balaban is the author of *The Hawk's Tale* (1988), a children's book. His poems have appeared in *Harper's*, *Ploughshares*, and other magazines.

Gerald Barrax was born in Attala, Alabama, in 1933. Since 1969 he has lived in North Carolina, where he teaches and edits *Obsidian II: Black Literature in Review* at North Carolina State University in Raleigh. Two of his three books of poetry are *The Deaths of Animals and Lesser Gods* (1984) and *Leaning Against the Sun* (1992).

Joe David Bellamy is director of the literature program for the National Endowment for the Arts. His first collection of poetry, *Olympic Gold Medalist* (1979), was a Walt Whitman Award finalist. In addition, he has published an anthology of interviews with poets, *American Poetry Observed* (1984).

Michael Benedikt continues to make his home in his native New York City. He has published three books of poems, one of which is *The Badminton at Great Barrington; Or, Gustav Mahler & The Chattanooga Choo-Choo* (1980). He has also edited five anthologies of twentieth-century literature and had his own work represented in at least forty anthologies and studies of contemporary American literature. Among a variety of awards he has received are grants from the Guggenheim Foundation and the National Endowment for the Arts.

Stephen Berg is founder and coeditor of the *American Poetry Review*. His *New and Selected Poems* was published in the fall of 1991.

Michael Blumenthal is the author of four books of poems, including *Against Romance* (1987), and editor of *Marriage: An Anthology* (1992).

Robert Bly's book *Iron John* (1990) is a product of his years of work with men, as a leader of workshops, conferences, retreats, and other gatherings. His *Selected Poems* was published in 1986. He has been a major force in American poetry since the 1950s as an author, editor, or translator of more than forty books.

James Broughton is a native Californian, raised in San Francisco. He has published twenty books, including *Special Deliveries: New and Selected Poetry* (1990), and made an equal number of experimental films. He has received two grants from both the Guggenheim Foundation and the National Endowment for the Arts. He lives in Port Townsend, Washington.

Eric Brown lives in Los Angeles and publishes a magazine called *Rats with Keys*. He describes himself as a "well-behaved young man, fun to work with and well motivated."

Michael Dennis Browne's fourth collection of poems is *You Won't Remember This*. He is author of many texts for music, including *Harmoonia* (1991), an opera for children with music by Stephen Paulus. He is director of creative writing at the University of Minnesota, Minneapolis.

Joseph Bruchac lives in the Adirondack foothills town of Greenfield Center, New York, with his wife and two sons. One of his books of poems is *Near the Mountains, New and Selected Poems* (1987). Over the last two decades he has held poetry and storytelling work-

shops in prisons from Alaska to Florida. Much of his writing draws on his Native American heritage.

Charles Bukowski was born in Germany in 1921, raised in Los Angeles, and now lives in San Pedro, California. He is internationally known for more than forty books of poetry and prose. Most have been translated and now appear in more than a dozen languages. His book of poems *You Get So Alone at Times That It Just Makes Sense* was published in 1986.

Raymond Carver's untimely death in 1988 brought to a close his distinguished career as a major short story writer and poet. *Where Water Comes Together with Other Water* (1985) and *Ultramarine* (1986) were his last books of poetry.

Cyrus Cassells is the author of *The Mud Actor*, a 1982 National Poetry Series winner, *Down from the Houses of Magic* (1991), and a play, *Soul, Make a Path Through Shouting*. He is a recipient of a grant from the National Endowment for the Arts and the Massachusetts Artists Fellowship, and his work has also been featured in *Under 35: The New Generation of American Poets*. He is poet-in-residence at Holy Cross College, Worcester, Massachusetts.

Philip Cioffari has had poems in *Southern Poetry Review, Worcester Review, Green Mountain Review,* and the *Anthology of Magazine Verse*. His fiction has appeared in *Northwest Review, Michigan Quarterly,* and *Playboy*. He teaches creative writing at Paterson College in New Jersey.

David Citino is the author of six collections of poetry, including *The House of Memory* (1990). He is a professor of

English and director of creative writing at Ohio State University.

Michael Cleary is a transplant to Fort Lauderdale from the Adirondacks of New York teaching English and creative writing at Broward Community College. He has published poems in such journals as *Texas Review, Negative Capability, Southern Poetry Review,* and *Apalachee Quarterly*.

Horace Coleman has an M.F.A. in creative writing from Bowling Green State University. A former Air Force officer, he has taught at the university level, been a writer-in-the-schools, and worked as a technical writer/editor. His work has appeared in *American Poetry Review, Black Scholar,* and *Carrying the Darkness* (1985), an anthology of Vietnam poems.

Victor Contoski has published three books of poetry and three books of translations of contemporary Polish poetry. He teaches American literature and poetry at the University of Kansas in Lawrence. He was United States Correspondence Chess champion a few years ago.

Sam Cornish was born and raised in Baltimore. He now lives in Brighton, Massachusetts, and teaches African-American literature and creative writing at Emerson College, Boston. He is the former literature director of the Massachusetts Council on the Arts and Humanities and writes book reviews for *Essence, Christian Science Monitor,* and other periodicals. His first volume of poetry is *Generations* (1971).

Robert Creeley is David Gray Professor of Poetry and Letters at the State University of New York at Buffalo. His *Collected Poems* was published in 1983.

He has since written four additional collections, including *Windows* (1990).

Philip Dacey was born in 1939 in St. Louis. One of his five books of poetry is *Night Shift at the Crucifix Factory* (1991). He is the recipient of two grants from the National Endowment for the Arts, two Pushcart prizes, and a Woodrow Wilson Fellowship. With Dave Jauss, he coedited *Strong Measures: Contemporary Poetry in Traditional Forms* (1985). He teaches at Southwest State University in Marshall, Minnesota.

Leo Dangel was born in South Dakota in 1941 and teaches English at Southwest State University in Marshall, Minnesota. His book of poems is *Old Man Brunner Country* (1987).

Glover Davis teaches in the creative writing program at San Diego State University. He is the author of three collections of poetry, one of which is *Legend* (1989).

Peter Davison is the author of nine volumes of poetry, including *The Great Ledge* and *New and Selected Poems*. He edits Peter Davison Books for Houghton Mifflin and since 1972 has been the poetry editor of *Atlantic Monthly*.

Michael Delp is chair of the creative writing division at Interlochen Arts Academy in Michigan. His poems, nonfiction, and fiction have appeared in such magazines as *Playboy, North Dakota Quarterly,* and *Southern Poetry Review*. His first book of poems is *Over the Graves of Horses* (1988).

James Dickey is poet-in-residence at the University of South Carolina. His many books of poetry include *Buckdancer's Choice* (1965), *The Strength of Fields,* and *The Eagle's Mile* (1981). His work is collected in *Poems, 1957–1967* (1967) and *The Central Motion: Poems 1968–1979* (1983).

Emanuel di Pasquale was born in Sicily and emigrated to the United States in 1957 at the age of fifteen. Since receiving his M.A. from New York University in 1966 he has taught college English. His poems have appeared in such magazines as *Sewanee Review, The Nation,* and *New York Quarterly;* his first book of poems is *Genesis* (1989). He also publishes poems for children.

Stephen Dobyns has published seven books of poems and thirteen novels, including *Body Traffic* (1990), a book of poems, and *After Shocks/Near Escapes* (1991), a novel. He directs the creative writing program at Syracuse University.

Joseph Duemer's collection of poems *Customs* was published in 1987. He teaches creative writing, literature, and humanities at Clarkston University in upstate New York and is poetry editor for the *Wallace Stevens Journal.*

Alan Dugan was born in Brooklyn in 1923. Among his many awards and honors are a Guggenheim Foundation Fellowship, a National Book Award, a Pulitzer Prize, and a Prix de Rome. Over the years, he has taught at many universities and colleges. Among his seven collections of poetry are *New and Collected Poems 1961–1983* and *Poems 6* (1989). At present, he is a staff member for poetry at the Fine Arts Work Center in Provincetown, Massachusetts.

Robert Duncan died in 1988, shortly after the publication of his two major collections, *Groundwork: Before the War* and *Groundwork II: In the Dark.* His life-long contribution to American poetry has been acknowledged by nu-

merous awards, including the Harriet Monroe Poetry Award, National Endowment for the Arts grants, a Guggenheim Foundation Fellowship, and the National Poetry Award.

Stephen Dunn's book *Landscape at the End of the Century* (1991) is his eighth collection of poetry. Among his many awards are fellowships from the National Endowment for the Arts and the Guggenheim Foundation. He teaches at Stockton State College in New Jersey.

Stuart Dybek, the author of two books, *Brass Knuckles* (1979), a collection of poetry, and *Childhood and Other Neighborhoods* (1986), a collection of stories, teaches at Western Michigan University.

Cornelius Eady is the author of three books of poetry: *Kartunes* (1986), *Victims of the Latest Dance Craze* (the 1985 Lamont Poetry Selection), and *The Gathering of My Name.* He is also a guitarist and a songwriter. He teaches at and directs the poetry center at the State University of New York at Stony Brook.

George Economou is a scholar of medieval literature, a translator of Greek and Roman classical literature, and, as a poet, the author of six books, including *harmonies and fits* (1987). He lives in Norman, Oklahoma, and Wellfleet, Massachusetts.

W. D. Ehrhart teaches at Germantown Friends School and lives in Philadelphia with his wife and daughter. His collections of poetry include *To Those Who Have Gone Home Tired* (1984) and *Winter Bells* (1988). He is also the author of three nonfiction books and the editor of the well-known Vietnam poetry anthologies *Carrying the Darkness* (1985) and *Unaccustomed Mercy* (1989).

Theodore Enslin, author of *Thoroughfare*, continues to live quietly in Millbridge, Maine, his favorite fishing village.

Don Eulert was born in 1935 in Paradise, Kansas. He is the founding editor of *American Haiku* magazine. Among his published works are four books of translations and four collections of poetry, including *Animal Plant Mineral* (1986). Married and the father of four sons and a daughter, he is the director of humanities at the California School of Professional Psychology and a farmer.

David Allan Evans was born in Sioux City, Iowa, in 1940. He has an M.F.A. from Arkansas University and has taught at South Dakota State University since 1968. One of his two books of poetry is *Real and False Alarms* (1985).

Donald Finkel is author of twelve volumes of poetry, including *The Wake of the Electron* and *Selected Shorter Poems* (1987). Among his awards are grants from the National Endowment for the Arts and the Guggenheim Foundation, and the Theodore Roethke Memorial Award. He is the translator of *Splintered Mirror: Chinese Poetry from the Democracy Movement*. He lives in St. Louis, Missouri.

Charles Fishman has published four volumes of poetry, one of which is *The Death of Mazurka* (1987). He is the director of programs in the arts and poet-in-residence at the State University of New York at Farmingdale, the founding editor of *Xanadu* magazine and Pleasure Dome Press, and the editor of *Blood to Remember: American Poets on the Holocaust* (1990).

Roland Flint has published four books and three chapbooks of poems, including *Stubborn* (1990), a National Poetry Series selection, and, with William Stafford, the chapbook *Hearing Voices* (1991). He teaches in the English department at Georgetown University.

Richard Flynn, author of the book *Randall Jarrell and the Lost World of Childhood* (1990), teaches contemporary poetry and children's literature at Georgia Southern University.

Kenneth Gangemi's books of poetry and fiction include *Olt* (1984), *The Interceptor Pilot* (1981), and *The Volcanoes from Puebla* (1979). He lives in New York City.

George Garrett is the vice chancellor of the Fellowship of Southern Writers in Charlottesville, Virginia. He is the author of seven books of poetry, five novels, six collections of short fiction, and two plays. His *Collected Poems* appeared in 1984.

Paul Gianoli lives in the hills of southwest Missouri and is a professor at the School of the Ozarks, a work-study college. His work appears regularly in literary magazines. His collection *Blueprint* was published in 1980.

Reginald Gibbons is the author of four collections of poetry, including *Maybe It Was So*. He is a professor of English at Northwestern University and has been the editor of *TriQuarterly* magazine since 1981.

Christopher Gilbert, a psychologist and poet, lives in Providence, Rhode Island, with his wife Barbara Morin, their son Robin, and Barbara's twin daughters, Heather and Tanya. His book *Across the Mutual Landscape* (1984) received the Walt Whitman Award; he has also received a Robert Frost Fellowship in

Poetry and a grant from the National Endowment for the Arts. He is the author of *Demos/Witnesses of the Striving That Was There.*

Jack Gilbert lives in the woods of western Massachusetts near Amherst, building fires and writing. He is the author of *Monolithos* (1982).

Gary Gildner was born in West Branch, Michigan, in 1938. A poet, short story writer, and novelist, he has published *Blue Like the Heavens: New and Selected Poems* (1984), *A Week in South Dakota* (1987), and *Warsaw Sparks* (1990)—the latter a memoir of the year he lived in Poland teaching at the University of Warsaw and coaching the city's baseball team, the Warsaw Sparks, who awarded him a sabre.

Allen Ginsberg, one of America's best known poets, published his *Collected Poems* in 1984. His social activism and his impact upon American poetry began with the publication of *Howl and Other Poems* in 1956 and continue with his book *White Shroud: Poems 1980–1985* (1987). He lives on New York City's Lower East Side.

Ray Gonzalez has published three volumes of poetry. His second book, *Twilights and Chants* (1987), won the 1988 Four Corners Book Award for Best Book of Poetry. He is the editor of six anthologies, including *After Aztlan: Latino Poets in the Nineties* and *Without Discovery: A Native Response to Columbus,* the poetry editor of *Bloomsbury Review,* and the literature director of the Guadalupe Cultural Arts Center in San Antonio, Texas.

Vince Gotera is an assistant professor of English at Humboldt State University in Arcata, California. He has won an Academy of American Poets Prize and the Mary Roberts Rinehart Award in Poetry. His poems have appeared in *Ploughshares, Caliban, Zone 3, Amerasia, Indiana Review,* and other journals.

Jack Grapes is the editor of *ONTHE-BUS,* a literary arts periodical published in Los Angeles, and the author of "eight and a half" books of poetry, including *Trees, Coffee, and the Eyes of Deer* (1987). He is also the recipient of grants from the National Endowment for the Humanities and the California Arts Council and an accomplished actor and playwright.

William Greenway has published two books of poetry, *Where We've Been* (1987) and *Pressure Under Grace* (1982). He is a Georgia native and teaches poetry and poetry writing at Youngstown State University in Ohio.

Donald Hall is a prolific writer and editor who lives in rural New Hampshire. His many awards and honors include the Lenore Marshall Memorial Poetry Award, the National Book Critics Circle Award, and his appointment as poet laureate of New Hampshire. Two of his books of poetry are *The One Day: A Poem in Three Parts* (1988) and *Old and New Poems, 1947–1990* (1990).

Michael S. Harper was born in 1938 in Brooklyn and attended high school and college in Los Angeles. He is I.J. Kapstein Professor at Brown University, where he has taught for two decades. He has edited magazines and books on Sterling A. Brown, Robert Hayden, and Ralph Ellison and has written nine books of poetry. He is the first poet laureate of Rhode Island.

Robert Hass's three books of poetry are *Field Guide* (1973), *Praise* (1980), and *Human Wishes* (1989). He is the recipient of both Guggenheim Foundation and MacArthur fellowships and teaches poetry at the University of California, Berkeley.

Robert Hayden was a professor of English at the University of Michigan in Ann Arbor. He published eight books of poetry during his lifetime, and his *Collected Poems* was published posthumously in 1985. Among his many awards were a Ford Foundation Grant and the First World Festival of Negro Arts Prize for Poetry.

Jim Heynen lives in Seattle but commutes to Portland, Oregon, where he is writer-in-residence at Lewis and Clark College. His works include *One Hundred Over 100* (1990), nonfiction; *A Suitable Church* (1982), poems; and *You Know What Is Right* (1985) and *The Man Who Kept Cigars in His Cap* (1979), fiction.

Norman Hindley lives in Hawaii and teaches at Punahou School. One of his two collections of poetry is *Living W/O John Rose.*

Anselm Hollo is a teacher in the writing and poetics program of the Naropa Institute in Boulder, Colorado. His books of poetry include *Outlying Districts* (1990) and *Near Miss Haiku.*

David Huddle has published his fourth book of short stories, *Intimates;* his third book of poetry, *The Nature of Yearning;* and his first book of essays, *The Writing Habit.* He teaches at the University of Vermont and the Bread Loaf School of English.

T. R. Hummer is the author of *The Passion of the Right-Angled Man* (1985),

coeditor, with Bruce Weigl, of *The Imagination as Glory: Essays on the Poetry of James Dickey* (1984), and senior editor of *New England Review* and *Bread Loaf Quarterly.* He teaches at Middlebury College.

David Ignatow's many books of poetry include *New and Selected Poems, 1970–1985* (1986). He lives in New York City and has taught in the writing program at Columbia University.

Lance Jeffers's book, *O Africa Where I Baked My Bread,* was published in 1977.

Louis Jenkins's poems have appeared in magazines, including *Kenyon Review, Poetry East, Paris Review,* and *Virginia Quarterly Review,* and anthologies. He has also published three chapbooks and two volumes of poetry, *An Almost Human Gesture* (1987) and *All Tangled Up With The Living* (1991). He lives in Duluth, Minnesota.

Nick Johnson attended Catholic University and received his M.F.A. from Brooklyn College. His poems have appeared in *Shenandoah, Epoch, Aileron, American Poetry Review,* and other literary magazines. He teaches part-time at the College of New Rochelle in New York.

Galway Kinnell is the recipient of grants from the Rockefeller, MacArthur, and Guggenheim foundations. One of his ten books of poetry is *When One Has Lived a Long Time Alone* (1990).

Michael Klein lives in Brooklyn and is the editor of *Poets for Life: 76 Poets Respond to AIDS* (1988). His poems have appeared in *Boulevard, Black Warrior Review, Pequod,* and *Sonora Review.*

Etheridge Knight's collected poems, *The Essential Etheridge Knight,* were published in 1986. He was awarded fellowships by the Guggenheim Foundation and the National Endowment for the Arts and in 1985 received the Shelley Memorial Award from the Poetry Society of America. He died in 1991.

Ron Koertge is the author of thirteen books of poetry, including *Life on the Edge of the Continent* (1982). He also writes and publishes novels for teenagers. He teaches at Pasadena City College, and "in his rarely ending quest to live forever he is currently a lap swimmer."

Yusef Komunyakaa was born in Bogalusa, Louisiana, in 1947. His books include *Lost in the Bonewheel Factory* (1979) and *Dien Cai Dau* (1988). He received an M.F.A. from the University of California.

Steve Kowit has been involved in the animal rights and antiwar movements over the last several years. He is the author of a number of books of poetry and translations, including *Lurid Confessions* (1982), *Passionate Journey* (1984), and *Pranks* (1990), and the editor of *The Maverick Poets: An Anthology* (1988). He teaches at Southwestern College in California near the Mexican border.

Jay Ladin lives in San Francisco. His poetry has appeared in a number of magazines, including *Parnassus, Sequoia, Minnesota Review, California Quarterly,* and in the anthology *Movieworks.*

David Lee has published five books of poetry, including *Day's Work* (1990). He lives "very quietly in St. George, Utah, with Jan, Jon, and Jodee" and heads the department of language and literature at Southern Utah University.

Li-Young Lee was born in 1957 in Indonesia to Chinese parents. His two books of poetry are *Rose* (1986) and *The City in Which I Love You* (1990). Among his awards are three Pushcart prizes, the 1990 Lamont Poetry Selection, and grants from the National Endowment for the Arts and the Guggenheim Foundation. He lives in Chicago with his wife, Donna, and their children.

David Lehman is the author of two collections of poems, *An Alternative to Speech* (1986) and *Operation Memory* (1990), and a critical work on deconstruction, *Signs of the Times* (1991). A Guggenheim Fellow in poetry for 1989–90, he has received an award in literature from the American Academy and Institute of Arts and Letters. He lives in Ithaca, New York.

Philip Levine's book *What Work Is* appeared in 1991. His many awards include grants from the National Endowment for the Arts, the National Institute of Arts and Letters, and the Guggenheim Foundation. As a teacher of creative writing at California State University, Fresno, since 1958 and as the author of more than fifteen books of poetry, he has influenced the work of several generations of American poets.

Gerald Locklin teaches English at California State University, Long Beach. He has published scores of books, including *The Rochester Trip* and *The Illegitimate Son of Mr. Madman.* His work appears regularly in *Wormwood Review* and *POETRY/LA.*

Clarence Major is the author of seven novels and eight books of poetry. He has received an award from the National Council on the Arts, a Fulbright grant, and two Pushcart prizes. For the last twenty-five years he has taught literature and creative writing at many leading universities. In 1991 he became the director of creative writing at the University of California, Davis.

Jack Marshall has published eight books of poetry, including *Arabian Nights* (1989). He has traveled widely in Europe, Africa, and Mexico and has taught at a variety of universities, including the Iowa Writers Workshop, U.S. International University, and the University of San Francisco. He lives in San Francisco.

J. D. McClatchy lives in New York City. He is the author of *White Paper* (1990), a critical study of contemporary poetry.

Thomas McGrath's *Collected Poems* was published in 1988, bringing him long-overdue recognition as an important American poet. He died in 1990 in Minnesota.

Wesley McNair teaches creative writing and literature at the Farmington campus of the University of Maine. He has received an award from the Devins for *The Faces of Americans in 1853* (1984), and grants from the Guggenheim Foundation and the National Endowment for the Arts. His other book of poems is *The Town of No* (1989).

William Matthews is the author of eight books of poems, including *Blues if You Want* (1989), and a book of essays, *Curiosities* (1989). He lives in New York City and teaches at City College.

Bill Meissner has three books of published poetry, including *The Sleepwalker's Son* (1987) and *Twin Sons of Different Mirrors* (1989), collaborative poems with Jack Driscoll. Among his many awards for poetry are a grant from the National Endowment for the Arts and a Min-

nesota State Arts Board Fellowship. He is the director of creative writing at St. Cloud State University in Minnesota.

James Merrill is the author of *The Changing Light of Sandover* (1982) and many other books. His many prizes and awards include the Bollingen Prize, the Pulitzer Prize, and the National Book Award. His book of poetry *The Inner Room* was published in 1988.

W. S. Merwin's *Selected Poems* appeared in 1988. A prolific poet and translator, he has introduced to American readers the work of poets from China, Japan, Spain, France, and other countries. He has received grants from the National Endowment for the Arts, the Rockefeller Foundation, and the Academy of American Poets, among many others. He lives in New York City.

Robert Mezey was born in Philadelphia in 1935 and educated at Kenyon, Iowa, and Stanford. His books include *The Lovemaker, A Book of Dying, The Door Standing Open,* and *Evening Wind* (1987), which won a PEN prize and the Bassine Citation. He edited *Poems from the Hebrew* (1973) and coedited *Naked Poetry*. He is the recipient of the Lamont Poetry Selection, grants from the National Endowment for the Arts, and Robert Frost and Guggenheim Foundation fellowships. Since 1976 he has been poet-in-residence and professor at Pomona College.

Richard Michelson is the author of *Tap Dancing for the Relatives* (1985) and, in collaboration with the artist Leonard Baskin, a study of the life of Edvard Munch. He is the recipient of the 1990 Felix Pollak Prize in Poetry and lives with his wife, Jennifer, and their two children in Amherst, Massachusetts, where he owns an art gallery.

Jim Wayne Miller has published seven collections of poetry, including *Brier, His Book* (1988). His essays, short stories, and poems have appeared in many textbooks and anthologies. He teaches at Western Kentucky University in Bowling Green.

John Minczeski lives in St. Paul, Minnesota. One of his books is *Gravity*.

Irvin Moen and his wife live near Glacier National Park in Montana. Poems of his have been published in *Ariel, Amelia, South Coast Poetry Journal, The Spirit that Moves Us,* and *West Branch*.

Fred Moramarco is coeditor of *Men of Our Time*. He teaches contemporary poetry at San Diego State University and is coauthor of *Modern American Poetry* (1990). His poetry and criticism have appeared in *American Poetry Review, New York Quarterly, Poetry East,* and other periodicals.

Robert Morgan teaches at Cornell University. His books of poetry include *At the Edge of the Orchard Country,* published in 1987, and *Sigodlin,* published in 1990. He is also a writer of fiction and a recipient of a grant from the Guggenheim Foundation.

David Mura is author of *Turning Japanese: Memoirs of a Sansei, A Male Grief: Notes on Pornography and Addictions* (1987), and *After We Lost Our Way* (1989), which won the 1989 National Poetry Series Contest. He lives in St. Paul, Minnesota, and teaches at St. Olaf College.

Peter Najarian is author of three published novels: *Daughters of Memory* (1986), *Wash Me On Home, Mama* (1978), and *Voyages* (1980). He still plays basketball with his peers every Monday night.

Leonard Nathan has published several books of poetry and translations, including *Carrying On: New and Selected Poems* (1985). He has been nominated for a National Book Award and has received a grant from the Guggenheim Foundation. He lives in Kensington, California.

Duane Niatum has published five volumes of poetry, including *Drawings of the Song Animals: New and Selected Poems,* published in 1990. He is the editor of the two widely known and praised anthologies of Native American poetry, *Carriers of the Dream Wheel* (1975) and *Harper's Anthology of 20th Century Native American Poetry* (1988). A roll member of the Klallam tribe of Washington State, he lives in Seattle.

John Frederick Nims's books include *The Kiss: A Jambalaya* (1982), *Selected Poems* (1982), and *The Six-Cornered Snowflake and Other Poems* (1990). He lives in Chicago.

Ed Ochester is the director of the writing program at the University of Pittsburgh. One of his books is *Changing the Name to Ochester* (1988).

Perry Oldham is author of *Vinh Long,* a book of poems, and *Higher Ground* (1987), a novel. He lives with his family in Oklahoma City, where he teaches at Casady School.

Antony Oldknow, who was born in Peterborough, England, has lived in North America since 1964 and teaches at Eastern New Mexico University. His poems and translations have appeared in *Poetry, Antaeus, The Nation,* and other magazines.

Patrick O'Leary lives in Detroit with his wife and two sons. He works as an advertising copywriter. His poetry has appeared in *Little Magazine, Taproot, Indian Scholar, Poetry East,* and *Iowa Review.*

Simon J. Ortiz, poet, short fiction writer, storyteller, teacher, is the author of *After and Before the Lightning* (poetry and prose). Among his books are *Going for the Rain, A Good Journey, Fight Back, Howbah Indians, From Sand Creek,* and *Fightin': New and Collected Stories* (1983). He received National Endowment for the Arts Fellowship awards in 1970 and 1980 and a New Mexico Humanitarian Award in 1989.

Mark Osaki has work published in *Georgia Review, South Carolina Review,* and *Carrying the Darkness* (1985). He has received awards from the Academy of American Poets and the National Endowment for the Arts. He lives in Berkeley, California.

Richard Oyama was born and raised in New York City. He is a lecturer in the Asian-American Studies department at the University of California, Berkeley. His work has appeared in such magazines as *Breaking Silence, Ayumi, Contact II, Quilt,* and *Y'Bird.* He is coeditor of *American Born and Foreign* (1979), an anthology of Asian-American poetry. In 1983 he was the recipient of a National Endowment for the Arts writer-in-residence grant.

Basil T. Paquet was born in 1944. He served in Vietnam from 1967 to 1968 and coedited an anthology of poetry, *Winning Hearts and Minds* (1972), and an anthology of short fiction, *Free Fire Zones.*

Walter Pavlich has published five books of poetry, including *Ongoing Portraits* (1985), a Pushcart Writer's Choice selection, and *The Lost Comedy,* a sequence on Laurel and Hardy. He divides his time between his native Oregon and California.

Mark Perlberg is the author of two books of poetry, one of which is *The Feel of the Sun,* published in 1981. He has won two Illinois Arts Council Literary Awards and is a founding member and current president of the poetry center at the Art Institute of Chicago.

George Perreault teaches at New Mexico Highlands University and has been published in such magazines as *High Plains Literary Review, Puerto Del Sol, Greenfield Review, The Fiddlehead,* and *Yankee.* His collection of poetry, *Curved Like and Eye* was published in 1988.

Robert Peters lives in southern California, where he teaches contemporary poetry and Victorian literature. Since his first books of poems, *Songs for a Son* (1967), he has published more than twenty-four books of poetry. He has won the Poetry Society of America prize, the Alice Fay di Castagnola Award, and fellowships from the Guggenheim Foundation and the National Endowment for the Arts. An iconoclastic and energetic critic of contemporary poetry, he is known for his *Great American Poetry Bake-off* series, *The Peters Black and Blue Guide to Current Literary Journals,* and the encyclopedic *Hunting the Snark* (1989).

Robert Pinsky teaches in the creative writing program at Boston University. His books of poetry and criticism include *The Situation of Poetry* (1977),

History of My Heart (1985), and *The Want Bone* (1990).

James Plath is the single custodial parent of four and teaches English at Illinois Wesleyan University in Bloomington. His stories and poems have appeared in *Modern Short Stories, Buffalo Spree, Amelia,* and *Kansas Quarterly.* He also edits *Clockwatch Review.*

Sterling D. Plumpp is a poetry editor of *Black American Literature Forum* and an associate professor in the departments of African and African American studies and English at the University of Illinois at Chicago. His poetry, essays, and reviews have appeared in such places as *TriQuarterly, Epoch, Obsidian II,* and *Greenfield Review.* He has published five books of poetry, one of which— *The Mojo Hands Call, I Must Go*—was awarded the Sandburg Literary Award for Poetry in 1983.

Charles Potts was born and raised in Idaho and now lives in Walla Walla, Washington. He has written and published numerous books of poetry, including *The Dictatorship of the Environment* and *Nature Lovers.*

Leroy V. Quintana, a native New Mexican, teaches in the English department of San Diego Mesa College. He is the author of *Now and Then, Often, Today* and *Interrogations,* poetry about the Vietnam experience.

Bin Ramke is the editor of the Contemporary Poetry Series for the University of Georgia Press and the author of four books of poems, the first of which was Richard Hugo's first selection for the Yale Younger Poets series. More recently he published *The Erotic Light of Gardens* (1990). He directs the graduate program in creative writing at the University of Denver.

Michael Rattee was born in Holyoke, Massachusetts, in 1953 and raised in Vermont. He has two books of poems, *Mentioning Dreams* (1985) and *Calling Yourself Home* (1986). He was the recipient of a grant from the National Endowment for the Arts in 1984. Since 1978 he and his wife have lived in Tucson.

David Ray has published more than a dozen books of poetry, including *The Maharini's New Wall,* poems about India, which appeared in 1989. He is a professor of English at the University of Missouri at Kansas City.

Eugene B. Redmond is the author of five volumes of poetry, including *Sentry of the Four Golden Pillars* and *In a Time of Rain & Desire.* He is cofounder and associate publisher/poetry editor of *The Original Chicago Blues Annual* and *Literati Internazionale,* a multicultural journal of literary and visual arts, and the author of *Drumvoices* (1976), a critical history of African American poetry. He has received grants from the National Endowment for the Arts and the National Endowment for the Humanities and the Award for Outstanding Contributions to Black Poetry from the Black Caucus of the National Council of Teachers of English. Named poet laureate of his native East St. Louis, Illinois, in 1976, he is a professor of English at Southern Illinois University at Edwardsville.

Ishmael Reed lives in Oakland, California. He is well known as a novelist, essayist, editor, and poet. His works include the novels *Mumbo Jumbo* (1989) and *Reckless Eyeballing* (1986). His *New* and *Collected Poems* was published in 1988.

Carlos Reyes has divided his time between County Clare, Ireland, and Portland, Oregon. When not writing, he works as a land surveyor in the western states and Alaska. He also teaches as a poet in an artist-in-the-schools program. He has published three books of poems, one of which is *Nightmarks*, published in 1989.

Jack Ridl is the son of the former University of Pittsburgh basketball coach C. G. Ridl. His poems have appeared in various magazines and journals, including *Poetry East, Poetry, Southern Review*, and *New York Quarterly*, and in his collection, *The Same Ghost* and *Between*. He lives in Ottawa Beach along Lake Michigan.

Alberto Rios teaches in the creative writing program at Arizona State University at Tempe. He received the Walt Whitman Award for *Whispering to Fool the Wind* (1982) and is a recipient of a grant from the National Endowment for the Arts.

Jerome Rothenberg is the author of more than forty books of poetry, two of which are *New Selected Poems, 1970–1985* and *Khurbn & Other Poems* (1989). He has edited six groundbreaking anthologies of experimental and traditional poetry, including *Technicians of the Sacred* (1985), *Shaking the Pumpkin* (1972), and *A Big Jewish Book* (1978). Actively engaged in poetry and performance since the late 1950s, he teaches at the University of California, San Diego.

Mark Rudman is a scholar and translator as well as a poet. He is the author of *The Nowhere Steps* (1990), a book of

poems, and *Diverse Voices,* a book of essays. He teaches in the creative writing programs at New York University and Columbia University.

Michael Ryan's book *God Hunger* was published in 1990. He lives in Irvine, California, and has been a recipient of the Yale Younger Poets Award.

Dennis Saleh has published four books of poems, including *This Is Not Surrealism* (1989). He is the editor of his own press, Comma Books, in Seaside, California.

Harvey Shapiro was born in Chicago but has lived in Brooklyn for the last thirty years. He is the author of seven books of poetry, including *National Cold Storage Company* (1988).

Richard Silberg was born in New York City in 1942. He has an M.A. in creative writing from San Francisco State University and has two books of poetry out, *Translucent Gears* (1982) and *The Fields*. He is the associate editor of *Poetry Flash* in Berkeley and codirector of the well-known poetry reading series at Cody's Bookstore.

Charles Simic was born in 1938 in Belgrade, Yugoslavia. He teaches at the University of New Hampshire. His *Selected Poems, 1963–1983* first appeared in 1985 and in a revised and expanded edition in 1990. Another of his books of poems is *The Book of Gods and Devils* (1990). In addition to the Pulitzer Prize in Poetry, he has received grants from the National Endowment for the Arts and the Guggenheim Foundation and was a MacArthur Fellow from 1984 to 1989.

W. D. Snodgrass teaches at the University of Delaware. His first book of poems, *Heart's Needle,* won the Pulitzer Prize. He has also published *Selected Poems: 1957–1987* (1987) and two collaborations with the painter Deloss McGraw, *W. D.'s Midnight Carnival* (1988) and *The Death of Cock Robin* (1989).

Gary Snyder is one of America's best known poets. A Pulitzer Prize winner, he is the author of more than a dozen books of poetry, including *Left Out in the Rain: Poems 1947–1984* (1986). He has been a tireless advocate for the well-being of the planet.

Gary Soto is the author of five collections of poetry, one of which is *The Portraits* (1989). He has received the Before Columbus Foundation American Book Award, *The Nation*'s Discovery Prize, and grants from the Guggenheim Foundation and the National Endowment for the Arts. He teaches Chicano studies and English at the University of California, Berkeley.

Peter Spiro was born, raised, and lives in Brooklyn, "the land of American poets." He is a playwright whose plays have been performed at the National Theatre in Washington, D.C., the Ensemble Studio Theatre in New York, and The Theatre for the Forgotten.

William Stafford was born in 1914 in Hutchinson, Kansas. Among his collections of poetry are *Smoke's Way* (1983) and *Things That Happen Where There Aren't Any People.* He has been a poetry consultant for the Library of Congress and an international traveler and lecturer on literature and writing for the United States Information Service. He lives in Oswego, Oregon.

Frank Steele is an editor of *Plainsong.* He teaches at Western Kentucky University and lives in Bowling Green, Kentucky. His work has appeared in *Zone 3* and *Louisville Review.*

Gerald Stern's *Leaving Another Kingdom: Selected Poems* was published in 1990. He teaches in the writing program at the University of Iowa and has received grants from the Guggenheim Foundation and the National Endowment for the Arts.

Barry Sternlieb lives with his family in Richmond, Massachusetts, where he started Mad River Press, printing broadsides and books by hand "the old way . . . [trying] to give valuable poems the attention they deserve." His work has been published by Brooding Heron Press and River Styx Press and in such journals as *Poetry* and *Poetry Northwest.*

Frank Stewart has lived in Hawaii for the past twenty years. He has published three books of poetry, one of which is *Flying the Red Eye,* published in 1986. He has edited four collections of fiction, poetry, drama, and poetics.

Austin Straus was born in 1939 in Brooklyn. He is a poet, artist, political activist, printmaker, and maker of one-of-a-kind artist's books. He is the founder and cohost of "The Poetry Connexion" (KPFK-FM, Los Angeles) and the author of *Laureate Without a Country,* a book of poems published in 1991. He teaches in the English department at Los Angeles City College.

Barton Sutter was born in Minneapolis in 1949 and raised in small towns in Minnesota and Iowa. His two collections of poems are *Cedarhome* and *Pine Creek Parish Hall and Other Poems.* A typesetter for ten years, Sutter now earns his living teaching at the University of Minnesota, Duluth.

Christopher Sweet teaches journalism, English, and creative writing at the local high school in Barrington, Illinois. His poems have appeared in *The Best of Hair Trigger* and *Writing from Start to Finish*.

Nathaniel Tarn has published more than twenty books of poetry and translations. *Seeing America First* (1989) and *Views from the Weaving Mountain: Selected Essays in Poetry and Anthropology* are among them. He lives near Tesuque Pueblo, New Mexico.

Henry Taylor is a professor of literature and the codirector of the graduate creative writing program at the American University in Washington, D.C. His books of poems include *The Horse Show at Midnight* (1966), *An Afternoon of Pocket Billiards* (1975), and *The Flying Changes* (1985), which was awarded the 1986 Pulitzer Prize in poetry.

David Trinidad was born and raised in southern California. He is the author of seven books and chapbooks, one of which is *Hand over Heart: Poems 1981–1988* (1991). His poems have appeared in numerous magazines and anthologies, including *Paris Review, City Lights Review,* and *American Poetry Since 1970: Up Late*. He lives in New York City.

Quincy Troupe teaches literature and creative writing at the University of California, San Diego and in Columbia University's graduate writing program. Winner of two American Book Awards, he is the author of four volumes of poetry, including *Weather Reports: New and Selected Poems* (1991), and the coauthor of *Miles: The Autobiography* (1989).

Lloyd Van Brunt is the founding poetry editor of the Pushcart Prize. His sixth collection is *Working Firewood for the Night* (1990). His seventh book is *La Traviata in Oklahoma: Selected Poems, 1960–1990*.

John Vernon is the author of a book of poems, *Ann* (1976), three books of literary criticism, and three novels: *LaSalle* (1986), *Lindbergh's Son* (1987), and *Peter Doyle*, which was published in 1991. He is a professor of English at the State University of New York at Binghamton.

Mark Vinz was born in North Dakota and grew up in Minneapolis and the Kansas City area. He has taught at Moorhead State University in Minnesota since 1968 and has published nine collections of poetry since 1975, one of which is *Mixed Blessings* (1989). He is a long-time editor of Dacotah Territory Press.

Ronald Wallace is the author of seven books, including *Vital Signs* (1989), *People and Dog in the Sun* (1986), and *Tunes for Bears to Dance To* (1983). He is the series editor for the Brittingham Prize in Poetry and director of creative writing at the University of Wisconsin, Madison.

Robert Ward lives in Seattle, where he specializes in antique photographica and historical documents. His poems have appeared in approximately fifty publications. His first chapbook, *Camera Obscura*, was published in 1987.

Michael Waters has published four books of poetry, including *The Burden Lifters* (1989) and *Bountiful*. He was awarded a grant from the National Endowment for the Arts in 1984. He teaches English at Salisbury State University in Maryland.

Charles Harper Webb has published two collections of poems, *Everyday Out-*

rages (1989) and *Zinjanthropus Disease,* which won a Wormwood Review Award. His book *Poetry That Heals* deals with self-help and self-exploration through creative writing. He is a licensed psychotherapist and teaches English at California State University, Long Beach.

Bruce Weigl was born in Lorain, Ohio, in 1949. He is the author of five collections of poetry, including *Song of Napalm,* published in 1988. He is also the author of *The Phenomenology of Spirit and Self: On the Poetry of Charles Simic.* He has been awarded the Pushcart Prize, a prize from the Academy of American Poets, and a grant from the National Endowment for the Arts. A past president of the Associated Writing Programs, he teaches at Penn State University.

Richard Wilbur has been Poet Laureate Consultant in Poetry to the Library of Congress and has won many awards, including a Guggenheim Foundation Fellowship, a Pulitzer Prize, and the National Book Award. His *New and Collected Poems* was published in 1988.

C. K. Williams's books include *Poems 1963–1983* (1988), which consists of his first five collections of poetry, and *Flesh and Blood* (1988) and *A Dream of Mind.* Among his awards are grants from the National Endowment for the Arts and

the Guggenheim Foundation, and the National Book Critics Circle Award for poetry in 1987. One of his works of translation is a version of Euripides' *Bacchae* (1990). He is a professor at George Mason University in Virginia.

Rob Wilson has published a book of poems on Korea entitled *Waking in Seoul* (1988). He is a native of Connecticut, a graduate of the University of California, Berkeley, and teaches in the English department at the University of Hawaii in Honolulu.

Gary Young lives in the mountains north of Santa Cruz with his wife and son. His books include *Hands* (1981), *In the Durable World* (1985), and *The Geography of Home.* A recipient of awards from the National Endowment for the Arts and the National Endowment for the Humanities, he designs, prints, and publishes limited edition books and broadsides at his Greenhouse Review Press.

Paul Zimmer has published six books of poetry, including *The Great Bird of Love* (1989). He is the director of the University of Iowa Press.

Al Zolynas, coeditor of *Men of Our Time,* has published one book of poems, *The New Physics* (1979). He teaches at United States International University and lives in Escondido, California.

INDEXES

INDEX OF POETS

INDEX OF TITLES

INDEX OF FIRST LINES